UNUSUAL SEXUAL BEHAVIOR

UNUSUAL SEXUAL BEHAVIOR

THE STANDARD DEVIATIONS

By

DAVID LESTER, Ph.D.
Richard Stockton State College
Pomona, New Jersey

CHARLES C THOMAS • PUBLISHER
Springfield • Illinois • U.S.A.

Published and Distributed Throughout the World by

CHARLES C THOMAS • PUBLISHER
Bannerstone House
301-327 East Lawrence Avenue, Springfield, Illinois, U.S.A.

This book is protected by copyright. No part of it
may be reproduced in any manner without written
permission from the publisher.

©*1975, by* CHARLES C THOMAS • PUBLISHER

ISBN 0-398-03343-9

Library of Congress Catalog Card Number: 74 20784

With THOMAS BOOKS careful attention is given to all details of manufacturing and design. It is the Publisher's desire to present books that are satisfactory as to their physical qualities and artistic possibilities and appropriate for their particular use. THOMAS BOOKS will be true to those laws of quality that assure a good name and good will.

Library of Congress Cataloging in Publication Data

Lester, David, 1942-
   Unusual sexual behavior.
   Includes index.
   1. Sexual deviation. I. Title. [DNLM: 1. Sex deviation. WM610 L642u]
RC577.L45   616.8'583   74-20784
ISBN 0-398-03343-9

Printed in the United States of America
A-2

INTRODUCTION

The purpose of this book is to review the literature on sexual deviations. Primarily the review is concerned with the research literature and not with clinical studies. However, occasional reference is made to the conclusions of clinical studies and, in particular, to psychoanalytic hypotheses about sexual deviations. The coverage of clinical and psychoanalytic ideas is by no means intended to be exhaustive, unlike the coverage of the research literature. The review does not cover the treatment of the sexual deviant.

The review is written from an unbiased a viewpoint as possible. Given my attempt to be unbiased, I dislike the term "sexual deviant." I much rather prefer the term "sexual variant." However, although the latter term is less judgmental, its meaning is less clear. It also leads to a more cumbersome terminology. For example, the meaning of terms such as "variant sexual behavior" and "sexual variant" are more ambiguous in their referent than the terms "deviant sexual behavior" and "sexual deviant." Thus, I have decided to continue to use the term "deviant."

I have adopted a classification of sexual deviations that proposes three kinds of deviant behavior.

1. *Variation in mode*: This refers to deviations in the manner or mode of obtaining sexual satisfaction and includes exhibitionism, obscene telephone calling, voyeurism, masochism and sadism, and rape.

2. *Variation in object*: This refers to deviations in the choice of stimulus that provides sexual stimulation and covers homosexuality, incest, pedophilia, bestiality, and fetishism. (Bestiality is not discussed here since no research study was found on the topic.)

3. *Variation in strength of the sexual response*: This refers to

deviations in the frequency and intensity of sexual behavior and includes impotence and frigidity on the one hand and nymphomania and satyriasis on the other. These topics are not included in this review. Impotence and frigidity are not usually considered to be sexual deviations, and their inclusion seemed out of place. Nymphomania and satyriasis are considered sexual deviations, but I was unable to find research conducted on either behavior.

4. *Miscellaneous*: Most classificatory systems have a miscellaneous category and it proved difficult to fit transvestism and transsexualism* into the three categories already described. I have placed these two behaviors in a separate category.

Obviously, there are cultural differences in what kinds of sexual behavior are considered to be deviant. This book deals with the perspective of the Twentieth Century and the United States, since this is the context in which the research reviewed here was conducted. Thus, heterosexuality is not considered as a deviation under the category "variation in object."

---

*This spelling is preferred over "transsexualism."

CONTENTS

Introduction v

Section I
DEVIATION OF MODE

Chapter
1. EXHIBITIONISM 5
2. THE OBSCENE TELEPHONE CALLER 19
3. VOYEURISM 22
4. SADISM AND MASOCHISM........................... 25
5. RAPE 27

Section II
HOMOSEXUALITY

6. GENETIC FACTORS IN HOMOSEXUALITY................ 39
7. PHYSIOLOGICAL AND CONSTITUTIONAL STUDIES OF HOMOSEXUALITY 46
8. THE CHILDHOODS OF HOMOSEXUALS.................. 57
9. THE PARENTS OF HOMOSEXUALS..................... 63
10. PSYCHOANALYTIC VIEWS OF HOMOSEXUALITY.......... 75
11. TYPES OF HOMOSEXUALS........................... 81
12. HOMOSEXUALITY AND OTHER PSYCHOLOGICAL DISTURBANCES 88
13. PSYCHOLOGICAL CORRELATES OF HOMOSEXUALITY....... 95
14. FEMALE HOMOSEXUALITY 112

Section III
OTHER DEVIATIONS OF OBJECT

15. INCEST 127
16. PEDOPHILIA 146
17. FETISHISM 158

Section IV
OTHER SEXUAL DEVIATIONS

18. TRANSVESTISM 169
19. TRANSEXUALISM 180

Section V
GENERAL STUDIES OF SEXUAL DEVIATION

20. THE DETECTION OF THE SEXUALLY DEVIANT 195
21. GENERAL STUDIES OF SEXUAL DEVIANTS 209

Section VI
CONCLUSIONS

22. REFLECTIONS 227

Index 233

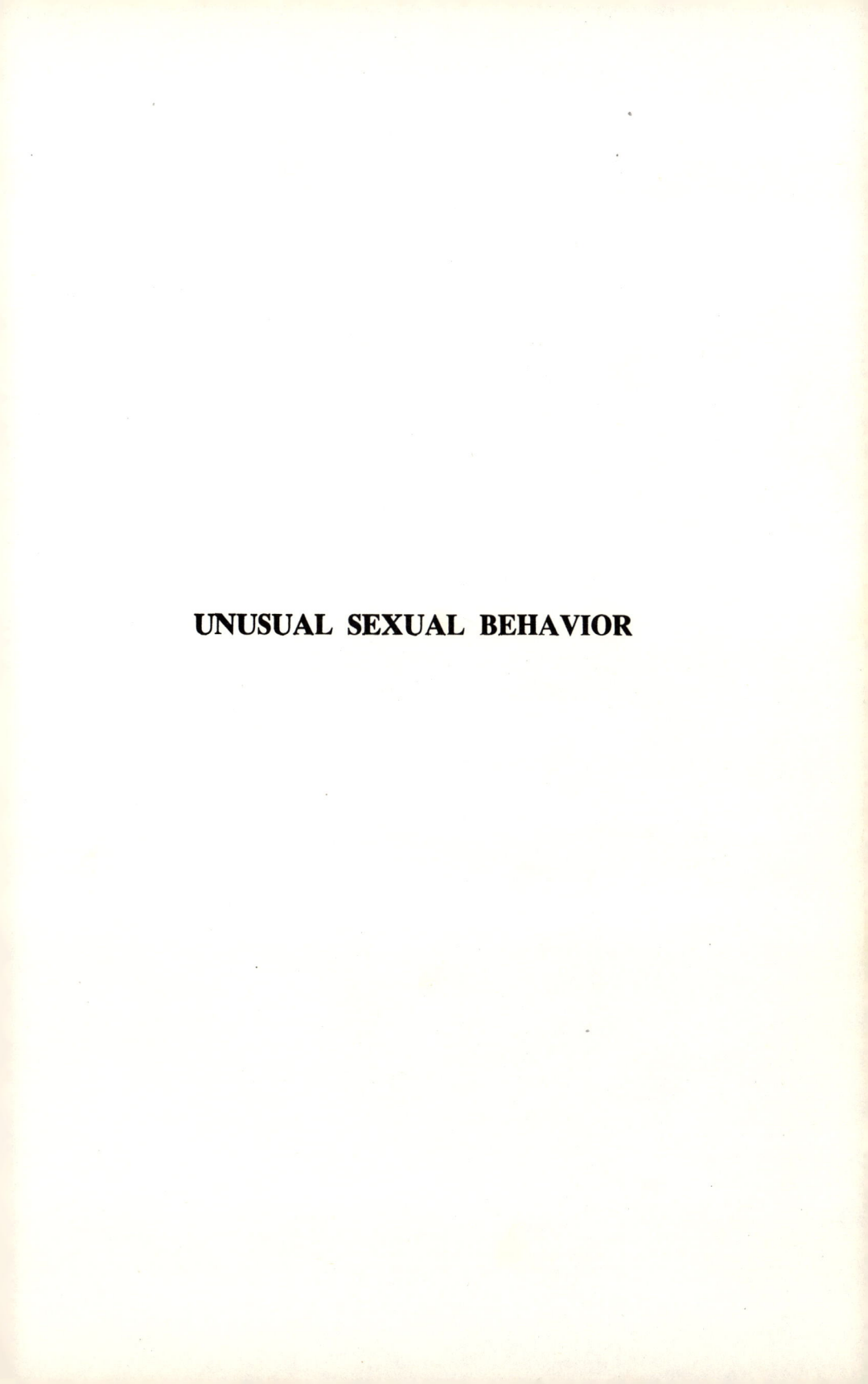

UNUSUAL SEXUAL BEHAVIOR

SECTION I
DEVIATION OF MODE

CHAPTER 1

EXHIBITIONISM

EXHIBITIONISM MAY BE DEFINED as an act of exposure of a part or the whole of the body for sexual or nonsexual rewards (Evans, 1970). This definition is not as broad as some that have been offered, such as that by Henry (1955) who defined exhibitionism as a self-display made for the purpose of winning approval. However, it is broader than some definitions that have been offered; in the narrowest sense, exhibitionism consists of exposure of the genitals to another who has not requested such a display.

The particular acts which are considered to constitute exhibitionism vary from culture to culture (Honigmann, 1944). In our culture, a common practice for males in groups is for one of the males to remove his trousers and present his bare arse to a female or group of females. Yohe (1950) described cases where a group of males gangs up on one male and removes his trousers, often in the presence of a female audience (which may be involuntarily observing the exposure). Yohe noted that in young boys aged eleven to fourteen, the female audience was not desired and the act had homosexual connotations, whereas in boys aged fourteen to seventeen the act assumed heterosexual connotations, and a female audience was desired. Our culture often excludes these acts from the narrow definition of exhibitionism.

Acts of exhibitionism are occasionally difficult to distinguish from (1) advances by pedophiles to children, (2) drunks, psychotics, or retarded males urinating without thought as to where they are, and (3) solicitation by males for females to engage in heterosexual intercourse. However, the majority of acts of exhibitionism do not fall into these three categories; they merely constitute acts in which the exposure of the genitals is the sole sexual aim of the male.

CHARACTERISTICS OF THE ACT

The incidence of exhibitionism is difficult to ascertain, for many cases remain unreported. It is found that some one third of all sexual offenses are acts of indecent exposure (Macdonald, 1973). The way in which the act is carried out varies greatly from person to person. The exhibitionist may be in a public or private place, at the window of a house, in a car, or in the open street. Macdonald reported that indecent exposure occurred most often outdoors and almost one half of these exposures were performed by males in cars. Some exhibitionists have an erection during the exposure while others do not. Masturbation may precede, accompany, or follow the act, or not occur at all. Macdonald (1973) reported that 7 percent of the exhibitionists that he examined undressed completely for their act of exposure.

The act seems to be impulsive in some cases and premeditated in others. Some men report no awareness of their actions until the act is completed; they appear to be dazed (in an altered state of consciousness). The majority of exhibitionists, however, develop a stereotyped pattern for the act. Occasionally, exhibitionists seem to carry out their act in a way that facilitates arrest. Some exhibitionists report feelings of guilt and shame, but others do not perceive their actions as a problem and are difficult to motivate toward treatment. Often only legal pressure can keep exhibitionists in psychotherapy (Mathis and Collins, 1970).

Quetelet's law states that crimes against the person are most common in warm months and warm climates, whereas crimes against property are most common in cold months and cold climates. Although it is claimed that acts of exhibitionism are more common in warm months (Evans, 1970), Macdonald (1973) found no seasonal variation in Denver. He discovered that acts of indecent exposure were most common between 8 AM and 6 PM, in particular between 8 AM and 9 AM and between 3 PM and 5 PM, and were more common on weekdays than on weekends. It might be noted that the temporal variation for exhibitionism is quite different from the temporal variation for rape.

Occasionally force or threat is used by the exhibitionist. Macdonald (1973) observed that four of 200 exhibitionists that he studied used force, three followed their victims, and two chased their victims. Macdonald also found a few cases of exhibitionists who brandished guns or knives and occasional cases of exhibitionists who forced victims to watch them masturbate.

The audience for the exhibitionist is usually a strange female. Most exhibitionists expose themselves to adult females (and particularly females who are alone). Exposure to children is also common (although not characteristic of the majority of exhibitionists) and, in these cases, exposure most often occurs in the presence of groups of children. Some exhibitionists are very particular in the choice of an audience, and this constitutes part of the stereotypy of the act. A few exhibitionists intend their act to be an invitation to further sexual involvement, but the great majority of exhibitionists do not want sexual involvement with the audience. They desire a particular reaction from the audience—fear and flight, indignation and abuse, or pleasure and amusement.

Acts of indecent exposure are rarely victim-precipitated, unlike many acts of rape.

THE EXHIBITIONIST

Most exhibitionists are male. Female cases have been reported but such reports are rare, and the females are usually judged to be retarded or psychotic. On the other hand, male exhibitionists are frequently judged to have personality disorders, although exhibitionism can be found in males with a variety of forms of psychopathology. Ellis and Brancale (1956) judged 72 percent of exhibitionists to be neurotic and 10 percent normal; a further 8 percent were judged to be borderline psychotic. Evans (1970) classified exhibitionists into two groups: organic (mentally retarded, epileptic, brain damaged, senile, and diabetic) and psychological (psychoneurotics, psychopaths, and psychotics). (Actually, Evans included the psychotics in the organic group, but such placement seems inappropriate.)

The usual onset of exhibitionism is in puberty, and the peak incidence occurs between the ages of fifteen and thirty. Its onset after the age of forty-five is rare except in cases of organic disease. Macdonald (1973) found little variation in the incidence of exhibitionism in different racial groups in Denver, although he did note that indecent exposure by whites was an intraracial act whereas indecent exposure by blacks was an interracial act. Macdonald also noted that exhibitionists came disproportionately from the lower social classes and tended to be married more than other sexual offenders, but had fewer children.

Rickels (1955) distinguished between three kinds of exhibitionists.

1. The depraved exhibitionist who exposes openly for sensual pleasure to stimulate an "impotent penis." He is immature, uses dark locations, exposes to children often as a means of solicitation for further sexual involvement, and tries to avoid arrest.

2. The exhibitionist who has organic brain disease and whose act is due to carelessness, loss of sense of social propriety, or an inability to distinguish right from wrong.

3. The exhibitionist who acts against his will, that is, one who acts under a compulsion. He is usually a tense, anxious man, conscious of his deed but unable to resist the impulse. Other investigators use the term "ego-dystonic" to describe such acts.

This latter kind of exhibitionist is usually modest and follows a strict moral code for behavior. He is embarrassed by his behavior and depressed after the act. He exposes himself before strange females and does not always masturbate. His tension is often relieved as soon as he is viewed. He tends to have voyeuristic tendencies. He frequently has been raised in a home where modesty is stressed and where there is a strict moral code, especially with regard to sex. As a child he tends to be judged as ideal and well-behaved. There is a close attachment to the mother which she will not allow to dissipate. The mother often insists on being called by some term of endearment (such as "honey"). The son often fails to make a good heterosexual adjustment. Marriage is not frequent and, if marriage is attempted, the sexual adjustment is poor. This kind of exhibitionist is overly reserved with women, with sexual contact infrequent and unsatisfactory. Exhibitionism often begins in puberty but is sometimes suppressed so that overt acts do not occur until later. The parents of the exhibitionist often have a lack of harmony and a good deal of tension in their marriage and they tend to fulfill their affectional needs through the son. The act of exhibiting is often precipitated by an emotional trauma such as engagement, the death of a relative, or marriage.

Mohr, et al. (1962) reported that the exhibitionist's urge to exhibit usually occurred during a time when he had a conflict with females (in adolescence his mother, in adulthood his finance/wife). At school, the exhibitionists were loners and isolated. They had few friends and either were bullied or frequently involved in fights. They had experienced difficulties in social relationships and in handling aggression.

The intelligence scores of the exhibitionists seemed to be average (although Ellis and Brancale [1956] found the intelligence of exhibitionists to be lower than that of the general population, yet higher than that of other sexual offenders). However, their educational achievement was quite poor. They were generally hard-working and conscientious (with a tendency to be compulsively conscientious), very sensitive to criticism, and easily upset if things went wrong. They preferred "manly" occupations and had good work records.

About a third of the exhibitionists had absent fathers during childhood. The fathers tended to have been distant emotionally and were more likely to be viewed negatively by their sons. The relationship of the exhibitionist to his mother was more emotional and there was strong love, resentment, or both. There were no differences in birth order, but there was an excess of male siblings over female siblings. Most of the exhibitionists idealized their relationships with their siblings, and they seemed unable to express resentment and hostility toward them.

About two thirds of the exhibitionists were married and the precipitating event was often the impending or recent marriage or the birth of a child. The wives seemed as disturbed as the husbands, with a struggle for dominance and dependency as the theme of the marriage relationship. Sexual intercourse with the wife was common, as was masturbation, and, although the men claimed that exposure often occurred after an absence of sexual activity, Mohr, et al. found that exposure frequently occurred after sexual intercourse with their wives.

Most of the exhibitionists had expressed a wish to have children soon after marriage, but once the children were born, there was no indication that there was a strong relationship between the father and his children. Only a small proportion of the exhibitionists were judged to be psychotic or neurotic.

McCawley (1965) and Macdonald (1973) reviewed a number of clinical studies of exhibitionists and noted that exhibitionists have been described as passive, compulsive, reticent, schizoid, morally strict, nonaggressive, shy, timid, retiring, conscientious, well-educated, highly intelligent, heterosexually immature, orally fixated, with feelings of inferiority, with a feminine identification, with poor impulse control, and occasionally (but not often) with sadistic and masochistic tendencies. (It might be noted that the good eucation and high intelligence is not borne up by surveys of arrested exhibitionists. Case studies from psychotherapy often produce different findings from surveys of arrested individuals.)

Zechnich (1971) proposed that exhibitionists suffered from a lack of privacy as children (particularly with regard to nudity) and that they deduced from this experienced that they have nothing which warrants covering. Their act of exhibitionism asserts that indeed they do have something worth covering, that they do have a life-space, and thus that they do exist. The exhibitionist attempts in his interpersonal relationships to correct for the experienced lack of privacy by being closed, guarded, hidden, secretive, and noncommittal. Zechnich noted that not only did the act of exhibitioning serve to get the exhibitionist arrested, it also satisfied the exhibitionist's need to avoid success which is manifest in other spheres of his life.

Gebhard, et al. (1965) classified exhibitionists into four groups: patterned-compulsive, drunks, mentally deficient, and miscellaneous. Gebhard, et al. noted that exhibitionists did not socialize much as children with their peers. After puberty, heterosexual difficulties were common. Masturbation was frequent among the married exhibitionists, although few married. Premarital sex began late and often was with prostitutes. The patterned-compulsive exhibitionists possessed a truly compulsive urge usually triggered by some emotional stress. The sexual availability of a wife or other female was not sufficient to reduce the urge.

Other investigators have pointed to narcissistic tendencies, organ inferiority, a history of stammering (both exhibitionism and stammering are primarily male behaviors), and a high utilization of fantasy, particularly with respect to sexual activity. Kopp (1962) described a subset of exhibitionists who were brash, loud, vulgar, and openly attention seeking. Some writers (for example, Selling, 1939) see the personalities of exhibitionists as quite variable, however. Many investigators state that exhibitionists are psychologically disturbed and perceive the exhibitionism as a secondary symptom of the psychiatric disorder. (It was noted above that the psychiatric disorder was frequently found to be mild or absent.) Other investigators view exhibitionism as a separate diagnostic entity (a compulsion or a form of acting-out, or both).

Macdonald (1973) reviewed other studies and concluded that 20 percent to 34 percent of exhibitionists had convictions for previous sexual offenses. However, 40 percent to 67 percent admitted previous sexual offenses. In addition, 15 percent to 23 percent had previous convictions for nonsexual offenses. The recidivism rate for exhibitionists has been estimated as 27 percent within five years, with a probable maximum of 30 percent (Frisbie, 1963). Mohr, et al. (1962) reported a recidivism rate for exhibitionists of 20 percent in three years as compared to 13 percent for pedophiles.

PSYCHOLOGICAL STUDIES OF EXHIBITIONISTS

Sjostedt and Hurwitz (1959) tried to assess the perceptual-cognitive maturity of exhibitionists, homosexuals, and controls using the Rorschach Test. (Perceptual-cognitive maturity was defined as form being dominant over color and immaturity as global undifferentiated responses.) The groups were matched for age, intelligence, and marital status. Sjostedt and Hurwitz found no differences between the groups (although the homosexuals were more variable than the exhibitionists in perceptual-cognitive maturity). In all groups the married subjects had greater perceptual-cognitive maturity than the unmarried subjects.

THE DEVELOPMENT OF THE BEHAVIOR

There is no research bearing on physiological, constitutional, or genetic factors in the etiology of exhibitionism. Many investigators view exhibitionism as a learned behavior. The act may initially occur intentionally (perhaps due to sexual frustration of sexual outlets or a desire to expose), accidentally, or through vicarious learning. McGuire, et al. (1965) reported cases of men who were surprised by females while surreptitiously urinating in public, for example, and who later developed into exhibitionists. The act of exhibitionism may continue to occur either through drive reduction mechanisms or simply because the first occurrence is incorporated into masturbatory (and possibly other sexual) fantasies. Evans (1968) tried treating exhibitionists with behavior therapy and found that those exhibitionists with normal masturbatory imagery were deconditioned faster than those with exhibitionistic masturbatory fantasies.

The development of exhibitionism, according to some writers, may also be the result of the individual's failing to learn society's rules well enough. Such a hypothesis is sufficiently reasonable as to be irrefutable. Schlegel (1963) classified the act of exhibitionism as a form of displacement (as understood by ethologists), but he felt it was unlikely that it was the result of a presently unknown innate releasing mechanism.

Rickels (1950) described the mothers of exhibitionists as important in the development of exhibitionism in their sons. The mothers were judged to have a high degree of penis envy which led to two possible outcomes: a masculine identification (a positive approach) or attempts to psychologically castrate men (a negative approach). These behaviors were made stronger if the mother hated her own father and feared him. The mothers tended to identify with their sons and to use the son to prove their equality with males. They possessed a penis through their sons, compensating for their lack of a penis and repairing the original injury to their narcissism. The sons exhibited themselves to prove their independence from their mother.

Rickels found two kinds of mothers: aggressive and masculine women and "clinging vines." The mothers rejected their husbands as soon as the son was born. The strong link between mother and son prevented the son's becoming schizophrenic.

The fathers of exhibitionists are often industrious, passive, meek, and ineffective, which serves to increase the son's dependence upon the mother. This leads to strong incestuous impulses in the son and castration anxiety based upon fear of the dominant mother. Some fathers of exhibitionists are strong and dominating which perpetuates the sons' feelings of weakness and impotence. The act of exhibitionism then is used to assert the sons' potence.

EXHIBITIONISM AND OTHER SEXUAL DEVIATIONS

Gebhard, et al. (1965) claimed that about 10 percent of exhibitionists had attempted or seriously contemplated rape. Mohr, et al. (1962) felt that other sexual deviations were rare with the exception of voyeurism. Many authors claim to detect a relationship between voyeurism and exhibitionism. The basis for this is not at all clear. In theory the actor can be seen as the exhibitionist and the audience as the voyeur, and the occurrence of an offense may be determined by ascertaining who is the unwilling person in the dyad and hence the victim. There is no data to indicate that the actor and audience find it easy to change roles. Hackett (1971) found one exhibitionist out of thirty-seven to also be a voyeur. (One other engaged in frotteurism and one other in homosexual acts. Nine were impotent.) Rooth (1973) found that only 20 percent of a sample of exhibitionists had engaged in voyeuristic acts. Frottage and homosexuality were more common. Rooth found that most of the exhibitionists had engaged in some other sexual deviation (only 13 percent had not), but of several hundred arrests only five were for indecent assault (usually in the exhibitionists' youth). Exhibitionists do not appear to engage in violence. Thus, the presumed relationship between exhibitionism and voyeurism may well be a myth.

Conceptual justification for the association comes most often from psychoanalysts. For example, Caprio (1948) claimed that exhibitionism was a passive form of voyeurism. Saul (1952) claimed that each act could be seen as the projection of the wish behind the other. Be this as it may, there are no good data to support the association.

PSYCHOANALYTIC VIEWS

Psychoanalysts have speculated upon the motivations behind exhibitionism. According to Christoffel (1936) the motivation is to persuade the audience to display her genitals in return. Fenichel (1946) felt that exhibiting gives the individual reassurance and reduces his castration anxiety. The audience confirms the presence of the penis. The exhibitionist also shows his own penis to contradict the idea that people can exist without penises, an idea that he cannot accept. (He originally has experienced the notion that people without penises can exist when he was a small child and viewed the genitals of little girls or his mother.) Fenichel felt that exhibitionism was rare in females since they do not have penises (and thus castration anxiety). Those females who exhibited their genitals were thought by Fenichel to have delusions of having a penis.

Rickels (1942) observed that exhibitionists used repression as a major defense mechanism, whereas Karpman (1948) emphasized regression. Rickels (1942) noted that the exhibitionist was usually dominated by his mother and/or wife and so the act served to prove the exhibitionist's virility and attractiveness and that his mother was not able to do everything for him. Exhibiting could be seen as an act of revenge.

Bromberg (1965) felt that the exhibitionist wished to arouse females sexually and to reassure himself of his own masculinity. The act expressed contempt for women and so was seen as hostile. It was also an act of sexual independence; a seduction without a finale. Exhibitionism can be both a defense against anger and a means of expressing anger. Exhibitionism has also been viewed as satisfying a desire to be punished (since so few exhibitionists take care to avoid arrest) and as a manifestation of narcissism (Stekel, 1952).

STRIPTEASERS

The profession of stripteasing bears many similarities to the act of exhibitionism. Most strippers are female, although occasionally males do perform (especially male transvestites). Skipper and McCaghy (1970) interviewed a number of strippers and reported that almost all were white and nineteen to forty-five years old, with the majority in their twenties. Compared to the average female and to "Playmates" (the centerfold nudes in *Playboy*) they were heavier, taller, and had larger hips and busts. The majority were brunettes (though many had dyed their hair).

Most were born or raised in the city. They came from all social classes, had a wide variety of schooling, and came from all religions. Some two thirds of those interviewed had been married but only about 6 percent were still married. Eighty-nine percent of those interviewed were first-borns. The majority (60 percent) came from broken homes. Their first menstruation had occurred earlier than that of the average female.

Skipper and McCaghy noted that the girls soon began using their bodies to get attention and recognition from others which they did not get from their nuclear family. (They received little affection from their parents, and their father was usually absent by the time they were adolescents.) They left home early (usually by the age of eighteen), often through marriage. Only rarely did siblings enter the profession. Most had had sexual intercourse by the age of sixteen, and most reported pleasing and easy relationships with males outside of the family.

Skipper and McCaghy felt that becoming a stripper had three sources: a tendency toward exhibitionistic behavior for gain, an opportunity structure that made stripping an accessible occupational alternative (for example, being a bar-girl and meeting those in the profession), and an awareness of the easy economic gain.

Some 20 percent of the strippers shared society's negative image about them. The rest either denied this image or used rationalization as a defense mechanism. These latter strippers had a positive self-image. Few strippers engaged in deviant behavior such as organized crime, alcoholism, drug addiction or use of marihuana, or pornographic posing. Their ideology was that stripping was an entertainment, a service (sexual catharsis for males), and a sex education service (for wives and females in general).

It was common for strippers to engage in prostitution (at least 50 percent admitted to so doing) and homosexuality. McCaghy and Skipper (1969) regarded homosexuality as an adaptation to their profession. The girls were isolated from affective social relationships, they had unsatisfactory relationships with males (since becoming strippers), and the opportunity structure allowed a wide range of sexual behavior, information as to access to gay bars, and fellow strippers. They usually became engaged in homosexual behavior only after becoming a stripper and most were bisexual. The career homosexual was rare.

NUDISM

Some writers see nudists as similar to exhibitionists, but studies of nudists (Blank, 1969; Casler, 1964; Weinberg, 1965) indicate little similarity between nudists and exhibitionists. Blank noted that nearly all nudists said that the sight of the body is not arousing. He felt that either they were lying, were undersexed, used conscious suppression of sexual responses, or were subject to involuntary suppression of sexual impulses.

Blank and Roth (1967) discovered few differences between nudists and control groups on the MMPI, but the differences that were found suggested more psychopathology in the nudists. On the Draw-A-Person Test, Blank and Roth concluded that the nudists were more likely to have a disturbed body image and sexual conflicts. One judge found indications of more severe psychopathology in the DAP protocols of the nudists, while a second judge found no differences in psychopathology between the DAP protocols of the nudists and the controls. Blank noted that the more severe disturbance of the nudists (if a valid conclusion) could be the result of being a nudist or merely a nonconformist.

Casler (1964) reported no differences between nudists and students of similar age and education on the California F Scale or the Wesley Self-Administered Rigidity Scale. Thus, nudists do not appear to be less rigid or moralistic than non-nudists.

SUMMARY

There has been a great deal of study of exhibitionists, and it is possible to describe the modal exhibitionist in terms of demographic and social variables and the modal exhibitionist act. However, with respect to psychological studies of exhibitionists, there is a paucity of research. Clinical studies have provided a rich array of hypotheses to test the personality of exhibitionists, but at present the results of these clinical studies must remain questionable.

Many interesting hypotheses about exhibitionists, such as their psychosexual immaturity and timidity and their involvement with other sexual deviations (especially voyeurism), remain untested. Behaviors such as stripteasing and nudism, while superficially similar to exhibitionism, appear upon investigation to be engaged in by individuals who differ greatly from the typical exhibitionist.

REFERENCES

Blank, L.: Nudity as a quest for life the way it was before the apple. *Psychol Today, 3*:18-23, 1969.

Blank, L., and Roth, R.: Voyeurism and exhibitionism. *Percept Mot Skills, 24*:391-400, 1967.

Bromberg, W.: Sex offense as a disguise. *Correct Psychiatry, 11*:293-298, 1965.

Caprio, F.S.: A case of exhibitionism with special reference to the family setting. *Am J Psychother, 2*:587-602, 1948.

Casler, L.: Some sociopsychological observations in a nudist camp. *J Soc Psychol, 64*:307-323, 1964.

Christoffel, H.: Exhibitionism and exhibitionists. *Int J Psychoanal, 17*:321-345, 1936.

Ellis, A., and Brancale, R.: *The Psychology of Sex Offenders*. Springfield, Thomas, 1956.

Evans, D.R.: Masturbatory fantasies and sexual deviation. *Behav Res Ther. 6*:17-19, 1968.

Evans, D.R.: Exhibitionism. In Costello, C.G.(Ed.): *Symptoms of Psychopathology*. New York, Wiley, 1970, pp. 560-573.

Fenichel, O.: On acting. *Psychoanal Q, 15*:144-160, 1946.

Frisbie, L.V.: *Recidivism among Treated Sex Offenders*. Sacramento, California, Department of Mental Hygiene Research Division, 1963.

Gebhard, P.H., Gagnon, J.H., Pomeroy, W.B., and Christenson, C.V.: *Sex Offenders*. New York, Har-Row, 1965.

Hackett, T.P.: The psychotherapy of exhibitionists in a court setting. *Sem Psychiatry, 3*:297-306, 1971.

Henry, G.W.: *All the Sexes*. New York, HRW, 1955.

Honigmann, J.J.: A cultural theory of obscenity. *J Crim Psychopathol, 5*:715-738, 1944.

Karpman, B.: The psychopathology of exhibitionism. *J Clin Psychopathol, 9*:179-225, 1948.

Kopp, S.B.: The character structure of sex offenders. *Am J Psychother, 16*:64-70, 1962.

Macdonald, J.M.: *Indecent Exposure*. Springfield, Thomas, 1973.

Mathis, J.L., and Collins, M.: Progressive phases in the group therapy of exhibitionists. *Int J Group Psychother, 20*:163-169, 1970.

McCaghy, C.H., and Skipper, J.K.: Lesbian behavior as an adaptation to the occupation of stripping. *Soc Prob, 17*:262-270, 1969.

McCawley, A.: Exhibitionism and acting out. *Compr Psychiatry, 6*:396-409, 1965.

McGuire, R.L., Carlisle, J.M., and Young, B.G.: Sexual deviations as conditioned behavior. *Behav Res Ther, 2*:185-190, 1965.

Mohr, J.W., Turner, R.E., and Ball, R.B.: Exhibitionism and pedophilia. *Correct Psychiatry, 8*:172-186, 1962.

Rickels, N.K.: Exhibitionism. *J Nerv Ment Dis, 95*:11-17, 1942.

Rickels, N.K.: *Exhibitionism*. Philadelphia Lippincott, 1950.

Rickels, N.K.: Exhibitionism. *J Soc Ther, 1*:168-181, 1955.

Rooth, G.: Exhibitionism, sex violence, and pedophilia. *Br J Psychiatry, 122*:705-710, 1973.

Saul, L.J.: A note on exhibitionism and scoptophilia. *Psychoanal Q, 21*:224-226, 1952.

Schlegel, W.: Der Exhibitionismus des Mannes. *Nervenarzt, 34*:365-368, 1963.

Selling, L.S.: Significant factors in the study and treatment of sex offenders. *Med Rec, 149*:173-175, 1939.

Sjostedt, E.M., and Hurwitz, I.: A developmental study of sexual functioning by means of a cognitive analysis. *J Proj Tech, 23*:237-246, 1959.

Skipper, J.K., and McCaghy, C.H.: Stripteasers. *Soc Prob, 17*:391-405, 1970.

Stekel, W.: *Patterns of Psychosexual Infantilism*. New York Liveright, 1952.

Weinberg, M.S.: Sexual modesty, social meanings and the nudist camp. *Soc Prob, 12*:311-313, 1965.

Yohe, C.: Observations on an adolescent folkway. *Psychoanal Rev, 37*:79-81, 1950.

Zechnich, R.: Exhibitionism. *Psychiatr Q, 45*:70-75, 1971.

CHAPTER 2

THE OBSCENE TELEPHONE CALLER

THE INCIDENCE OF OBSCENE telephone calls is quite high. Murray (1967), in a survey of undergraduates, found that 46 percent of the females reported having received such calls. In a subsequent study, Murray and Beran (1968) reported that 75 percent of female undergraduates and 39 percent of male undergraduates surveyed had received obscene calls. Nadler (1968) noted that the telephone company in New York City received 65,500 complaints in a nine-month period of which 19 percent concerned obscene calls. Brockopp and Lester (1969) reported a high incidence of males' calling a suicide prevention center who desired to masturbate while talking to a female counselor.

The obscene caller is often regarded as gratifying voyeur and exhibitionist desires. The exhibitionist's desires seem more evident. Many case histories of obscene callers report a history of other exhibitionist behaviors (for example, Nadler, 1968).

Nadler noted the dependence upon others for reassurance and the low self-esteem in these men. In each of the three cases he described there was evidence of anger toward women which seemed to stem from their relationship with the mother. Their mothers were described as bossy, overprotective, and dominating. The fathers tended to be meek toward the mother and uninterested in the sons. Nadler noted schizoid and depressive tendencies in the men and that the use of the telephone eliminated the anxiety felt in face-to-face confrontation. The men felt safer from retribution, and they were less likely to be laughed at. Telephoning also prevented them from getting too involved with the female and protected them from the danger of physically acting out their rage and murderous fantasies.

Like the exhibitionist, the obscene caller attempts to gain

a sense of mastery through the reactions of others. Yet he clearly is more timid than the exhibitionist since he lacks the courage to physically confront another person.

Gebhard, et al. (1965) found six obscene telephone callers in their sample of 1356 white males convicted for sexual offenses. The men usually called total strangers selected randomly from the telephone book. The men often masturbated while calling. While most of the sex offenders came from broken homes, the obscene callers did not. Their relationships with parents, siblings, and peers were normal, and they had had an adequate frequency of heterosexual activity. They had had some homosexual experiences, but these experiences were infrequent.

The men were above average in the number of orgasms experienced per week and so appeared to have a greater need for sexual outlets; therefore, they were perhaps less able to delay gratification. Telephoning provided a readily available, safe means for gratification. The hypothesis of a strong drive was buttressed by their continuing to call after being arrested and by the fact that alcohol and drugs were rarely used (to overcome inhibitions and anxieties). Of the six men, three had no previous arrest record while the other three had been convicted in the past for exhibitionism. Two of the latter group also had been arrested for burglary and theft.

SUMMARY

Although obscene telephone calling is a common behavior no adequate research studies have appeared on the topic. The information obtained from case reports suggests that obscene callers resemble exhibitionists. Different investigators disagree, however, on the kinds of family backgrounds from which obscene telephone callers come.

REFERENCES

Brockopp, G.W., and Lester, D.: The masturbator. *Crisis Intervention, 1*:10-13, 1969.

Gebhard, P.H., Gagnon, J.H., Pomeroy, W.B., and Christenson, C.V.: *Sex Offenders.* New York, Har-Row, 1965.

Murray, F.S.: A preliminary investigation of anonymous nuisance telephone calls to females. *Psychol Rec, 17*:395-400, 1967.

Murray, F.S., and Beran, L.C.: A survey of nuisance calls received by males and females. *Psychol Rec, 18*:107-109, 1968.

Nadler, R.P.: Approach to the psychology of obscene telephone calls. *New York State J Med, 68*:521-526, 1968.

CHAPTER 3

VOYEURISM

Yalom (1960) has defined voyeurism as an exaggerated desire to see, by stealth, a member of the opposite sex in some stage of undress, in the sexual act, or in the act of excretion; a desire which is so intense that it surpasses in importance the normal sexual act. Yalom viewed voyeurism as an ego-syntonic compulsion, a compulsion that the patient does not object to. Voyeurs rarely, if ever, seek treatment of their own accord.

PSYCHOANALYTIC VIEWS

Obendorf (1939) believed that the voyeur was trying to reassure himself (unconsciously) that the fantasized penis of the female exists. The female whom he observes is symbolic of his mother. The reassurance is necessary to reduce his castration anxiety. Yalom (1960) regarded the act as a direct fulfillment of an infantile wish to see the female genitals and the sexual act. This wish was once repressed, but now it is conscious and satisfied. It assuages the person's castration anxiety through re-experiencing the frightening scenes viewed as a child that led to the intensification of the child's castration anxiety. Sexual gratification is obtained through identification with the person viewed. Almansi (1960) had speculated that voyeurism was linked with early visual sensitization due to feelings of oral deprivation and object loss.

CHARACTERISTICS OF VOYEURS

Most voyeurs are male, and they seek to view females. Female voyeurs and homosexual voyeurs seeking to view a person of the same sex are rarely reported.

Yalom (1960) commented upon eight patients, most of whom had been arrested for other crimes, but who were voyeurs. They ranged in age from fifteen to thirty-three. The activity was persistent. Five began by peeping at their mother. Five masturbated while peeping. Five of the patients had been married but were separated or divorced at the time of the study. The intelligence quotients of the patients ranged from 105 to 125. Yalom noted that seven of the eight had no older brother (three were only children, two only sons, and two the oldest sons).

Yalom noted the elements of sadism involved in the act. The act of being viewed was often seen by the voyeur as a punishment for the person viewed. Voyeurs often referred to the women viewed as their "prey," and the act enabled the voyeur to feel superior. Yalom observed that voyeurs often turned to rape, assault, burglary, and arson, but there was no evidence to test this assertion. The masochistic elements in voyeurism are minimal. The voyeur does suffer social ostracism if caught, and he may suffer from the weather in pursuing his goals. Yalom commented upon the lure of the forbidden and noted that voyeurs rarely visited burlesque shows or made use of pornography.

Gebhard, et al. (1965) observed that voyeurs were a mixed group, including sociosexual underdevelopment, mental deficiency, situational cases, and drunks. The majority of the voyeurs that they studied had inadequate heterosexual lives. Those with more adequate heterosexual outlets were less habitually voyeurs. Gebhard, et al. also noted that voyeurs usually spy on strangers.

They tend to be the only or the youngest child and to have few sisters. They got on relatively well with their parents, although the parents did not always get on well together. The voyeurs lacked female friends when they were children. This poverty of female companionship persisted into adolescence. Voyeurs petted relatively infrequently. Few married. The picture is of a somewhat stunted heterosexuality with a rather strong homosexual component. They tend to have an extensive criminal record, especially as adolescents, but most of the record stems from voyeurism and occasionally exhibitionism.

The association between voyeurism and exhibitionism is frequently commented upon, but there have been no data advanced to support such an association.

SUMMARY

There have been no adequate research studies of voyeurs. There are a number of case reports that indicate the presence in voyeurs of strong castration anxiety, a stunted heterosexuality (arising from inadequate contact with females when young), strong homosexual trends, and exhibitionist tendencies.

REFERENCES

Almansi, R.J.: The face-breast equation. *J Am Psychoanal Assoc,* 8:43-70, 1960.

Gebhard, P.H., Gagnon, J.H., Pomeroy, W.B., and Christenson, C.V.: *Sex Offenders.* New York, Har-Row, 1965.

Obendorf, C.P.: Voyeurism as a crime. *J Crim Psychopathol, 1*:103-111, 1939.

Yalom, I.D.: Aggression and forbiddenness in voyeurism. *Arch Gen Psychiatry, 3*:305-319, 1960.

CHAPTER 4

SADISM AND MASOCHISM

VERY LITTLE RESEARCH has been conducted on sadism and masochism in sexual behavior, although psychologists have discussed sadism and masochism in general terms (for example, Brown, 1965; Shore, et al. 1971).

A phenomenon in which death is associated with sexuality has been described. Young males (often transvestites) hang themselves (occasionally masturbating during the hanging) to facilitate erections and sexual orgasm (Resnick, 1972). Weisman (1967) described females who heighten sexual orgasms by partially suffocating themselves.

Litman and Swearingen (1972) studied a small group of males (but with no comparison group) who were white, middle class, living in the community, and who found erotic pleasure in being bound, restrained, and rendered helpless. They noted that occasional deaths occur as a result of the bondage. (Accidental deaths also occur during the self-hangings and self-suffocations mentioned above.) Litman and Swearingen could find no common family patterns of interaction or early traumatic experiences. They found frequent evidence of depression and suicidal ideation/behavior in the men. They felt that the men had homosexual trends and, with age, these homosexual trends became stronger and the bondage was indulged in with a partner rather than alone. The men differed in the liking for pain, some disliking it and others enjoying it. Most of the men were impotent without props, for fantasy alone was incapable of producing an orgasm. They needed fetish objects and a scenario. About half of the men would take the sadist role, but only with reluctance.

Marks, et al. (1965) noted that masochism is treatable using aversion techniques. They cured a fetish with masochistic trends by using electric shock aversive therapy. Thus, pain per se is not pleasurable to the masochist. The shock was aversive to the patient even though the patient fantasized masochistic acts and liked his wife to kick him and stand on him.

SUMMARY

Far too little research has been conducted on masochism and sadism for any conclusions to be drawn. Some scenarios for the behaviors have similarities to fetishism, but this may not be true for the majority of sadomasochistic acts. The fact that the masochist may enjoy pain does not preclude the use of pain in aversion therapy to cure the behavior.

REFERENCES

Brown, J.: A behavioral analysis of masochism, *J Exp Res Person,* 1:65-70, 1965.

Litman, R., and Swearingen, C.: Bondage and suicide. *Arch Gen Psychiatry,* 27:80-85, 1972.

Marks, I., Rachman, S., and Gelder, M.: Methods for the assessment of aversion treatment in fetishism with masochism. *Behav Res Ther,* 3:253-258, 1965.

Resnick, H.: Erotized repetitive hangings. *Am J Psychother,* 26:4-21, 1972.

Shore, M., Clifton, A., Zelin, M., and Myerson, P.: Patterns of masochism. *Br J Med Psychol,* 44:59-66, 1971.

Weisman, A.: Self-destruction and sexual perversion. In (Ed.): E. Shneidman, *Essays in Self-destruction.* New York, Science, 1967, p. 265-299.

CHAPTER 5

RAPE

RAPE INVOLVES sexual contact between two individuals in which one of those individuals uses force or compulsion upon the other in order to carry out the sexual act. Usually, rape is a heterosexual offense, but it can be a homosexual offense. Legally, this behavior is called forcible rape in order to distinguish it from statutory rape in which one of the two individuals involved in the sexual act is under some stipulated age.

The problem for the psychologist is that rape (both forcible rape and statutory rape) is a legal term. Force may obviously occur in some acts of sexual intercourse but yet not be called rape. The legal definition of rape does not fit into a psychologically meaningful categorization of sexual behavior. This is not the place to explore the general use of aggressiveness in heterosexual (or homosexual) intercourse, but suffice it to say that some investigators (for example, Kanin, 1967) have studied normal males who are aggressive or nonaggressive in their heterosexual intercourse.

Leaving these caveats aside, this review will focus upon legally defined acts of rape. Insofar as is possible, studies on statutory rape will be reviewed in the chapter on pedophilia (Ch. 16). Most of the research on rape has confined itself to heterosexual acts. Thus, this review will focus upon heterosexual forcible rape.

SOCIOLOGICAL STUDIES

There have been a number of sociological studies of rape. Goldner (1972) noted that cases of statutory rape were often more common than cases of forcible rape (in New York in the 1930s by about four to one), and that the incidence of forcible rape increased roughly with the size of the city. Female rapists, although rare, are encountered, but their victims are usually young male children. MacDonald (1971) noted that females who assist male rapists may also be charged with rape.

Chappell, et al. (1971) compared rapists in Boston and Los Angeles and found many differences. They noted a high frequency of young married men in both cities, and they discovered a high frequency of physical handicaps in the offenders. In Los Angeles, rapes occurred more on weekends, with an even monthly distribution (in Boston the peak was in the summer), more often in groups, with fewer total strangers as victims, and with more young victims. In Los Angeles there were more pick-ups (in cars and bars), while in Boston there were more rapes after breaking and entering and, although rare in both cities, more injury to the victim in Boston.

The most thorough study of patterns in forcible rape has been reported by Amir (1971) who studied all rapes occurring in Philadelphia in 1958 and 1960. He reported that rape was more common among blacks than whites (and this was true for both offenders and victims), that most rapes were intraracial, that the modal age of both offender and victim was fifteen to nineteen, but that victims tended to be younger than the offenders in general. Offenders tended to be single whereas victims tended to be single and/or dependents. Rapists tended to be from the lower classes even when racial differences were controlled for. Rapes were more common in July and August, on weekends (and especially on Saturdays), and in the evenings (8 PM to 2 AM). In 82 percent of the rapes, the offender and victim lived in the same neighborhood.

Alcohol was present in 24 percent of the offenders and 31 percent of the victims. Alcohol was more common in white participants than in black participants. If alcohol were present, the rape was more likely to be planned and the sexual acts more deviant; and if the offender were black there was more violence accompanying the rape.

About half of the offenders had previous arrest records (as compared to only 19 percent of the victims), but only 12 percent of the arrests were for sex offenses. For the victims with arrest records, 38 percent of the arrests were for sexual misconduct.

Offenders met victims most often on the street (48 percent)

or at the victim's home (26 percent). Most of the rapes were planned (71 percent) rather than impulsive (16 percent). Of the various kinds of nonphysical force, intimidation was most common (42 percent), followed by coercion (25 percent), intimidation with a weapon (21 percent), and temptation (12 percent). Physical force was used in 85 percent of the rapes, but brutal beating or choking (as compared to roughness or nonbrutal beatings) was used in only 35 percent of the rapes.

Sexual deviations (fellatio, cunnilingus, and anal intercourse) occurred in only 53 percent of the rapes and multiple intercourse in 43 percent.

Most of the victims submitted (55 percent), 27 percent resisted, and 18 percent fought. Younger victims were more submissive. The more physical force used, the less submission, although which is cause and which is effect is disputable here. Also, the more nonphysical force used, the more submission.

Felony rape (that is, rape during the commission of a felony) was quite rare, occurring in only 4 percent of the cases. Multiple rape (that is, with two or more offenders) was quite common. Multiple rapes accounted for 43 percent of the rapes and 71 percent of the offenders. Multiple rapes tended to occur more on weekends, to involve more planning, and to involve more travel by the offenders to the place where they met the victim. Alcohol was used more often, and the offenders tended to have more prior arrests for offenses against the person and for sex offenses. Force was more common in multiple rapes, sexual deviations less common, and multiple intercourse more common.

In 42 percent of the rapes, the victim and offender were strangers and in 14 percent they were intimates (relatives and friends). Some 19 percent of the rapes were judged to be victim-precipitated.

Amir reported the second-order associations for most of the variables he studied, but there is little to be gained from summarizing these here.

SOCIOLOGICAL THEORIES OF RAPE

Amir (1971) proposed a sociological theory to account for his results. He adopted the notion of Ferracuti and Wolfgang (1964) of a subculture of violence which is hypothesized to exist in some societies. This subculture of violence leads to a variety of behaviors, including homicide and rape. This subculture in Philadelphia clearly consists of single black males aged fifteen to twenty-four. It should be noted that Amir's study was descriptive and his explanation was a post hoc one. He did not delineate where the subculture of violence existed and then explore the incidence of rape. He noted that single black males had a high incidence of rape and, therefore, inferred that theirs was the subculture of violence. Further, this theory does not enable predictions to be made about which members of the subculture will murder, which will rape, and which will do neither. It enables only rates of rape to be predicted, not individual acts.

LeVine (1959) felt that four factors were necessary (although not sufficient) for a high incidence of rape in a society. (1) There must be severe formal restrictions on the nonmarital sexual relations of females. (2) There must be moderately strong sexual inhibitions on the part of the females. (3) Barriers to marriage must exist that prolong the bachelorhood of some of the males into their late twenties. (4) There must be an absence of physical segregation between the sexes.

Chappell, et al. (1971) hypothesized that the more restricted and rare the opportunities for cooperative sexual intercourse in a society, the higher the incidence of rape. Also, the more permissive the sexual mores in the society, the higher was the incidence of rape, since there would be greater frustration in the male (since his self-image was damaged if he were rejected, even though there might be fewer rejections). They felt that Los Angeles was more permissive in sexual mores than Boston and so should have the higher rape rate. This was found, even after correcting for the fact that the police in Los Angeles used a broader definition of rape than those in Boston.

Von Hentig (1947) felt that rape was more common in times of prosperity, and this might reflect the greater frustration of the lower classes in times of prosperity. (See Henry and Short [1954] for an illustration of this reasoning for homicide in the lower classes.)

Svalastoga (1962) argued that if the ratio of males to females in a society was too high, then there would not be sufficient sexual outlets for the males and rape would be more common. The high status males would have more potential for legal outlets and would eschew violence. But groups of lower class males would turn to rape. He compared rural-urban areas to test his hypothesis, but the comparison was confounded by the rural-urban variable. Lester (1974) tested the assumption in the states of the United States and found no support for the hypothesis. When Lester examined the sex ratio for the blacks in each state the result was in a direction opposite to that predicted, that is, the higher the sex ratio for black males in a state, the lower the incidence of rape.

PSYCHOLOGICAL CHARACTERISTICS OF RAPISTS

A number of unrelated psychological studies of rapists have been reported and, although it is quite difficult to integrate their findings, it is worthwhile to review them briefly.

Hammer (1954a) found no difference between rapists and pedophiles (who were in jail) in the tendency to draw the opposite sex first on the Draw-A-Person Test. On the House-Tree-Person Test, the trees of the rapists were judged to be older by their artists than the trees of heterosexual pedophiles, but there was no difference in the age of the persons drawn (Hammer, 1954b). The age of the female figures drawn was older than the age of the male figures, but this difference reached statistical significance only for the pedophiles. The age assigned to the tree by its artist supposedly reflects the psychosexual age of the artist, and so Hammer concluded that the pedophiles were psychosexually less mature than the rapists. If the female figure has a greater age than the male figure, this supposedly indicates inferiority feelings in its artist or the maternalization of the female figure (and hence a perception of her as forbidden). This did not seem, therefore, to be characteristic of the rapists. In a further analysis of these data (Hammer, 1955), the trees of the rapists were least often judged to be dead by their artists, the trees of the heterosexual pedophiles more often, and the trees of the homosexual pedophiles most often. Judging the tree to be dead supposedly indicates serious psychopathology, and Hammer noted that the increase in the occurrence of judgments of dead trees in the three groups paralleled the increasing distance from an appropriate sex object.

In a final study on these subjects, Hammer and Jacks (1955) examined the movement responses given to the Rorschach Test. The rapists gave more extensor responses and more often failed to report a human on Card III as compared to the pedophiles. This was thought to reflect greater self-assertiveness and hostility and a dehumanized approach to people in the rapists. There were no differences in the production of flexor responses to Card III (supposedly indicative of passivity and dependency) or blocked movement responses (indicating indecisiveness). It should be borne in mind that the validity of the interpretations of the differences made by Hammer is open to question.

Pascal and Herzberg (1952) compared prisoners convicted for nonsexual crimes, rape, homosexual acts, and heterosexual pedophilic acts. The prisoners were given the Rorschach Test twice: once in the usual fashion and once when asked to point out any male and female genitals seen in the cards. The groups did not differ in the total number of responses given to the standard Rorschach nor in the number of genital organs seen in the modified Rorschach task. Using the criteria of rejecting a card and the number of times a genital was seen in an unusual location (defined statistically), Pascal and Herzberg were unable to distinguish the rapists from the nonsexual criminals and the pedophiles from the homosexuals. However, the rapists/nonsexual criminals differed significantly from the pedophiles/homosexuals. Thus, deviant sex behavior seemed to be associated with deviant responding on the Rorschach.

Perdue and Lester (1972) found no differences between the Rorschach protocols of rapists in jail and nonsexual offenders on the standard Rorschach categories. Burton (1947) compared teenage rapists, homosexuals, and nonsexual offenders in jail for their scores on the *Mf* scale of the MMPI. Neither the rapists nor the homosexuals differed from the nonsexual offenders. Goldner (1972) claimed that the intelligence test scores of rapists were below the average for the general population.

Palm and Abrahamsen (1954) in a clinical study of rapists concluded that they had been overstimulated by their mothers, often in a frustrating manner (since no satisfaction could be obtained and since they were often beaten). The rape was seen as an attempt to force the seductive/rejecting mother figure to give in. (The wives of the rapists resembled the rapists' mothers in this seductive/rejecting characteristic; therefore the victim could symbolically represent the wife/mother figure.)

In an old (and possibly methodologically inadequate) study, Hooton (1939) claimed to find unique physical characteristics in rapists as compared to other criminals. Black rapists were described as short in stature, with a small head breadth and head circumference, long noses and ears, short and broad faces, and thick eyebrows. White rapists had blue-grey eyes, deflected nasal septa, facial asymmetries, short stature and sitting height, excessive chest depth, and excessive shoulder breadth.

Kercher and Walker (1973) examined the reactions of rapists in jail and nonsexual offenders to heterosexual and nonsexual pictures. No differences were found in penile volume changes to the pictures. However, the rapists showed generally higher galvanic skin responses to the heterosexual stimuli; and, on a Semantic Differential rating of the slides, the rapists rated the heterosexual pictures as less appealing. Kercher and Walker concluded that heterosexual stimuli* were unpleasant for the rapists, and so they were not able to get vicarious pleasure from pornography. Thus, they had to have sexual intercourse, even if force had to be used.

Gebhard, et al. (1965) distinguished between heterosexual offenders against adults and heterosexual aggressors against adults. The former group seemed to Gebhard, et al. to be similar to ordinary lower class males, save for an inability to foresee the consequences of their actions and a reduced concern with moral issues. In childhood, parental background, and sexual development, the heterosexual offenders against adults seemed normal and healthy. Their inappropriate sexual behavior stemmed from their impulsiveness. Gebhard, et al. described them as simple, unimaginative, impulsive opportunists, uneducated and basically goodhearted souls who take their pleasure where they find it and let the future take care of itself. Their lives are disorderly, continually involving trouble over property and women, but rarely involving serious crime. They may make a pass at anything in skirts, but rarely attempt forcible rape or pedophilia. They are prone to minor crimes such as petty theft, stealing cars, and

---
*or possibly sexual activity itself.

general disorderly conduct.

The aggressors against adults (a group that includes males convicted of forcible rape) were found to be criminal men who take what they want. Their sex offenses are by-products of their general criminality. Gebhard, et al. distinguished several varieties: the sadistic/assaultive, the amoral delinquent, the drunk, the explosive, the double-standard variety (pick-ups can be forced to keep the implicit promise), and a mixed group of psychotics and defectives. The heterosexual adjustment of these men seems normal and healthy. They get involved in crime quite early in life, and there are occasional hints of underlying violence and sadism in a minority of the men. However, the sex offense often involves unnecessary violence, bizarre behavior, and self-delusion, all of which suggests pathology. A minority are not antisocial individuals but merely ordinary citizens who erupt under stress or who misjudge the situation.

THE WIVES OF RAPISTS

Palm and Abrahamsen (1954) studied the wives of a number of rapists in a clinical study and noted that they had had threatening and sexually aggressive fathers, which perhaps accounted for their apparent fear of men (and of rape). The fears against rape were thought to reflect an unconscious wish to be raped.

The wives related to the males in a passive-submissive masochistic manner. They clung to their husbands despite the infidelity of their husbands and the social disgrace of the arrest. If they ran away from the home, they usually returned out of fear and guilt. Their hostility to men was felt to be unconscious.

It was felt that either the wives had identified with their fathers (since female figures were absent from the wives' Rorschach protocols) or alternatively that they had identified with aggressive mothers (since the female figures, if present in the Rorschach protocol, were aggressive). These wives competed with men, negated their own femininity, and were felt to have latent homosexual inclinations. The rapists felt their wives to be frigid and not sexually spontaneous or receptive. Often sexual frustration had preceded the rape. The wives were seen as stimulating sexual aggression in their husbands but then meeting this sexual aggression with rejection.

GANG RAPE

Blanchard (1959) speculated that homosexual factors play a part in gang (or multiple) rape. There tended to be eroticized adulation between the members of the group, a sharing of the girl among each other, and sexual stimulation taking place in a group setting, all of which pointed to homosexual underpinnings to the act. Blanchard studied the leaders of two groups of gang rapists and felt them to be quite sadistic.

SUMMARY

There has been at least one good sociological study of rapists and their victims, and it is possible to describe the modal offender, victim, and act of rape. Psychologically, the research has been quite poor. There has been a reliance on possibly invalid projective tests which makes an adequate description of the rapist quite difficult. In general, however, the rapist appears more like the nonsexual offender than any other group of sexual deviants. On psychological tests, the protocols of rapists usually do not differ from those of nonsexual criminals, and their sexual history appears to be normal. Their acts of rape appear to stem from their impulsiveness and their general criminal tendencies. Unfortunately, it appears that they may be attracted to women who exacerbate their conflicts and increase the stress that they are under by acting both seductive and rejecting.

REFERENCES

Amir, M.: *Patterns in Forcible Rape.* Chicago, U of Chicago Pr, 1971.
Blanchard, W.H.: The group process in gang rape. *J Soc Psychol, 49*:259-266, 1959.
Burton, A.: The use of the M-F scale of the MMPI as an aid in the diagnosis of sexual inversion. *J Psychol, 24*:161-164, 1947.
Chappell, D., Geis, G., Schafer, S., and Siegel, L.: Forcible rape. In Henslin, J. (Ed.): *Studies in the Sociology of Sex.* New York, Appleton, 1971, pp. 169-190.
Ferracuti, F., and Wolfgang, M.: The prediction of violent behavior. *Correct Psychiatry, 10*:289-301, 1964.
Gebhard, P.H., Gagnon, J.H., Pomeroy, W.B., and Christenson, C.V.: *Sex Offenders.* New York, Har-Row, 1965.
Goldner, N.S.: Rape as a heinous but understudied offense. *J Crim Law Criminol Police Sci, 63*:402-407, 1972.
Hammer, E.F.: Relationship between diagnosis of psychosexual pathology and the sex of the first drawn person. *J Clin Psychol, 10*:168-170, 1954a.
Hammer, E.F.: A comparison of H-T-P's of rapists and pedophiles. *J Proj Tech, 18*:346-354, 1954b.
Hammer, E.F.: A comparison of H-T-P's of rapists and pedophiles. *J Clin Psychol, 11*:67-68, 1955.
Hammer, E.F., and Jacks, I.: A study of Rorschach flexor and extensor human movement responses. *J Clin Psychol, 11*:63-67, 1955.
Henry, A., and Short, J.: *Suicide and Homicide.* Glencoe, Free Pr, 1954.
Hooton, E.: *Crime and the Man.* Cambridge, Harvard U Pr, 1939.
Kanin, E.J.: An examination of sexual aggression as a response to sexual frustration. *J Marr Family, 29*:428-433, 1967.
Kercher, G.A., and Walker, C.E.: Reactions of convicted rapists to sexually explicit stimuli. *J Abnorm Psychol, 81*:46-50, 1973.
Lester, D.: Rape and social structure. *Psychol Rep, 35*:146, 1974.
LeVine, R.A.: Gusii sex offenses. *Am Anthropol, 61*:965-990, 1959.
MacDonald, J.: *Rape.* Springfield, Thomas, 1971.
Palm, R., and Abrahamsen, D.: A Rorschach study of the wives of sex offenders. *J Nerv Ment Dis, 119*:167-172, 1954.
Pascal, G.R., and Herzberg, F.C.: The detection of deviant sexual practice from the Rorschach. *J Proj Tech, 16*:366-373, 1952.
Perdue, W.C., and Lester, D.: Personality characteristics of rapists. *Percept Mot Skills, 35*:514, 1972.
Svalastoga, K.: Rape and social structure. *Pac Sociol Rev, 5*:48-53, 1962.
Von Hentig, H.: *Crime.* New York, McGraw, 1947.

SECTION II

HOMOSEXUALITY

CHAPTER 6

GENETIC FACTORS IN HOMOSEXUALITY

THE INFLUENCE OF GENETIC FACTORS upon the development of sexual deviation has been explored in a variety of ways, some direct and others indirect. In the review that follows, the subjects are male unless it is stated to the contrary.

TWIN STUDIES

The basic study comparing monozygotic and dizygotic twins was reported by Kallman (1952) in which he found 100 percent concordance in monozygotic twins for homosexuality as compared to only 8 percent in dizygotic twins (where homosexuality was defined as a Kinsey rating of 3 to 6). Since then, only one other study has been reported (Heston and Shields, 1968), and this study used a much smaller sample than Kallman's. Nonetheless, Heston and Shields found two of five monozygotic twins concordant for homosexuality and one of seven dizygotic twins concordant. (Another one of the monozygotic twins exhibited a sexual deviation other than homosexuality.) This difference does not reach statistical significance. Heston and Shields reviewed foreign data and these supported the existence of a difference. Nine of fourteen monozygotic twin pairs were concordant while zero of seven dizygotic twin pairs were concordant (Fisher $p < 0.05$).

Kallman reported that the twins in his concordant monozygotic pairs developed their homosexual behavior independently of each other, although mutuality has been reported (Pardes, et al., 1967).

Mesnikoff, et al. (1963) suggested that it would be of interest to compare the homosexual and nonhomosexual twins in discordant twin pairs. However, their attempt to do this was methodologically inadequate.

CHROMOSOMAL STUDIES

Pare (1956) examined fifty male homosexuals, twenty-five female controls, and twenty-five male controls and found that all the homosexuals were male as defined by their chromosomes. There were no differences in the number of chromatin spots between the male homosexuals and the male controls, while both of these groups differed from the female controls. Pritchard (1962) studied six male homosexuals who had male chromosome patterns and found no autosomal aberrations.

Raboch and Nedoma (1958) compared male homosexuals with males who had a female type of chromatin. Most of the men with the female type of sex chromatin had hypoplastic testicles and a reduced volume of ejaculate. Only nine of the 194 homosexuals had hypoplastic testicles. The nuclear pattern of their sex chromosomes was found to be normally male.

Randell (1959) found the chromosomal structure of thirty-five male transvestites and transexuals to be normal, and Barr and Hobbs (1954) found a normal structure in five male transvestites. Hoenig and Torr (1964) studied ten male and three female transexuals and found their chromosomes to be normal. Many single cases of homosexuals and transvestites have been reported with normal chromosomes. No case of a homosexual, transvestite, or transexual with abnormal chromosomes has been reported in the literature.

SEXUAL DEVIATIONS AND KLINEFELTER'S SYNDROME

Money and Pollitt (1964) studied sixteen males with Klinefelter's syndrome (47,XXY) and found two to be transvestites, two others to be homosexuals, and one other to be an arsonist. They suggested that Klinefelter's syndrome might constitute a genotype with a disposition to defective psychosexual differentiation. (This might, of course, be related to the mental retardation and passive-dependent personality often found in males with Klinefelter's syndrome.)

Baker and Stoller (1968) reviewed forty cases from the literature and found a high incidence of a variety of psychosexual disturbances and deviations. (Although most of the cases reviewed by Baker and Stoller were Klinefelter's syndrome, some were hypogonadal as a result of other causes.)

Mosier, et al. (1960) compared Klinefelter's males with controls matched for intelligence and found that more sexual offenses had been committed by the Klinefelter's males. They also studied 600 sexual psychopaths and found that 1 percent gave a positive sex chromatin test, which Mosier, et al. felt to be indicative of Klinefelter's syndrome. These six males had normal hair, penis, scrotum, and prostate gland. There was no gynocomastia, a normal or low/normal 17-ketosteroid excretion rate, normal gonadotrophin excretion, and small but firm testes. Their bodies, however, were judged to enuchoid.

McKerracher (1971) claimed that among the criminally insane sexual offenses were more common in both males with XXY sex chromosomes and with XYY sex chromosomes. Sexual aggression, however, was not more common in these males.

SEX RATIO OF SIBLINGS

Kallman (1952) reported that male homosexuals had more brothers than sisters (and more so than controls). This finding was confirmed by Lang (1940) and Darke (1948). Kallman found no difference in the sex ratio of the siblings for homosexuals less than twenty-five years old as compared to those older than twenty-five. Lang, however, found the sex ratio of the siblings to be greater in the older homosexuals and for the unmarried homosexuals. Darke found the excess of male siblings to be statistically significant only for the older homosexuals and only when he included all homosexuals rather than only the exclusive homosexuals.

Darke found no significant excess of males among the half-siblings. Both Darke and Lang reported an excess of male half-siblings through the father and an excess of female half-siblings through the mother. Darke also examined the effect of active-passive homosexuality and anal-oral activity: passive anal homosexuals tended to have an excess of sisters whereas passive oral homosexuals had significantly more brothers.

Lang utilized a control group for the half-sibling data and found the sex ratio of the control siblings (107) to be less than that for the half-siblings of the homosexuals through the father (143) and greater than that for the half-siblings through the mother (93).

Lang argued that the excess of male siblings for homosexuals meant that some of the homosexuals were actually transformed females, who, had they not been transformed, would have made the sex ratio of the siblings normal. This is, of course, very indirect evidence for genetic factors in homosexuality.

There are several objections that can be made here. First, it is worth noting that many of the results reported above were not subjected to tests of statistical significance, and usually no control group was used. Furthermore, Morrow, et al. (1965) proved mathematically that any set of male children will have more brothers than sisters, and similarly any set of female children will have more sisters than brothers if the proportion of new or entirely unisexual families exceeds the expected proportion*. They found a sex ratio for siblings of male students of 125 which was significantly higher than the national average of 106.

Thus, the validity of Lang's method for measuring genetic factors in homosexuality is severely questioned by the data of Morrow, et al. However, it must be noted that the argument of Morrow, et al. does not account for the differences reported by Lang, Darke, and Kallman for old and young, anal and oral, passive and active, married and single homosexuals, nor those reported by Lang and Kallman for homosexuals versus controls.

James (1971) noted that Lang reported that the maternal half-siblings of homosexual males had more females while the paternal half-siblings of homosexual males had more males. James noted that this could be explained if (1) the offspring of broken marriages were more likely to live with the same sex parent, and (2) the half-siblings were sometimes unaware of one another if they were not living together. Thus, there was no necessity for a speculative genetic explanation. James noted that the use of control groups would eliminate this possibility. An alternative suggested by James was to compare young and old half-siblings. The effect reported by Lang would be found only for the older half-siblings if James' explanation is correct.

However, the original findings themselves have been questioned. Nash and Hayes (1965), for example, found no differences in the sex ratio of siblings of active and passive homo-

*Westoff and Rindfuss (1974) found unisexual families to be in excess of chance expectations in the United States.

sexuals in jail. It is clear that the research into these effects must be replicated with adequate methodology before confidence can be placed on the validity of the results. Even then, there may be alternative explanations for any phenomena so discovered.

As for the offspring of homosexuals, Lang (1940), Kallman (1952), and Hemphill, et al. (1958) found the sex ratio to be normal.

THE AGE OF THE PARENTS OF HOMOSEXUALS

Slater (1962) found that the mothers of male and female homosexuals were older than expected when the homosexuals were born. The homosexuals tended to be more often later-born. (Exhibitionists and transvestites did not differ in these two variables from the general population.) Kendrick and Clarke (1967) found that the fathers of male homosexual psychiatric patients were older than their wives and more so than the fathers of heterosexual normal controls. Evans (1972), however, found no differences between the ages of the mothers of homosexuals and heterosexuals in the community at the birth of their sons.

Data on the birth order of homosexuals and heterosexuals is somewhat relevant here and the research is reviewed in Chapter 8. Suffice it to say here that the research is quite inconclusive.

Abe and Moran (1969) took Slater's data and showed that even with better controls, the mothers of male homosexuals were older than chance expectations. However, they found also that the fathers of the male homosexuals were older than chance expectations, and more so than the mothers. They carried out a multiple regression analysis and concluded that the maternal age difference could be explained by regression on the paternal age but not vice versa. Thus, Abe and Moran concluded that the father's age was the critical factor. In addition, they showed that catchment area and social class were not confounding factors in this analysis.

The relevance of this to genetic factors is by implication. Older mothers are more likely to produce children with genetic abnormalities than younger mothers, as in Down's syndrome. Thus, if the parents of homosexuals are older than the average parents, then there may well be some genetic aberration in the homosexual offspring. Obviously, this evidence is very indirect.

SUMMARY

The data from twin studies supports the existence of genetic factors in homosexuality, but clearly the level of sophistication in the twin studies has not reached that of, say, twin studies in schizophrenia. Data from direct examination of chromosomes has proven that most, if not all, homosexuals have normal chromosomes as far as we can tell. Studies of males with Klinefelter's syndrome indicate a high incidence of psychosexual disturbance. Finally, data from the sex of siblings and parental age, although suggestive, is only indirectly related to the existence of genetic factors in homosexuality.

REFERENCES

Abe, K., and Moran, P.A.: Parental age of homosexuals. *Br J Psychiatry, 115*:313-317, 1969.

Baker, H.J., and Stoller, R.J.: Sexual psychopathology in the hypogonadal male. *Arch Gen Psychiatry, 18*:631-634, 1968.

Barr, M.L., and Hobbs, G.E.: Chromosomal sex in transvestites. *Lancet, 1*:1109, 1954.

Darke, R.A.: Heredity as an etiological factor in homosexuality. *J Nerv Ment Dis, 107*:251-268, 1948.

Evans, R.: Physical and biochemical characteristics of homosexual men. *J Consult Clin Psychol, 39*:140-147, 1972.

Hemphill, R., Leitch, A., and Stuart, J.: A factual study of homosexuality. *Br Med J, 1*:1317-1323, 1958.

Heston, L.L., and Shields, J.: Homosexuality in twins. *Arch Gen Psychiatry, 18*:149-160, 1968.

Hoenig, J., and Torr, J.: Karyotyping of transexualists. *J Psychosom Res, 8*:157-159, 1964.

James, W.H.: Sex ratios of half-sibs of male homosexuals. *Br J Psychiatry, 118*:93-94, 1971.

Kallman, F.J.: Twin and sibship study of overt male homosexuality. *Am J Hum Genet, 4*:136-146, 1952.

Kendrick, D., and Clarke, R.: Attitudinal differences between heterosexually and homosexually oriented males. *Br J Psychiatry, 113*:95-99, 1967.

Lang, T.: Studies in the genetic determination of homosexuality. *J Nerv Ment Dis, 92*:55-64, 1940.

McKerracher, D.: Psychological aspects of a sex chromatin abnormality. *Can Psychol, 12*:270-281, 1971.

Mesnikoff, A., Rainer, J.D., Kolb, L.C., and Carr, A.C.: Intra-familial determinants of divergent sexual behavior in twins. *Am J Psychiatry, 119*:732-738, 1963.

Money, J., and Pollitt, E.: Cytogenetic and psychosexual ambiguity. *Arch Gen Psychiatry, 11*:589-595, 1964.

Morrow, J.E., Cupp, M.E., and Sachs, L.B.: A possible explanation of the excessive brother-to-sister ratios reported in siblings of male homosexuals. *J Nerv Ment Dis, 140*:306-306, 1965.

Mosier, H.D., Scott, L.W., and Dingman, H.F.: Sexually deviant behavior in Klinefelter's syndrome. *J Pediatr, 57*:479-483, 1960.

Nash, J., and Hayes, F.: The parental relationships of male homosexuals. *Aust J Psychol, 17*:35-43, 1965.

Pardes, H., Steinberg, J., and Simons, R.C.: A rare case of overt and mutual homosexuality in female identical twins. *Psychiatr Q, 41*:108-133, 1967.

Pare, C.M.B.: Homosexuality and chromosomal sex. *J Psychosom Res, 1*:247-251, 1956.

Pritchard, M.: Homosexuality and genetic sex. *J Ment Sci, 108*:616-623, 1962.

Raboch, J., and Nedoma, K.: Sex chromatin and sexual behavior. *Psychosom Med, 20*:55-59, 1958.

Randell, J.B.: Transvestism and transexualism. *Br Med J, 2*:1448-1452, 1959.

Slater, E.: Birth order and maternal age of homosexuals. *Lancet, 1*:69-71, 1962.

Westoff, C., and Rindfuss, R.: Sex preselection in the United States. *Science, 184*:633-636, 1974.

CHAPTER 7

PHYSIOLOGICAL AND CONSTITUTIONAL STUDIES OF HOMOSEXUALITY

STUDIES OF PERSONS WITH HORMONAL ABNORMALITIES

Masculinized Females

EHRHARDT AND MONEY (1967) STUDIED TEN CASES OF PROGESTIN-INDUCED HERMAPHRODITISM IN GIRLS (caused by the mothers receiving progestin while pregnant). They had abnormal genitals but all were raised as females. In many psychological and behavioral traits, the girls behaved as tomboys (for example, athletic energy, playing with boy's toys). However, their behavior did not exclude conceptions of eventual romance, children, and home and family care.

In fifteen cases of early-treated adrenogenital syndrome (caused by excessive androgen manufactured by the fetus which masculinizes the external genitalia) in patients raised as girls, Ehrhardt, et al. (1968a) noted that these girls (whose average age was ten-and-one-half) were tomboys but had expectations of a normal female role. They were more interested in a career than a comparison group of normal girls and less interested in infant care.

Ehrhardt, et al. (1968b) studied twenty-three females with adrenogenital syndrome who were treated late in life. Their median age was twenty-eight with treatment begun at the median age of eighteen. Some 18 percent had had active homosexual experience and 48 percent had shown homosexual inclinations in dreams and fantasies. However, without a control group these figures were difficult to interpret. No case of exclusive lesbianism or transexualism was noted.

Delayed Puberty

Bobrow, et al. (1971) followed up thirteen males from childhood to adulthood who had delayed puberty (hypogonadotrophic hypogonadism) and who were treated with hormonal therapy. None reported homosexual fantasies, homosexual imagery, or repeated homosexual behavior before or after treatment. Two had had a single teenage homosexual experience but neither had the desire to repeat it.

Androgen Insensitivity

Two syndromes, Turner's syndrome (XO) and the testicular feminizing or androgen-insensitivity syndrome lead to babies born with female external genitals, the former having neither ovaries nor testes and the latter having testes which produce androgens and estrogens for a body that is sensitive only to estrogens. A sample of these girls, although sterile, had adopted a heterosexual orientation and had had no homosexual experiences or dreams (Masica, et al., 1971).

General Hermaphrodites

Money, et al., (1957) studied seventy-six hermaphrodites of various kinds and found that seventy-two of the seventy-six had adopted the gender role assigned to them at birth and with which they had been reared without difficulty. This occurred despite the fact that some of the gender-assigned males acted like "sissies" and some of the gender-assigned females were "tomboys" during their development (Money, 1971).

Effeminate Boys

Green and Money (1961) studied eleven boys with signs of effeminacy, and they noted that there was no evidence of effeminacy or overt homosexuality in their fathers. The parents did not report homosexual (or heterosexual) behavior in the boys; nor did the boys report any. However, the boys were still young when studied. The onset of symptoms was from ages. one-and-one-half to six with a median of five. The causes of this behavior have not been studied adequately and are not presently clear.

Precocious Puberty

Money and Alexander (1969) found homosexuality virtually

absent in a group of sexually precocious male children (both idiopathic sexual precocity and adrenal hyperplasia).

Conclusions

Money noted that there were nine variables involved here: assigned sex and sex of rearing, external genital morphology, internal accessory reproductive structures, pubertal hormones, fetal hormones, gonadal variables, chromosomal variables, neural (hypothalamic) variables, and gender role.

Money argued that the gender role was primarily established by the assigned sex and sex of rearing with minimal inputs from the other variables. He also espoused a kind of imprinting theory in which the gender role was determined by experiences in the first two years of life.* For example, Money, et al. (1957) noted that sex reassignment by edict was usually psychologically possible without psychological damage if the child was less than two years old, but not if the child was older. (Zuger [1970] found the evidence for this wanting, although not contradictory.)

MORPHOLOGICAL STUDIES

Old studies claimed that homosexuals had different morphology from heterosexuals. For example, Henry and Galbraith (1934) claimed that male homosexuals had feminine carriage of their arms; large muscles; deficient hair on their face, chest, and back; a high-pitched voice; small penis and testicles; and a scrotal fold. They supposedly had softer fat in greater amounts on their shoulders, abdomen, and buttocks. Henry and Galbraith noted, however, that some male homosexuals had abnormally large penises. Henry and Galbraith found no differences in shoulder-hip and leg-torso measurements but claimed that homosexuals showed more variation in these measurements than heterosexuals.

Barahal (1939) compared homosexual psychiatric patients to other psychiatric patients and found no differences in height, weight, arm span, or in the measurements of torso, leg, shoulder, or hip. However, he claimed that a female distribution of pubic hair was more common in the homosexuals (40 percent versus 29 percent) and that their facial hair was more scanty (24 percent versus 17 percent).

*The signs that determine the gender role include pronouns differentiating gender, hair cut, dress, etc.

More recent studies continue to suggest that there are differences in morphology of homosexuals, even though the differences are not as extreme or so crude as suggested by the earlier studies. For example, Evans (1972) found that homosexual males in the community were more linear, less muscular, and had less fat on Parnell's body-typing system than heterosexual males in the community. Thus, homosexual males are more ectomorphic. The homosexuals were less broad-shouldered and had less muscular strength. Spencer (1959) found no differences in Sheldonian typology between homosexual and heterosexual college students.

Housden (1965) reviewed cases of transvestites in the literature and found that of thirty-six cases, four were judged to have feminine physique, one was judged to have a feminine body hair distribution, and one was judged to have a feminine facial hair distribution. Two were judged to have abnormal endocrine performance, although none had gynocomastia or abnormal sexual organs. Housden noted that one cannot rule out the possibility of self-administered hormonal therapy in these cases.

Although morphological differences are still found occasionally, many reports are conflicting or report no differences. Gibbens (1957) found that homosexual delinquents were more likely to be endomorphs than heterosexual delinquents, but his samples were small. Coppen (1959) looked at homosexual and heterosexual psychiatric patients and normals and found that there were no differences in the fat-bone index or height-weight ratios. The homosexuals had a lower biacromial diameter but so did the heterosexual psychiatric patients. Thus, although the androgyny scores (thrice the biacromial diameter minus the bi-iliac distance) were lower in the homosexuals, Coppen concluded that it was the psychiatric disturbance rather than the homosexuality that was responsible for the difference. (Coppen found no differences between homosexuals with and without psychiatric symptoms.)

Hemphill, et al. (1958) found enlarged breasts in 3 percent of a sample of male homosexual prisoners, abnormal testes in 3 percent, and a female distribution of pubic hair in 6 percent. Hoenig and Torr (1964) found no evidence of hermaphrodism or any other physical abnormality in ten male and three female homosexuals, and Kolodny, et al. (1971) found that homosexual and heterosexual males in the community did not differ in testicular size or texture or in secondary sex characteristics. Braaten and Darling (1965) found no differences in physical appearance between homosexual and nonhomosexual college students seen at a counseling center, but the homosexual students did have more effeminate gestures.

BIOCHEMICAL STUDIES

Sex Hormone Studies

Neustadt and Myerson (1940) studied the urine excretion of androgens and estrogens in male homosexuals (obtained from private practice and a state hospital). They compared the data to norms rather than a control group. They reported that twenty-five of the twenty-nine homosexuals had a low level of androgen excretion and a high level of estrogen excretion. They also reported that a small sample of impotent males had low excretion rates of both, while a small sample of chronic masturbators had a high level of excretion of both. A later report (Myerson and Neustadt, 1942) confirmed this earlier report.

Wright (1935, 1941) reported low testosterone levels in a sample of jailed homosexuals (again without looking at a control group) and high estrogen and gonadotrophin levels. Wright, throughout his studies, claimed to find endocrine abnormalities in all sexual deviants, but his data presentation and methodology were usually quite poor. In a study that employed a control group, Glass, et al. (1940) did find a lower androgen/estrogen ratio in jailed homosexuals, although Kinsey (1941) attacked both their laboratory technique and statistical analyses.

Sevringhaus and Chornyak (1945) studied overt male homosexuals and controls and found that some 50 percent of the homosexuals showed no gonadotrophic hormone in their urine as compared to 0 percent of the controls. There were no differences in the excretion of 17-ketosteroids (although the homosexuals might have shown greater variability).

Garst and Stobin (1955) compared sex offenders to medical students and found no differences in 17-ketosteroid excretion, nor in day-to-night excretion ratios. There were no differences between aggressive and nonaggressive sex offenders. There were also no differences in the ratio of alph to beta 17-ketosteroids.

It has been customary to dismiss these older studies and to claim that their methods of estimating the critical chemical substances are too crude to be reliable. However, more recent studies continue to report differences.

Margolese (1970) found that the 17-ketosteroid level excreted by overt male homosexuals was normal in nine of the ten male homosexuals he studied. However, the ratio of androsterone to etiocholanolone was less than 1.4 in the homosexuals and greater than 1.4 in the heterosexual controls. Margolese noted that four heterosexuals in poor health (with diabetes and depression) had ratios similar to those of the homosexuals.

Kolodny, et al. (1971) compared male homosexuals in the community with heterosexual controls and found that the mean levels of plasma testosterone were lower in the homosexuals. Some 13 percent of the homosexuals were azoospermic, and the higher the Kinsey rating the lower the sperm count. From buccal-smear examinations, all the homosexuals were judged to be males, although no karyotyping was done.

Loraine, et al. (1970) studied three male homosexuals and found low testosterone levels but normal luteinizing hormone levels. Evans (1972) compared male homosexuals and heterosexuals in the community and found no differences in the 17-ketosteroid levels (products of androgen metabolism) or estrogen levels. The homosexuals had lower levels of creatinine (an index of the amount of active muscle), a lower androsterone-etiocholanolone ratio, lower levels of 17-ketogenic steroids (metabolites of hydrocortisone, reflecting adreno-cortical activity), and many differences in blood serum lipids (such as cholesterol and lipoproteins).

Doerr, et al. (1973) compared homosexuals and heterosexuals and found no differences in the plasma testosterone level, even when the Kinsey rating, activity-passivity, and orgasm frequency were taken into account. However, the homosexuals did have higher estradiol levels. (The estradiol level was not related to the Kinsey rating, activity-passivity, or orgasm frequency.) No differences were found in sperm count, sperm motility, sperm morphology, and the initial fructose concentration of the ejaculate.

Hemphill, et al. (1958) studied male homosexual prisoners without controls and found no abnormalities in the ketosteroid output or the androgen-estrogen ratio.

Dewhurst (1969) studied one homosexual and found no relationship between sexual activity over a ninety-day period (all by masturbation) and the excretion of estrone (an estrogen) in the urine, even if the data were lagged. The length of the cycle of steroid excretion was similar to heterosexual male controls. It is of interest to note that patients with cyclic changes of sexual orientation have been noted (for example, Lief, et al., 1962).

The different reports are clearly most inconsistent in their findings, and the reasons for these inconsistencies are by no means clear at the present time.

In a similar fashion, reports from before the Second World War on the effects of castration and hormone therapy on homosexuality (and other sexual deviations) were similarly inconsistent, although diagnosis (Hackfield, 1935) and the degree of establishment of the sexual choice (Rosenzweig and Hoskins, 1941) were suggested as mediating factors.

Other Studies

Rosanoff and Murphy (1944) found no differences between male homosexuals and norms in basal metabolic rate, fasting blood sugar levels, glucose tolerance tests, and X-ray lateral views of skull to measure pituitary fossae.

Marsh, et al. (1954) studied sexual deviants and looked at the rennin inhibitor concentration in blood serum analyses. For minor sex offenders (undefined) there was less change under stress, but the concentrations were abnormal (age did not affect this result). For the more deviant sex offenders (again undefined) the rennin concentrations were also abnormal. No control subjects were analysed.

Williams (1944) injected prostigmine into males and noted the drop in serum cholinesterase activity. Using addicts from a federal penitentiary, he found that active homosexuals and heterosexuals (and heterosexual nonaddicts) almost all showed a drop, while passive homosexuals did not show a drop. Williams noted, however, that lack of a drop was not characteristic of females.

Selling (1938) claimed that glandular disease was uncommon in sex offenders.

THE CENTRAL NERVOUS SYSTEM

Silverman and Rosanoff (1945) reported finding abnormal EEG patterns in 75 percent of homosexuals in a federal penitentiary but failed to utilize a control group.

Many authors have speculated upon a possible relationship between brain damage, and in particular temporal lobe damage, and sexuality. Cases have been reported in fetishists and transvestites (for example, Ball, 1968). Mitchell, et al. (1954) reported a case in which viewing the fetish triggered a temporal lobe seizure. Hooshmand and Brawley (1969) felt that some automatic behavior seen in patients with temporal lobe seizures resembled exhibitionism. Newnham (1966) reported a case of pedophilia that seemed to be associated with a fronto-parietal tumor.

It is interesting to note that homosexuality has not been seen as associated with brain damage in the same way as these other sexual deviations.

SUMMARY

In contrast to the reports of many secondary sources, there is a good deal of evidence for the existence of physiological differences between homosexuals and heterosexuals, particularly in physique and endocrine function. However, it may be that the physiological differences are not responsible for the sexual orientation. As Kolodny, et al. (1971) have suggested, the physiological differences could be a result of psychological factors (and we might add actual sexual activity) via some mechanism not presently clear. It may also be that many homosexuals take drugs that affect the physiology of their body.

Whatever the explanation of these differences, it cannot be maintained in the light of current knowledge that no differences exist. However, a good deal of research is needed to check upon the reliability of the differences and their causes.

REFERENCES

Ball, J.: A case of hair fetishism, transvestism and organic cerebral disorder. *Acta Psychiatr Scand, 44*:249-254, 1968.

Barahal, H.S.: Constitutional factors in male homosexuals. *Psychiatr Q, 13*:391-400, 1939.

Borrow, N.A., Money, J., and Lewis, V.G.: Delayed puberty, eroticism and sense of smell. *Arch Sex Behav, 1*:329-344, 1971.

Braaten, L., and Darling, C.: Overt and covert homosexual problems among male college students. *Genet Psychol Monogr, 71*:269-310, 1965.

Coppen, A.J.: Body-build of male homosexuals. *Br Med J, 2*:1443-1445, 1959.

Dewhurst, K.: Sexual activity and urinary-steroids in man with special reference to male homosexuality. *Br J Psychiatry, 115*:1413-1415, 1969.

Doerr, P., Kockott, G., Vogt, H., Pirke, K., and Dittmar, F.: Plasma testosterone, estradiol, and semen analysis in male homosexuals. *Arch Gen Psychiatry, 29*:829-833, 1973.

Ehrhardt, A., Epstein, R., and Money, J.: Fetal androgens and female gender identity in the early treated adrenogenital syndrome. *Johns Hopkins Med J, 122*:160-167, 1968a.

Ehrhardt, A., Evers, K., and Money, J.: Influence of androgen and some aspects of sexually dimorphic behavior in women with the late-treated adrenogenital syndrome. *Johns Hopkins Med J, 122*:115-122, 1968b.

Ehrhardt, A., and Money, J.: Progestin-induced hermaphroditism. *J Sex Res, 3*:83-100, 1967.

Evans, R.B.: Physical and biochemical characteristics of homosexual men. *J Consult Clin Psychol, 39*:140-147, 1972.

Garst, J.B., and Stobin, E.K.: Trends in the 17-ketosteroid excretion of male sex offenders. *Arch Neurol Psychiatry, 74*:125-130, 1955.

Gibbens, T.C.N.: The sexual behavior of young criminals. *J Ment Sci, 103*:527-540, 1957.

Glass, S.J., Duel, H.J., and Wright, C.A.: Sex hormone studies in male homosexuality. *Endocrinology, 26*:590-594, 1940.

Green, R., and Money, J.: Effeminacy in prepubertal boys. *Pediatrics, 27*:286-291, 1961.

Hackfield, A.: The ameliorative effects of therapeutic castration in habitual sex offenders. *J Nerv Ment Dis, 82*:15-29, 1935.

Hemphill, R., Leitch, A., and Stuart, J.: A factual study of homosexuality. *Br Med J, 1*:1317-1323, 1958.

Henry, G.W., and Galbraith, H.M.: Constitutional factors in homosexuality. *Am J Psychiatry, 13*:1249-1270, 1934.

Hoenig, J., and Torr, J.B.D.: Karyotyping of transexualists. *J Psychosom Res, 8*:157-159, 1964.

Hooshmand, H., and Brawley, B.W.: Temporal lobe seizures and exhibitionism. *Neurology (Minneap), 19*:1119-1124, 1969.

Housden, J.: An examination of the biologic etiology of transvestism. *Int J Soc Psychiatry, 11*:301-305, 1965.

Kinsey, A.: Homosexuality. *J Clin Endocrinol Metab, 1*:424-428, 1941.

Kolodny, R., Masters, W., Hendryx, J., and Toro, G.: Plasma testosterone and semen analysis in male homosexuals. *N Engl J Med, 285*:1170-1174, 1971.

Lief, H., Dingman, J., and Bishop, M.: Psychoendocrinological studies in a male with cyclical changes in sexuality. *Psychosom Med, 24*:357-368, 1962.

Loraine, J., Ismail, A., Adamopoulos, D., and Dore, G.: Endocrine function in male and female homosexuals. *Br Med J, 4*:406-409, 1970.

Margolese, M.S.: Homosexuality. *Horm Behav, 1*:151-155, 1970.

Marsh, J., Hilliard, J., and Liechti, R.: Proteolytic enzyme system in sexual deviates. *Arch Neurol Psychiatry, 72*:341-347, 1954.

Masica, D., Money, J., and Ehrhardt, A.: Fetal feminization and female gender identity in the testicular feminizing syndrome of androgen insensitivity. *Arch Sex Behav, 1*:131-142, 1971.

Mitchell, W., Falconer, M., and Hill, D.: Epilepsy with fetishism relieved by temporal lobe lobectomy. *Lancet, 2*:626-630, 1954.

Money, J.: Differentiation of gender identity and gender role. *Psychiatr Ann, 1*:44-49, 1971.

Money, J., and Alexander, D.: Psychosexual development and absence of homosexuality in males with precocious puberty. *J Nerv Ment Dis, 148*:111-123, 1969.

Money, J., Hampson, J., and Hampson, J.: Imprinting and the establishment of gender role. *Arch Neurol Psychiatry, 77*:333-336, 1957.

Myerson, A., and Neustadt, R.: Bisexuality and male homosexuality. *Clinics, 1*:932-957, 1942.

Neustadt, R., and Myerson, A.: Quantitative sex hormone studies in homosexuality, childhood and various neuropsychiatric disturbances. *Am J Psychiatry, 97*:524-551, 1940.

Newnham, W.H.: Sexual perversion associated with cerebral tumor. *Int J Neuropsychiatry, 2*:633-636, 1966.

Rosanoff, W.R., and Murphy, F.E.: The basal metabolic rate, fasting blood sugar, glucose tolerance, and size of the Sella Turcica in homosexualss. *Am J Psychiatry, 101*:97-99, 1944.

Rosenzweig, S., and Hoskins, R.: A note on the ineffectualness of sex-hormone medication in a case of pronounced homosexuality. *Psychosom Med, 3*:87-89, 1941.

Selling, L.S.: The endocrine glands and the sex offender. *Med Rec, 147*:441-444, 1938.

Sevringhaus, E.L., and Chornyak, J.: Homosexual adult males. *Psychosom Med, 7*:302-305, 1945.

Silverman, D., and Rosanoff, W.R.: Electroencephalographic and neurological studies of homosexuals. *J Nerv Ment Dis. 101*:311-321, 1945.

Spencer, S.: Homosexuality among Oxford undergraduates. *J Ment Sci,* *105*:393-405, 1959.

Williams, E.G.: Homosexuality. *J Nerv Ment Dis, 99*:65-70, 1944.

Wright, C.A.: Endocrine aspects of homosexuality. *Med Rec, 142*:407-410, 1935.

Wright, C.A.: Results of endocrine treatment in a controlled group of homosexual men. *Med Rec, 154*:60-61, 1941.

Zuger, B.: Gender role determination. *Psychosom Med, 32*:449-468, 1970.

CHAPTER 8

THE CHILDHOODS OF HOMOSEXUALS

ALTHOUGH A GOOD DEAL OF RESEARCH HAS BEEN CONDUCTED on the parents of homosexuals (see Ch. 9), very little research has been conducted on the childhoods of homosexuals. A few studies have looked at data which can be easily obtained, such as sibling position and sibship composition, and a few studies have asked the homosexual about his childhood.

What would be ideal in this area would be studies of children, with a subsequent follow-up study to compare those becoming homosexual and those becoming heterosexual. The only study of this type has been reported by McCord, et al. (1962) and is discussed below. A number of papers have been published on boys who behave effeminately (for example, Green and Money, 1961), but as yet no follow-up studies on these boys have appeared. Furthermore, since most investigators of effeminate boys view the "effeminacy" as a problem, therapy is usually instituted for these boys and so the follow-up studies will not be very useful for finding antecedents for sexual-object choice and gender-role choice.

FAMILY CONSTELLATION

Siegelman (1973) has reviewed the many studies that report birth order data, and he noted that the reports are quite inconsistent in their findings.

With respect to family size, two studies report no differences in the number of brothers of male homosexuals and heterosexuals, two report no differences in the number of sisters, and one reports no difference in whether the subject has an older brother or sister. Similar results are found for female homosexuals: two studies report no differences in the number of siblings, three studies report no differences in the number of sisters, while one study reports that the homosexuals had more sisters, one study reports no differences in the number of younger brothers and sisters, and one final study reports that homosexuals have fewer older brothers and sisters.

Siegelman (1973) in a study of male and female homosexuals and heterosexuals in the community found no consistent difference in the number and kind of siblings.*

With respect to birth order, five studies report no differences between male homosexuals and heterosexuals in sibling position, five report that homosexuals are more likely to be the youngest child, one that they are more likely to be an only child, and one that they are less likely to be an only child. For females, one study found no differences, three report that female homosexuals are more likely to be only children, one that they are more likely to be the youngest, one that they are more likely to be the youngest or the oldest, and one that in small families they are more likely to be the oldest whereas in large families they are more likely to be the youngest.

Again, Siegelman (1973) using nonclinical samples of male and female homosexuals and heterosexuals found no consistent differences.

The sex ratio of the siblings of homosexuals has been discussed in Chapter 6, where it was noted that the use of such data to throw light on possible genetic influences in homosexuality was probably quite invalid. It was noted, however, that there was some evidence that differences existed in the sex ratio of the siblings of sexual deviants. Many studies report no differences. For example, O'Connor (1964) found no differences between homosexuals and neurotic males in the Air Force, and Kendrick and Clarke (1967) found no differences between male homosexual psychiatric patients and heterosexual normals. However, other studies find striking differences. For example, Spencer (1959), studying college males, found no differences between homosexuals and heterosexuals who were psychiatric patients, but the nonclinical homosexuals had a sex ratio for their siblings of 170 whereas the homosexual psychiatric patients had a sex ratio of only 95.

Gebhard, et al. (1965) found wide variations in the sex ratio of the siblings of various kinds of sexual offenders. The sex ratio

---

*With the exception of an inconsistent tendency for the male homosexuals to have more sisters.

was lowest for heterosexual aggressors and highest for voyeurs and incest offenders against children. Lack of sisters also varied widely among the different offender groups, with homosexual offenders and voyeurs most often lacking sisters and heterosexual offenders against children and minors least often lacking sisters. Lack of brothers was least common in incest offenders against minors and adults and most common in homosexual offenders against adults.*

It should be noted that Gebhard, et al. did not carry out statistical tests on their data, but, be that as it may, it is difficult to identify meaningful trends over the different offender groups.

RELATIONS WITH SIBLINGS

In Bieber's (1962) study of homosexuals and heterosexuals in psychoanalysis, the psychoanalysts reported that the homosexuals were more often their mother's favorite while a sibling was more often the father's favorite. The homosexuals disliked their brothers and admired their sisters more, and they more often wished to be like a sibling (and more often a brother than a sister). The homosexuals had more homosexual siblings, but the homosexuals and heterosexuals did not differ in the number of siblings seeking psychiatric treatment.

Stephan (1973) compared homosexual males in a homophile university group with students in an introductory psychology course and found that the homosexuals had been closer to their sisters in childhood but did not differ with respect to their brothers. Lewis and Schoenfeldt (1973) found that homosexual males in an activist group had experienced more sibling friction than male freshmen.

HOMOSEXUALS AS CHILDREN

Bieber's (1962) study of male homosexuals and heterosexuals in psychoanalysis revealed that the homosexuals were reported by their psychoanalysts to have been more dependent as children, less social, more effeminate and less aggressive, and to have wanted to be female more often.

Thompson, et al. (1973) found that male homosexuals in the community had more feminine interests as children and more

---

*The sibling position of heterosexual offenders, incest offenders, homosexual offenders, voyeurs, and exhibitionists was as expected, but heterosexual aggressors tended to middle born less often than expected. The number of siblings varied widely from an average of 3.5 for heterosexual aggressors against children to 6.1 for incest offenders against adults.

doubts about their bodies as compared to male heterosexuals. The female homosexuals had more often been tomboys than the female heterosexuals.

Evans (1969) compared male homosexuals in a homophile organization with volunteers for a cardiovascular disease study and found that the homosexuals described themselves as more frail, more clumsy, less athletic, more often loners, more often avoiding fights, and more often playing with girls in childhood. Evans felt that his results replicated those of Bieber using a nonclinical sample and self-report rather than reconstruction by a psychoanalyst.

Stephan (1973), in his comparison of male homosexuals in a university homophile association with introductory psychology students, found that the homosexuals were more socially isolated as children, more feminine, rejected more by male peers, and had more female friends. (Incidentally, they had had homosexual experiences earlier and orgasms earlier than the heterosexuals, and their heterosexual experiences were less often enjoyable. There were no differences in the age of puberty.)

Spencer (1959), studying male undergraduates, found no differences in psychiatric patients between homosexuals and heterosexuals in experience of day versus boarding school. However, in the nonclinical sample, the homosexuals had been to boarding school more.

McCord, et al. (1962) in a study of sexually deviant and nondeviant adolescents found that the feminine/homosexual boys were more often viewed as "oddballs," were more unfavorably compared with peers, and were more often judged to have neurological disorders. The perverted boys (meaning those who engaged in other sexual deviations) were more often found to have had early heterosexual experiences.

The sexually deviant boys had more abnormal fears, more sexual anxiety, more grandiose fantasies, more suicidal tendencies, and more sado-masochistic traits. The feminine/homosexual boys more often had inferiority feelings, excaped from frustrating situations, wet their beds, and disliked both parents.

Incidentally, in a follow-up study, the sexually deviant and nondeviant boys did not differ in the incidence of alcoholism, psychiatric admissions, and nonsexual crimes, but the deviant boys had committed more sexual offenses (11 percent of them had done so versus 6 percent of the nondeviant boys).

In Green and Money's (1961) study of effeminate boys, there were no reports or complaints of homosexual play or homosexual experiences in the boys and no signs of overt homosexuality or effeminacy in their fathers.

SUMMARY

The studies reviewed in this chapter do no more than point to some potentially interesting areas for future research. Furthermore, if the future research is to be meaningful, it must move from an examination of distal variables (such as sibling position and reports of childhood experiences) to an examination of proximal variables, such as the study of children prior to pubertal sexual choices (and without so-called therapeutic interference), and the study of homosexuals and heterosexuals interacting with their siblings and parents in laboratory situations where careful observation of the social interactions can take place.

REFERENCES

Bieber, I.: *Homosexuality*. New York, Basic, 1962.

Evans, R.: Childhood parental relationships of homosexual men. *J Consult Clin Psychol, 33*:129-135, 1969.

Gebhard, P., Gagnon, J., Pomeroy, W., and Christenson, C.: *Sex Offenders*. New York, Har-Row, 1965.

Green, R., and Money, J.: Effeminacy in prepubertal boys. *Pediatrics, 27*:286-291, 1961.

Kendrick, D., and Clarke, R.: Attitudinal differences between heterosexually and homosexually oriented males. *Br J Psychiatry, 113*:95-99, 1967.

Lewis, M., and Schoenfeldt, L.: Developmental-interest factors associated with homosexuality. *J Consult Clin Psychol, 41*:291-293, 1973.

McCord, W., McCord, J., and Verden, P.: Family relationships and sexual deviance in lower class adolescents. *Int J Soc Psychiatry, 8*:165-179, 1962.

O'Connor, P.: Aetiological factors in homosexuality as seen in Royal Air Force psychiatric practice. *Br J Psychiatry, 110*:381-391, 1964.

Siegelman, M.: Birth order and family size of homosexual men and women. *J Consult Clin Psychol, 41*:164, 1973.

Spencer, S.: Homosexuality among Oxford undergraduates. *J Ment Sci, 105*:393-405, 1959.

Stephan, W.: Parental relationships and early social experiences of activist male homosexuals and male heterosexuals. *J Abnorm Psychol, 82*:506-513, 1973.

Thompson, N., Schwartz, D., McCandless, B., and Edwards, D.: Parent-child relationships and sexual identity in male and female homosexuals and heterosexuals. *J Consult Clin Psychol, 41*:120-127, 1973.

CHAPTER 9

THE PARENTS OF HOMOSEXUALS

THERE HAVE BEEN A NUMBER OF STUDIES of the parents of homosexuals and the results have been, on the whole, strongly indicative of characteristic parent-child relationships and parental qualities. It is difficult to review the studies, however, because the studies have usually explored large numbers of variables. For example, the study by Bieber (1962) explored seventy variables relevant to the mother-son relationship. To report the findings in detail would bore the reader and present too much data for easy digestion. On the other hand, to summarize the findings of each study briefly is to fail to do justice to the studies. However, I shall adopt the latter approach, and the reader must consult the original reports if he wants a more detailed exposition of the results.

PARENTAL LOSS

Moran and Abe (1969) examined psychiatric patients and found no differences in the incidence of parental loss, comparing the homosexual with the chance incidence for the general population.

Greenstein (1966) compared delinquent boys with and without fathers and found no differences in overt homosexual behavior, in TAT or Rorschach indices of homosexuality, or in scores on the MMPI *Mf* scale. Social workers rated the fathers of those boys who had fathers, and no association was noted between father dominance and homosexuality in the boys. However, the closer the fathers were to the boys, the more likely overt homosexuality was to be found in the boys and the more likely homosexual signs were to be present in the Rorschach protocol. (However, father closeness was not associated with homosexual signs on the TAT or scores on the MMPI *Mf* scale.) Greenstein concluded that his study gave little support for theories of homosexuality that stress problems in identification with the father.

Bieber (1962) compared homosexual and heterosexual males in psychoanalysis and found that the psychoanalysts reported a greater incidence of absent fathers in the childhoods of the homosexuals. McCord, et al. (1962) in their study of sexually deviant and nondeviant adolescents found that the feminine/homosexual boys had more often had an absent father. Stephan (1973) compared homosexuals in a university association with students in an introductory course on psychology and found that the homosexuals had more father absences due both to death and divorce.

The studies clearly contradict one another, and it is not readily apparent at the present time where the source of these contradictions lies.

IDENTIFICATION

Chang and Block (1960) had homosexual and heterosexual males in the community rate themselves, their ideal selves, their mothers, and their fathers on an adjective checklist. By looking at the correspondences between these ratings, Chang and Block decided that the homosexuals had a stronger identification with their mothers than with their fathers and a stronger identification with their mothers than the heterosexuals had with their mothers. (The weaker identification of homosexuals with their fathers was almost statistically significant, too.)

Krieger and Worschel (1960) performed a similar study using a small group of homosexuals of both sexes and neurotic and normal control groups. Rather than having the subjects rate their mothers and fathers, however, the investigators had the subjects rate the "father as seen by himself" and the "mother as seen by herself," a procedure which appears to be less appropriate for a test of identification. The results indicated no significant differences between the groups in their identification with either parent, but the tendency was for the homosexuals to identify more with the same sex parent and for the neurotics and normals to identify more with the opposite sex parent.

Thompson, et al. (1973) had male and female homosexuals in the community rate themselves, their mothers, and their fathers on the Semantic Differential. The heterosexuals saw themselves as more similar to the same sex parent than the opposite sex parent, but there were no significant differences for the homosexuals. Thompson, et al. concluded that the homosexuals seemed alienated. A similar pattern of results was obtained for ratings of similarity to the concepts of the two biological sexes.

FAMILIES THAT PRODUCE HOMOSEXUALS

Few studies have taken different kinds of families and explored the incidence of homosexual offspring (as opposed to taking samples of homosexuals and heterosexuals and looking back at the families). Two minor studies have appeared which do utilize this different methodology.

Opler (1957) compared Irish-American and Italian-American schizophrenics and noted that overt homosexuality was much more common in the Italian-Americans whereas latent homosexuality was much more common in the Irish-Americans. Opler attributed these results to the traditional differences in the Irish and Italian family interaction patterns and sex roles.

Kearney and Taylor (1969) studied boys who had alcoholic parents and found that the boys showed a great deal of acting-out behavior. Their behavior tended to be impulsive and uncontrolled. Two of the twenty boys were homosexuals, one was a murderer, four had attempted suicide, and eight had been arrested. However, the incidence of homosexuality does not seem unduly high and obviously cannot be assessed without the presence of data from a control group.

The Parents of Homosexuals

Bieber (1962) gave questionnaires to the psychoanalysts of a large number of male homosexuals and heterosexuals and had the psychoanalysts rate the mothers and fathers of the subjects for some seventy items. Twenty-seven of the seventy items differentiated the mothers, and Bieber concluded that the mothers of the homosexuals were more often close-binding and intimate, less often controlling and dominating, and less often remarkable. Twenty of the items differentiated the fathers, and Bieber concluded that the fathers of the homosexuals were more often detached and more often hostile and indifferent.

Evans (1969) gave homosexual and heterosexual males in the community a short questionnaire based on that used by Bieber. His results supported those of Bieber. The homosexual males saw their mothers more as being puritanical, being cold toward men, insisting upon being the center of the son's attention, making him her confidant, being seductive toward him, allying with him against the father, interfering with his heterosexual activities during adolescence, discouraging masculine attitudes, and encouraging feminine attitudes. The fathers of the homosexuals were seen in retrospect as less likely to encourage masculine attitudes and activities, spending little time with their son and less often being accepted by him. The homosexuals hated their fathers more, were afraid more that their fathers would harm them, were less likely to accept or respect their fathers, and were less often his favorite child. Evans found no relationship between the responses of the homosexuals and their Kinsey rating of the degree of homosexuality. The homosexuals from better family backgrounds did, however, consider themselves as more masculine.

Mosberg, et al. (1969) compared homosexuals and heterosexuals in military service on their responses to a questionnaire based on Bieber's one. The mothers of the homosexuals were seen by their sons as more controlling, closer to their sons, and more often strong. The family relationships provided a negative model for the son and gave little satisfaction to the parents. The mother was more persuasive and powerful in the triad. The homosexual sons had a poor relationship with their fathers, and the father was more rejecting and detached.

Ullman (1960) studied a group of sexually deviant and nondeviant criminals and found no differences in family structure, residential background, economic status, and personality characteristics. He had the men rate their mothers and fathers for maintenance behavior and training behavior. In all of the comparisons, the rapists, pedophiles, and sexual psychopaths did not differ from the controls in the ratings of their parents. But the homosexuals rated their mothers as relatively harsh, hostile, and critical in their training behavior and relatively unfriendly and unloving in their maintenance behavior. (The homosexuals did not view their mothers differently from the controls in their indulgence.) The homosexuals also rated their fathers as deficient in positive feelings in their maintenance behavior; for example, the fathers of the homosexuals played less with their sons and gave them less love and attention.

West (1959) compared homosexual and heterosexual psychiatric patients and rated their relationships with their parents on two dimensions. He found that the mother-son relationship of the homosexuals was more intense and the father-son relationship of the homosexuals was more unsatisfactory as compared to the parent-child relationships of the heterosexuals. The homosexuals were more likely to have both of these characteristics.

McCord, et al. (1962) compared adolescent boys who were feminine/homosexual, perverted (that is, engaged in other kinds of sexual deviations), repressed, and normal. They found that the mothers of the sexually deviant boys in general were more often authoritarian and sexually anxious while the fathers were more often punitive. The fathers of the feminine/homosexual boys were more often rejecting, grandiose, psychiatrically disturbed, and aggressive; the mothers were also more psychologically disturbed, and the parents used threats more often with their sons. The perverted boys, on the other hand, had mothers who strongly encouraged dependency behavior and had fathers who drank to excess and who were sexually promiscuous. The parents of the repressed deviants were not characterized by any special qualities.

Thompson, et al. (1973) gave male and female heterosexuals and homosexuals in the community a parent-child interaction questionnaire and found that the male homosexual pattern was one of rejection by the father and seduction by the mother. The male homosexuals also rejected their own fathers more. (The female homosexual pattern was of overacceptance by the father and rejection by the mother; the female homosexuals also rejected their fathers more.)

O'Connor (1964) found that homosexuals in the Air Force had more often had foster parents than neurotics in the Air Force. Greater attachment to the mother than to the father was more common in the homosexuals. The homosexuals had poorer relationships with the father and had absent fathers more often. Kendrick and Clarke (1967) compared male homosexual patients with normal heterosexuals and found no differences in the incidence of broken homes or strict upbringings. Spencer (1959) studied college males and found no differences in the incidence of broken homes, disharmony between the parents, or in disturbed relationships with the father both for normal and psychiatric patient samples. However, for the psychiatric patients only, the homosexuals did have more disturbed relationships with the mother. Lewis and Schoenfeldt (1973) compared male homosexuals in an activist group with male freshmen and found no differences in the warmth of the parental relationship or in parental control over their sons.

Stephan (1973) compared male homosexuals in a university association with male students in an introductory psychology course and found that the homosexuals had been rejected more by distant and hostile fathers who were less encouraging of masculine behavior in their sons. The mothers of the homosexuals were more dominant but less liked and respected by their sons. They encouraged feminine attitudes and behavior. The parents of the homosexuals tended to regard sex as shameful more often than the control parents.

Bene (1965) compared male homosexuals and heterosexuals in the community and found that homosexuals had a more negative view of their fathers and felt that the greater hostility and less affection was a reciprocal feeling. The relationship with the mother was also more negative, but less so than the relationship with the father. Bene found no differences in maternal overprotection, maternal overindulgence, or paternal overindulgence, but the homosexuals felt more overprotected than their siblings. The fathers were seen as being less overindulgent toward the homosexuals than toward the siblings of the homosexuals. The homosexuals and heterosexuals saw the mothers as equally competent, but the homosexuals saw their fathers as less competent. Although the groups did not differ in how frequently they chose their mother as a model, the homosexuals chose their father as a model significantly less often.

Apperson and McAdoo (1968) compared homosexuals and heterosexuals in the community and schizophrenics on a checklist of which things the children did that bothered each of their parents. The homosexuals had less restrictive mothers who emphasized integrity less but emphasized sexuality more. The fathers of the homosexuals were less strict, but more cold and impatient and more concerned with performance in school. Thus, the parents of the homosexuals seemed to be overpermissive, and the relationship between son and father was less close. The authors concluded that the homosexuals were not taught basic respect for others and attitudes which would promote good interpersonal relationships.

Rubins (1969) noted that the traditional portrait of the homosexual's parents closely resembled the portrait described for self-mutilators, schizophrenics, sociopaths, drug addicts, and so on. The study by Apperson and McAdoo was unique in that they tried to differentiate between the portraits of different disturbed groups. Compared to the mothers of schizophrenics, the mothers of the homosexuals were less restrictive, emphasized authority less, were less overprotective, made fewer performance demands, and emphasized integrity more. The fathers of the homosexuals were less restrictive and protective but had more difficulty discussing sexual matters.

These studies suggest two alternative patterns for the parents of homosexuals. First, several of the studies lend support to the notion that the mothers of male homosexuals are close-binding, intimate, and controlling; this has been found for both clinical samples (for example, Bieber, 1962) and nonclinical samples (for example, Evans, 1969). On the other hand, several studies using clinical (Ullman, 1960) and nonclinical samples (Bene, 1965) reported that the mothers of the homosexuals were not close-binding and intimate but rather hostile and rejecting. Nearly all of the studies agree, however, that the fathers of male homosexuals are detached, hostile, and rejecting.

Siegelman (1974) attempted to explore these discrepancies in greater depth using nonclinical samples of homosexuals and heterosexuals in the community. Siegelman took care to match his subjects on a number of variables (such as age, percentage in therapy, education, social class, sibling position, and the tendency to respond to questionnaires with the socially desirable response). Each subject was administered a parent-child relations questionnaire, and Siegelman found that the homosexuals reported both their mothers and fathers to be less loving and more rejecting than did the heterosexuals. The homosexuals felt less close to their fathers but did not differ from the heterosexuals in closeness to the mother, mother versus father dominance, or parental protective and demand behavior.

Siegelman then selected samples low in neuroticism as measured by a psychological test and compared the homosexuals and heterosexuals. No differences were found in their perception of their parents. Siegelman also compared homosexuals and heterosexuals who obtained low femininity scores on a psychological test and found that the homosexuals described their fathers as less protecting and loving and as more rejecting and demanding; the mothers of the two groups did not differ.

Two things are noteworthy here. First, the results supported the conclusion that both the mothers and the fathers of homosexuals were rejecting, hostile, and less loving. However, more importantly, these differences were not found when the degree of neuroticism was controlled. This suggests that the differences between the parents of homosexuals and heterosexuals hitherto reported may be a result of the differences in psychopathology of the two groups. Merely because the two samples may both be clinical samples does not ensure an absence of differences in psychopathology. Siegelman's data on this would have been more convincing had he presented comparison data for homosexuals and heterosexuals with high neuroticism scores.

The Mother-Father Relationship

In Bieber's (1962) study of homosexuals and heterosexuals in psychoanalysis, the mother-father relationship was rated by the psychoanalysts as similar for both groups. The parents of the homosexuals tended to share fewer interests and to spend less time together, and if one parent was judged inferior it was more likely to be the father. On the other hand, in Evans' (1969) study of homosexuals and heterosexuals in the community, there were no differences in the amount of time the parents of each group spent together or in the similarity of the interests of the parents. McCord, et al. (1962) in their study of adolescents found that the sexually deviant adolescents as a group were more likely to have had parents who were in intense conflict.

Parental Correlates of Homosexual Style

In Bieber's (1962) study of homosexuals and heterosexuals in psychoanalysis, the insertees tended to fear their fathers more and hate and respect them less, to be their mother's confidant more often, to have had overprotective mothers more often, and to have felt more guilt over masturbation. Evans (1969), in his study of homosexuals and heterosexuals in the community, found no relation between the Kinsey rating of the homosexuals and their parents' behaviors. However, the homosexuals with families resembling the heterosexual model tended to describe themselves as more masculine.

Nash and Hayes (1965) compared active and passive homosexuals in jail (defining activity/passivity in a broad manner, using both the role in sexual activity and life-style). The groups did not differ in experience of parental death, maternal care, absence of a parent, whether the mothers were worrying and fussy, or institutional experiences during childhood. The active homosexuals got along better with their fathers, judged their fathers as less neglectful, felt that they lacked affection less often, disliked their fathers less, and were less afraid of their fathers. The passive homosexuals more often preferred the mother to the father, wanted affection from the mother, admired their mothers more, felt that their parents wanted a daughter instead of a son, and wished more often to have been born a girl. The mixed homosexuals were felt to be more similar to the active homosexuals, but no data were given on this point. Overall, then, the active homosexuals resembled the heterosexuals more than the passive homosexuals did.

CONCLUSIONS

Several things are noteworthy in this body of research. First, although the data are inconsistent, several trends are clearly identifiable. For example the fathers of homosexuals are more distant and rejecting. The mothers appear either overprotective and intimate or as rejecting and hostile. There is some evidence for an increase in paternal absences. It is remarkable that despite the fact that the evidence on these points is not consistent, the description of the parents of the homosexual has become standardized and appears with great frequency in textbooks. Not only is this remarkable, it is worrisome, since the study of Siegelman indicates that the differences may result from a methodological artifact—the failure to control for neuroticism. With a control for neuroticism, Siegelman found no differences in the parents of homosexuals and heterosexuals.

A second point is that, of course, these correlational studies do not indicate cause and effect. We fall too easily into the error of assuming that the parent causes the child's behavior. We must remember that there is evidence that the infant's behavior has been shown to affect the parents' behavior too (Bell, 1968).

A third point is that almost all of the studies reviewed are based on the adult homosexual's perception of his past and his parents. No study looks at the parents of homosexuals. It is obviously difficult to contact the parents of people and interview them, more difficult than interviewing the subjects about their parents. But difficult studies are conducted in other areas of psychology. It becomes, therefore, a serious omission in research on homosexuality. Because of the seeming importance and relevance of parental behavior to the development of homosexual behavior, it is perhaps inexcusable that no investigator has studied the parents firsthand rather than relying on the possibly distorted recollections and perceptions by the homosexual of his parents.

REFERENCES

Apperson, L., and McAdoo, W.: Parental factors in the childhood of homosexuals. *J Abnorm Psychol, 73*:201-206, 1968.

Bell, R.Q.: A reinterpretation of the direction of effects in studies of socialization. *Psychol Rev, 75*:81-95, 1968.

Bene, E.: On the genesis of male homosexuality. *Br J Psychiatry, 111*:803-813, 1965.

Bieber, I.: *Homosexuality.* New York, Basic, 1962.

Chang, J., and Block, J.: A study of identification in male homosexuals. *J Consult Psychol, 24*:307-310, 1960.

Evans, R.: Childhood parental relationships of homosexual men. *J Consult Clin Psychol, 33*:129-135, 1969.

Greenstein, J.: Father characteristics and sex typing. *J Pers Soc Psychol, 3*:271-277, 1966.

Kearney, T., and Taylor, C.: Emotionally disturbed adolescents with alcoholic parents. *Acta Paedopsychiatr,* (Basel) *36*:215-221, 1969.

Kendrick, D., and Clarke, R.: Attitudinal differences between heterosexually and homosexually oriented males. *Br J Psychiatry, 113*:95-99, 1967.

Krieger, M., and Worchel, P.: A test of the psychoanalytic theory of identification. *J Individ Psychol, 16*:56-63, 1960.

Lewis, M., and Schoenfeldt, L.: Development-interest factors associated with homosexuality. *J Consult Clin Psychol, 41*:291-293, 1973.

McCord, W., McCord, J., and Verden, P.: Family relationships and sexual deviance in lower class adolescents. *Int J Soc Psychiatry, 8*:165-179, 1962.

Moran, P., and Abe, K.: Parental loss in homosexuals. *Br J Psychiatry, 115*:319-320, 1969.

Mosberg, L., Snortum, J., Gillespie, J., Marshall, J., and McLaughlin, J.: Family dynamics and homosexuality. *Psychol Rep, 24*:763-770, 1969.

Nash, J., and Hayes, F.: The parental relationships of male homosexuals. *Aust J Psychol, 17*:35-43, 1965.

O'Connor, P.: Aetiological factors in homosexuality as seen in Royal Air Force psychiatric practice. *Br J Psychiatry, 110*:381-391, 1964.

Opler, M.: Schizophrenia and culture. *Sci Am, 197*:103-110, 1957.

Rubins, J.: Sexual perversions. *Am J Psychoanal, 29*:94-105, 1969.

Siegelman, M.: Parental background of male homosexuals and heterosexuals. *Arch Sex Behav, 3*:18, 1974.

Spencer, S.: Homosexuality among Oxford undergraduates. *J Ment Sci, 105*:393-405, 1959.

Stephan, W.: Parental relationships and early social experiences of activist male homosexuals and male heterosexuals. *J Abnorm Psychol, 82*:506-513, 1973.

Thompson, N., Schwartz, D., McCandless, B., and Edwards, D.: Parent-child relationships and sexual identity in male and female homosexuals and heterosexuals. *J Consult Clin Psychol, 41*:120-127, 1973.

Ullman, P.: Parental participation in child rearing as evaluated by male social deviates. *Pacific Sociol Rev, 3*:89-95, 1960.

West, D.: Parental figures in the genesis of male homosexuality. *Int J Soc Psychiatry, 5*:85-97, 1959.

CHAPTER 10

PSYCHOANALYTIC VIEWS OF HOMOSEXUALITY

THE APPROACH OF PSYCHOANALYTIC THEORY TO HOMOSEXUALITY has been summarized well by Saul and Beck (1961). At the basis of psychoanalytic theory is the notion that humans are basically bisexual. Not only are there anatomical and physiological similarities between the sexes, but also every child usually has a mother (or mother substitute) and a father (or father substitute) with whom to identify. However, given this, it is still necessary to determine what factors lead to a homosexual choice and what role the homosexuality plays in the person's behavior.

THE GENESIS OF MALE HOMOSEXUALITY*

Three major kinds of hypotheses have been suggested for the genesis of male homosexuality: faulty or inadequate identifications, unusual infantile fixations, and homosexuality as a defense or adaptive mechanism.

Faulty or Inadequate Identifications

Two major kinds of faulty identifications have been suggested.

1. Positive identification with women (a mother, a sister, or some other important female) perhaps due to the father's being absent or the females' being overwhelming.

2. A failure to identify with men perhaps due to a strong feeling of fear or hatred of a sadistic or overpowering father.

Unusual Infantile Fixations

Unusual infantile fixations can occur in two ways.

1. An exaggerated exclusive libidinal investment in the father if the mother is absent.

2. An excessive genital attachment to the father if overt sexual behavior occurs between father and son.

---

*Although most psychoanalytic views pertain to males, much of the hypothesizing can be transposed for females quite easily.

Homosexuality as a Defense or Adaptive Mechanism

Homosexual behavior is often viewed as a means of defending against unconscious impulses.

1. Homosexuality may be a defense against castration anxiety which may be caused, for example, by viewing the female genitals and noting the absence of a penis. Such anxiety may be exacerbated by the Oedipal conflict.

2. Related to this, homosexuality may be a defense against incestuous attachment to the mother.

3. Homosexuality may a way of appeasing a mother who does not want her son to be aggressive and masculine.

4. Homosexuality may be chosen to overcompensate for the son's hatred and destructive wishes for his father (or brother or some other important male figure).

5. Homosexuality may be an attempt to appease a father by assuming a noncompetitive feminine role.

Homosexuality as a Way of Expressing Pregenital Drives

A variety of unconscious wishes may be gratified through homosexuality. The genital system (used heterosexually or homosexually) may be used to express a wide variety of wishes such as infantile dependency wishes and needs for love, narcissistic-omnipotent wishes, sadistic-castrating wishes, defiance and rebellion against superego standards, and masochistic drives. These wishes may be gratified through homosexuality as in the following illustrations.

1. The infantile dependency wishes and needs for love may lead to powerful receptive, dependent, and passive wishes that may be gratified through taking the passive role in homosexual acts. The homosexuality may also represent a generalization of the homosexual's early dependence on his father for "knowledge," with these dependency needs becoming eroticized.

2. Homosexuality may gratify the person's narcissistic self-love by allowing him to receive love from his partner or by identifying with the partner and bestowing love on him. The homosexual may satisfy his need to achieve eminence, power, prestige, and social status by taking a successful man as a sexual partner.*

3. Homosexuality may represent a wish to please a parent's unconscious wishes for deviant sexual behavior, or alternatively may represent a defiance of superego standards.

4. Since homosexuals often find themselves in degrading and puritive situations, homosexuality can serve to satisfy masochistic drives.

5. Homosexuality can satisfy sadistic and castration wishes (possibly upon a lover who is a father substitute) by degrading the sexual partner

---

*Kaplan (1967) saw homosexuality as a search for an ego-ideal with whom to identify (see Karp, et al. [1970] for a description of this process in heterosexual mate selection).

or inflicting pain upon him or merely by unconsciously fantasizing the homosexual act as a castration of the sexual partner.

6. Homosexuality may also express a wish to incorporate the fantasized lost penis by accepting it into the body from another.

Several psychoanalysts (for example, Weissman, 1962; Gillespie, 1964) have noted that passive homosexual wishes can be of two kinds: regressions from the Oedipal level and those that originate in pre-Oedipal identifications (and in particular oral fixations relating to the mother, her breasts, and the trauma of weaning).

In a similar vein, Ovesey (1954) noted that the choice may have a constitutional basis with the person fixating at the homosexual stage of psychosexual development and failing to progress to the heterosexual stage. Ovesey argues that the homosexual stage of development may have stronger instinctual urges for the individual, or perhaps the gratification then obtained is stronger than that obtained in later stages.

THE CONCEPT OF LATENT HOMOSEXUALITY

The concept of latent homosexuality is common in psychoanalytic writings but, as Salzman (1957) noted, the definition of latent homosexuality can easily become circular or meaningless. Latent homosexuality is a wish for sexual relations with someone of the same sex which is not manifest in overt homosexual behavior. The absence of overt homosexual behavior proves its existence while the presence of overt homosexual behavior means that the latent homosexual wishes are now manifest. It is clear that this is a poor definition since it implies that there are only two states: latent and overt homosexuality, with all men falling into one or the other category. It is also clear that a definition of latent homosexuality depends upon one's definition of overt homosexuality.

Freud proposed that wishes which are unconscious may disappear and reappear after a time unchanged. During this time, the wishes were unconscious and latent, that is *dormant*. Salzman noted, however, that often the term latent is used to mean *potential* (or predisposition), which is quite different. Salzman argued that a term for potential is not needed since psychologists who accept the notion of environmental determinants of behavior would see any behavior as potential or possible, given the appropriate circumstances. Only a dormancy concept is needed.

Given that Freud believed in the bisexual nature of humans, Salzman pointed out that Freud saw every person as having dormant sexual needs. However, all of us have to form a satisfactory relationship with someone of the same sex before we can form a satisfactory relationship with someone of the opposite sex. Those who manage to form a satisfactory relationship with someone of the same sex and who manage the transition well rarely have problems with members of the opposite sex and will rarely experience homosexual wishes. Other people never manage this and become overt homosexuals. Some manage it only with difficulty and never become overtly homosexual. However, they may have fleeting homosexual wishes or some feminine identification; these are the people for whom the term latent homosexual is applicable, even though it may be assumed to be present in all men. Thus, withdrawal from or difficulty with the opposite sex (or feminine behavior and interests) may be seen as a criterion for a definition of latent homosexuality.

Salzman concluded however that the concept of latent homosexuality is meaningless. It connotes dormancy rather than potentiality. As a dormancy concept, it requires us to accept Freud's theory of bisexuality as the explanation for the development of homosexuality. There is no good evidence for any preexisting state which has become dormant. As a potentiality concept, it is unnecessary. Thus, Salzman advocated the abandonment of the concept unless it could be defined more precisely in order to make it more meaningful and useful for personality theory.

A TEST OF PSYCHOANALYTIC VIEWS

Silverman, et al. (1973) have attempted to test some psychoanalytic views of homosexuality. They noted that two unconscious motives were commonly posited to lie behind male homosexuality: incestuous wishes toward the mother and a wish for a symbiotic union with the pre-Oedipal mother (Socarides, 1971). These wishes are not necessarily stronger in homosexuals, but they are *the* unconscious motives behind the behavior.

To test whether these wishes were motives for male homosexuals, Silverman, et al. took a sample of male homosexuals and heterosexuals who were neither in psychotherapy nor in jail and presented them with subliminal stimuli representing incest, symbiosis, and neutral topics. Each subject was tested three times, once with each kind of subliminal stimulus. After being presented with the subliminal stimulus, the sexual orientation of the subjects was tested by having them rate male and female faces, and the degree of threat experienced as a result of the subliminal perception was measured using a threat index from the Rorschach Test.

After viewing the incest subliminal stimulus, the heterosexual males showed no change in sexual orientation or threat. The male homosexuals, however, showed an increased preference for the male faces. After viewing the symbiotic subliminal stimulus, the heterosexual males showed no change in sexual orientation or threat. The male homosexuals, however, showed a decrease in the threat index. The directions of these differences were in accordance with expectations from psychoanalytic views. Subliminal incestuous stimuli increased homosexual wishes in homosexuals and subliminal symbiotic stimuli decreased homosexual wishes in homosexuals. To reiterate the point of Silverman, et al., it is not that the particular wishes are necessarily stronger in homosexuals; rather it is that those wishes are the motivating wishes in homosexuals for their behavior.

SUMMARY

Various psychoanalytic views on homosexuality were reviewed and the limited experimental research available was found to support some of these views. The concept of latent homosexuality was discussed and arguments were presented for its abandonment.

REFERENCES

Gillespie, W.H.: Symposium on homosexuality. *Int J Psychoanal, 45*:203-209, 1964.

Kaplan, E.A.: Homosexuality. *Arch Gen Psychiatry, 16*:355-358, 1967.

Karp, E., Jackson, J., and Lester, D.: Ideal-self fulfillment in mate selection. *J Marriage Fam, 32*:269-272, 1970.

Ovesey, L.: The homosexual conflict. *Psychiatry, 17*:243-250, 1954.

Salzman, L.: The concept of latent homosexuality. *Am J Psychoanal, 17*:161-169, 1957.

Saul, L.J., and Beck, A.T.: Psychodynamics of male homosexuality. *Int J Psychoanal, 42*:43-48, 1961.

Silverman, L.H., Kwawer, J.S., Wolitzky, C., and Coron, M.: An experimental study of the psychoanalytic theory of male homosexuality. *J Abnorm Psychol, 82*:178-188, 1973.

Socarides, C.W.: Psychoanalytic therapy of a male homosexual. *Psychoanal Q, 38*:173-190, 1971.

Weissman, P.: Structural considerations in overt male bisexuality. *Int J Psychoanal, 43*:159-168, 1962.

CHAPTER 11

TYPES OF HOMOSEXUALS

There have been several attempts to classify homosexuals into different types. An adequate classification system allows us to recognize that all homosexuals are not alike and to organize them in a meaningful way. However, as yet the attempts at classification have not been completely satisfactory, and there are several possible dimensions of behavior along which homosexuals may be described. The relative usefulness of the different dimensions cannot presently be assessed. The present chapter describes the most promising dimensions of homosexual behavior that have been described in recent years.

SEXUAL BEHAVIOR

Kinsey, et al. (1948) classified homosexuals in terms of the degree of homosexual behavior engaged in by the person as compared to the degree of heterosexual behavior. The classification is a continuum, but for convenience Kinsey, et al. divided the continuum into seven discrete points, with the exclusive heterosexual at point zero and the exclusive homosexual at point six.

Another common categorization is in terms of the mode of sexual gratification. Does the homosexual prefer masturbation, anal intercourse, or oral intercourse? For example, Carrier (1971) studies urban Mexican male homosexuals and found that some 90 percent preferred anal intercourse, a much higher percentage than is found in American male homosexuals.

A distinction is often made as to whether the homosexual is an insertor or an insertee. The insertor places his penis into the anus or mouth of his sexual partner; the insertee receives the penis. A number of studies have compared insertors and insertees. For example, Carrier (1971) found no differences in insertors and insertees from urban areas of Mexico in the age at their first ejaculation, the age at their first homosexual contact, their education, their sibship size, or how feminine and masculine they rated their mothers and fathers. The insertees had had less heterosexual intercourse and, if they had experienced such intercourse, it was at a later age than the insertors. The insertees had had more contact with older male homosexuals prior to their first ejaculation and they rated themselves as more feminine both currently and as children.

With respect to the manner of sexual gratification, occasional reports have appeared of incidental physiological abnormalities that may facilitate particular modes of sexual activity. For example, MacAlpine (1953) suggested that *pruritis ani* (which produces an itching sensation in the anus) may lead to a preference for anal stimulation. Gioscia (1950) reported that homosexuals who practice fellatio occasionally are found to have the gag reflex absent or considerably reduced. (These abnormalities may, of course, result from homosexual activity rather than antedate it.)

Gebhard, et al. (1965) classified homosexuals by the age of their preferred kind of partner. In their study of sexual offenders they found a number of differences that differentiated the groups.

The homosexual offender who chose children had an early life characterized by poor relationships with both parents and broken homes. Their prepubertal sex play, which was frequent and homosexual, seemed to be a way of finding emotional gratification outside the home. As adults they emphasized masturbation and, like the other homosexuals, deemphasized heterosexual intercourse. The frequency of homosexual contacts exceeded that of the other groups and, although attracted primarily to children, they were reasonably flexible with regard to sex and species. They were distributed somewhat evenly over the diagnostic categories of pedophile, mental defective, drunks, and situational.

The homosexual offenders against minors had poor relationships with both parents (and especially the father). As a child, they socialized well with both sexes and engaged in much prepubertal sex play, somewhat more homosexually than heterosexually directed. After puberty, their heterosexual activity declined and their homosexual orientation became stronger. Their choice of minors appeared to reflect a retreat from adult homosexual competition or to result from a lapse of judgment or situational factors that led to them taking a sexual partner younger than was customary for them.

The homosexual offenders against adults had poor relationships with their fathers but tended to be partial to their mothers. Their social lives with both sexes during childhood were good. As children, they were ill a good deal. They reached puberty early and thus they were faced with strong sexual urges at an age when society does not provide outlets for expression of these urges. These homosexuals had the strongest sex drive in terms of frequency of orgasm, and they masturbated a good deal. Their heterosexual interest was weak. They ended up in jail through having been caught in police raids or else they were cruisers or flaunters.

LIFE-STYLE

A common categorization for homosexuals is that of active versus passive. The active-passive categorization may be based on the dimension of insertor-insertee, in which case the latter distinction is semantically more correct. Alternatively, the active-passive categorization is extended to social roles and may resemble a dominant-submissive distinction or a masculine-feminine distinction. Hooker (1965) has argued that the active-passive distinction is meaningless (because it is confused with these other distinctions). She has argued for the use of the more basic and semantically clearer dimensions. (Incidentally, Hooker claimed that there were no associations between the dimensions of insertor-insertee and masculine-feminine, but her data on this point were quite poor.)

Brown (1958) distinguished between homosexuality, which he saw as sexual activity with or desire for someone of the same sex, and inversion, which he saw as identification with or adoption of the psychological identity of the opposite sex and which involved the total personality structure.* This distinction is similar to the masculine-feminine distinction already mentioned. The notion that identification may be involved is a presently untested hypothesis.

*This role reversal has been institutionalized in many societies, for example, the Berdache in the Winnebago (Sonenschein, 1966).

Brown argues that in normal development the male child has to identify with his father after being attached to his mother whereas the female child identifies with her mother. Thus, the process of development can more easily go awry with the male child. Brown therefore predicted that inversion would be more common in males than in females, since more boys would not switch from mother to father, but rather identify with their mother instead. Brown noted that in general public opinion polls females more often wish to have been born males than males wish to have been born females, but he saw this as due to the greater ease and latitude that females have in expressing preference for the opposite sex role in our society. Brown noted that fewer females apply for sex change operations as compared to males.

Holemon and Winokur (1965) compared homosexual prisoners who were homosexual before being imprisoned and classified them as effeminate versus noneffeminate. The effeminate homosexuals tended to be more exclusively homosexual but the difference was not significant. However, the effeminate homosexuals did show more feminine traits as children than the noneffeminate homosexuals, who in turn did not differ from heterosexual controls. The effeminate homosexuals had had more homosexual experiences before the age of twelve (whereas the noneffeminate homosexuals did not differ from the heterosexual controls). Holemon and Winokur noted that the effeminate homosexuals learned their homosexuality earlier and their heterosexuality later. Their first homosexual partners tended to be older; their homosexual acts were repeated more and with a greater continuity of partners. They had been passive more often in their first homosexual encounter and their awareness of their homosexuality had occurred at an earlier age. After their first homosexual encounter, the effeminate homosexuals had been more active sexually and had engaged more in cross-dressing. The effeminate and noneffeminate homosexuals did not differ in their frequency of heterosexual intercourse. The homosexuals as a group did not differ from the heterosexual controls in birth order, maternal age, or psychiatric illness, but the siblings of the homosexuals were more often judged to be psychopaths.

Although homosexual behavior can occur in persons with

all kinds of diagnoses, some writers use diagnosis as a way of categorizing homosexuals. For example, Adler (1967) distinguished between sociopathic homosexuals (the prostitutes), the schizoid homosexuals (those who get caught in public places for homosexual behavior), and compulsive neurotic homosexuals (mainly married men who give into irresistible impulses).

Sociologists have devised a variety of classifications based on a composite picture of the homosexual's life-style. Humphreys (1970) described five kinds. The *trades* are males who consider themselves to be heterosexual and who take the insertor role in the sexual act. Most of them are married. The *ambisexual* is found in the upper strata of society and describes men (often married) who like to participate in deviant sexual activity, but who are not exclusively homosexual. The *gay* describes the younger, autonomous, unmarried segments of society who participate in the homosexual social life and who are visible. Their self-identification is homosexual. The *closet queen* describes those men who know they are homosexual but fear involvement in the more overt visible activities of homosexual society. They are frequently unmarried teachers, salesmen, and factory workers. Finally, there is the *hustler,* the homosexual prostitute who may maintain a heterosexual self-image.

FORCED HOMOSEXUALITY

Many writers distinguish between freely chosen homosexual behavior by those living in normal society and homosexual behavior adopted because of a lack of opposite sex partners (as in jails). Clearly, many individuals engage in homosexual behavior under conditions where partners are limited. A good index of how "forced" the behavior is may be the fantasies that accompany the sexual act and the daydreams that the participants have.

A number of studies have been conducted on situational or forced homosexuality in jails. Guze, et al. (1969) followed up a number of felons after eight to nine years. They found that whereas only 10 percent had been homosexual prior to being imprisoned, some 14 percent were homosexual at the time of follow-up. However, Guze, et al. felt that homosexuality was probably no more common in jails than in the general population.

Tittle (1969) studied male and female addicts in prison and found homosexual activity to be equally common in both sexes. The female homosexual relationships in jail were more stable and affected the total relationship more, whereas for the males, homosexual activity was more for physical gratification, more casual, and more as part of an economic exchange. More of the female prisoners exchanged letters with the male prisoners than vice versa. (However, the jail had more males than females, and so this latter finding may have been a result of this sex ratio.)

Devereux and Moos (1942) noted that homosexual behavior served many functions for the prisoners. For example, it was a defense against isolation, it led to social negativism (the in-group, out-group phenomenon), and it led to social stratification which made for social stability. Devereux and Moos saw homosexual behavior as regressive and infantilistic, but they noted that the sexual isolation made it the only available alternative.

Kirkham (1971) noted that heterosexual deprivation might result in abstinence and masturbation rather than homosexuality. Thus, deprivation is not sufficient as an explanation of why some persons turn to homosexual behavior in segregated situations. Kirkham presented a description of the different social roles for homosexuals in jails, much as Humphreys has done for homosexuals in the community. Kirkham described the *Queen Fag* (the homosexual is so by choice), the *punk* who who engages in homosexual acts for gain (rewards or aggrandisement or as a result of threats), and the *wolf* who uses force on others (and whom Kirkham saw as motivated by deprivation and power motives).

It has been suggested that the rapist homosexuals (wolves) who command territories within the jail in fact prevent much violence from taking place by setting up stable social rankings and territories (Roth, 1971).

SUMMARY

Several classificatory schemes have been proposed and some appear to have potential usefulness for understanding homosexuality. They do appear to be a little simple given the complexities of sexual behavior and attitudes, and it would be of interest to explore the associations between the different classificatory schemes. It is doubtful that they are completely independent of one another. It would seem clear that research on homosexuals in general would be limited in usefulness, and that meaningful research can only proceed if the different kinds of homosexuals are carefully distinguished.

REFERENCES

Adler, K.: Life-style, gender role, and the symptom of homosexuality. *J Individ Psychol, 23*:67-78, 1967.

Brown, D.G.: Sex role development in a changing culture. *Psychol Bull, 55*:232-242, 1958.

Carrier, J.: Participants in urban Mexican male homosexual encounters. *Arch Sex Behav, 1*:279-291, 1971.

Devereux, G., and Moos, M.: The social structure of prisons and the organic tensions. *J Crim Psychopathol, 4*:306-324, 1942.

Gebhard, P., Gagnon, J., Pomeroy, W., and Christenson, C.: *Sex Offenders.* New York, Har-Row, 1965.

Gioscia, N.: The gag reflex and fellatio. *Am J Psychiatry, 107*:380, 1950.

Guze, S., Goodwin, D., and Crane, J.: Criminality and psychiatric disorders. *Arch Gen Psychiatry, 20*:583-591, 1969.

Holemon, E., and Winokur, G.: Effeminate homosexuality. *Am J Orthopsychiatry, 35*:48-56, 1965.

Hooker, E.: An empirical study of some relations between sexual pattern and gender identity in male homosexuals. In Money, J. (Ed.): *Sex Research.* New York, HRW, 1965, p. 24-52.

Humphreys, L.: *Tearoom Trade.* Chicago, Aldine, 1970.

Kinsey, A., Pomeroy, W., and Martin, C.: *Sexual Behavior in the Human Male.* Philadelphia, Saunders, 1948.

Kirkham, G.: Homosexuality in prison. In Henslin, J. (Ed.): *Studies in the Sociology of Sex.* New York, Appleton, 1971, p. 325-349.

MacAlpine, I.: Pruritis ani. *Psychosom Med, 15*:499-508, 1953.

Roth, L.: Territoriality and homosexuality in a male prison population. *Am J Orthopsychiatry, 41*:510-513.

Sonenschein, D.: Homosexuality as a subject of anthropological inquiry. *Anthropol Q, 39*:73-82, 1966.

Tittle, C.: Inmate organization. *Am Soc Rev, 34*:492-505, 1969.

CHAPTER 12

HOMOSEXUALITY AND OTHER PSYCHOLOGICAL DISTURBANCES

Homosexuality has been hypothesized to be associated with other disturbed behaviors, in particular paranoia and alcoholism. The research on this topic will be reviewed in this chapter.

HOMOSEXUALITY AND PARANOID DELUSIONS

The psychoanalytic theory of paranoid delusions argues that the potential paranoid has strong unconscious homosexual wishes. When he is in a situation in which the possibility of gratification of these wishes is likely, he becomes anxious. He resolves (and/or explains) this anxiety by projecting the unconscious homosexual wishes onto another. He does not become conscious of the homosexual aspects of the wishes that he has projected onto the other; he is aware only of the nonsexual elements. The potential paranoid has thus become paranoid by coming to believe that the other person is "after" him or is "out to get" him. Alternatively, the potential paranoid can be viewed as using reaction formation to turn the unconscious homosexual impulses toward another into unconscious hatred of the other person. It is this hatred which is then projected onto the other so that now the other is seen as hating the potential paranoid.* When this process happens in a short period of time, the process is often called homosexual panic (Glick, 1959).

Lester (in press) has reviewed the considerable body of research that has been conducted to test this hypothesis, and only the major points of his review will be summarized here.

The existence of overt homosexuals with paranoid delusions causes difficulties for the simple Freudian position, and such individuals have been reported (for example, Rosenfeld, 1949). To explain this, various authors have suggested that blocked (as

*Karon and Rosberg (1958) have generalized these ideas to schizophrenia in general.

opposed to repressed) homosexual impulses can be projected, that some aspect of homosexual impulses can be projected (for example, the active homosexual may project his unconscious passive homosexual impulses), and that the paranoia may develop before the individual becomes overtly and consciously homosexual.

Grauer (1955) wondered why, since Freud claimed that everyone has unconscious homosexual wishes, only a few individuals develop paranoid delusions. Knight (1940) asked why the unconscious homosexual wish in some individuals was so strong that it must be defended against and denied. Knight suggested that the homosexual wishes were so strong because they were a reaction formation against strong hate which had to be denied, hate originally directed toward the individual's father and which could not be expressed.

Several studies have found that those with paranoid delusions are more overtly homosexual then those without paranoid delusions, that they have more homosexual preoccupations than those without paranoid delusions, that they are judged by psychiatrists to have more latent homosexual impulses than those without paranoid delusions, and that they have more unconscious homosexual wishes (as manifest in sexual impotence, fear of castration or genital injury, homosexual dreams, excessive masturbation, or feelings that males make homosexual advances toward themselves).

These studies suffered from several inadequacies: a poor choice of control group in some of the studies, the use of criteria for assessing unconscious homosexual impulses whose validity was open to question, and the use of clinical judgments about homosexual preoccupations which were susceptible to experimenter bias. Furthermore, there is no reason to except that those with paranoid delusions will show an increased incidence of overt homosexual behavior and conscious homosexual preoccupation. The Freudian hypothesis is that they should show more *unconscious* homosexual preoccupation.

These problems resolve themselves, therefore, to the assessment of unconscious homosexual impulses. Several psychological studies have attempted to deal with this problem by attempting to assess unconscious impulses by indirect methods, such as particular responses given to the Rorschach test; fixation time when presented with pictures of males and females simultaneously, and perceptual defense to homosexual, heterosexual and neutral words. The studies are not completely in agreement but the majority show that paranoid patients resemble overt homosexuals on these tasks more than they resemble non-paranoid patients.

The evidence then seems to suggest an association between both conscious and unconscious impulses and paranoia, a finding not in accordance with the simple Freudian position.

It is worth noting that Scott and Lyman (1968) have proposed an interactional analysis that accounts for the association between homosexuality and paranoid delusions. The individual who has repressed homosexual impulses might have fears for his masculinity. This may lead to behavior categorized as "strange" and which would make people suspicious of him. This in turn may reinforce his concerns about the reactions of others toward him. The behavior of his peers gives him a basis for his paranoid delusions. Similarly, the overt homosexual is often in a heterosexual environment which, for him, is stressful and would lead to heightened suspiciousness by him of the thoughts and reactions of others toward him. He will tend to interpret events in a paranoid fashion and adopt strategies of disavowing and concealing his deviance. This may make him appear "odd" to his peers and so, as in the case of the repressed homosexual, a vicious circle is set up. We might predict from this analysis that homosexuals who spend more time in homosexual circles would be less paranoid. This prediction has not yet been tested.

HOMOSEXUALITY AND THE PRE-MORBID SCHIZOPHRENIC

Chapman and Reese (1953) compared six patients developing schizophrenia and six controls and found that the preschizophrenic patients gave more homosexual signs on the Rorschach Test. Chapman and Reese argued that in the process of a schizophrenic break, the patient passes through a period when homosexual drives are significant and prominent. The study, and therefore the conclusion, would obviously have been more sound had the patients been followed for a longer period both before and after the schizophrenic process began.

HOMOSEXUALITY AND ALCOHOLISM

Several studies have explored the association between homosexuality and alcoholism. For example, both alcoholics and hysterics gave some of Wheeler's signs from the Rorschach that were indicative of homosexuality, although not as often as overt homosexuals (Reitzell, 1949). Norman (1948) found that paranoid schizophrenics had significantly more homosexual experiences than catatonic schizophrenics and alcoholics, but he judged the alcoholics and paranoid schizophrenics to have had more unconscious homosexual impulses than the catatonic schizophrenics. Ericksen (1951) found that both paranoid schizophrenics and alcoholics showed more perceptual defense to homosexual stimuli as compared to other psychiatric patients.

Botwinick and Machover (1951) hypothesized that alcoholism might be a defense against or an expression of underlying homosexual motivation. They gave a sample of male alcoholics the MMPI *Mf* scale and the Terman-Miles inversion scale. The alcoholics did not differ from norms on the *Mf* scale and they were found to be less inverted on the Terman-Miles scale. Thus, the hypothesis was not supported.

Machover, et al. (1959) identified a number of Rorschach signs that differentiated homosexuals from heterosexual controls. The alcoholics did not differ from the controls in the number of homosexual signs given, but the alcoholics in remission did give more of the homosexual signs than the alcoholics currently drinking. Similarly, on the Draw-A-Person Test, a number of signs were found to differentiate homosexuals from heterosexual controls. The Alcoholics gave more of these signs, a difference due to the alcoholics in remission giving a large number of the signs. The *Mf* scale of the MMPI gave similar results. Machover, et al. concluded that homosexual trends were not present in all alcoholics, but that homosexual trends were most marked in alcoholics in remission.

Gibbins and Walters (1960) hypothesized that alcoholics were latent homosexuals, and they explored the perceptual defense of alcoholics, homosexuals, and heterosexuals to homosexual words. They found no differences between the groups. In a replication study, they found the most perceptual defense in heterosexuals, next most in the alcoholics, and least in the homosexuals. In a third study, they gave the subjects male and female symbols in pairs and asked each subject to choose the symbol they most preferred in each pair. The homosexuals and alcoholics chose more male symbols than the heterosexuals. Although these studies were methodologically poor (for example, the homosexuals in the first two studies were volunteers from the community while the homosexuals in the third study were offenders, there was no psychiatric control group, and the demand characteristics of the experiment were different for the groups) the data support the hypothesis to some extent.

HOMOSEXUALITY AND ULCERATIVE COLITIS

A couple of studies have looked for homosexual trends in patients with ulcerative colitis. Engel (1955) found no homosexual activity but occasional homosexual fantasies in patients with ulcerative colitis. Castelnuovo-Tedesco (1962) felt that ulcerative colitis would be rare in homosexuals since they were accustomed to submission. However, should a person be forced to have anal intercourse against his will, then ulcerative colitis could occur, and Castelnuovo-Tedesco reported such a case.

HOMOSEXUALITY AND MIGRAINE

Monsour (1957) felt that for males migraine could result from homosexual impulses that have been repressed, especially passive homosexual desires. For women, Monsour felt that the sexual conflicts that could lead to migraine were more likely to be heterosexual desires that revived feelings of competition and anger toward other women.

HOMOSEXUALITY AND NEUROSIS

Vetter (1955) found that obsessive-compulsive neurotics gave more of Wheeler's Rorschach signs of homosexuality than undifferentiated neurotics, who in turn gave more of the signs than normals. Vetter concluded that conflicts between male and female identifications constituted the focal conflict in obsessive-compulsive neuroses.

HOMOSEXUALITY AND PEPTIC ULCER

Marguis, et al. (1952) found a tendency for peptic ulcer patients to give more of Wheeler's signs of homosexuality on the Rorschach test than did other psychosomatic patients, but the difference failed to reach statistical significance.

SUMMARY

There is some clear tentative evidence that patients with some disturbances (such as paranoia, alcoholism, peptic ulcer, and obsessive-compulsive neurosis) do have homosexual conflicts or repressed homosexual desires. However, apart from the association between paranoia and homosexuality, the evidence is not presently convincing for the association between homosexuality and the other disorders discussed.

REFERENCES

Botwinick, J., and Machover, S.: A psychometric examination of latent homosexuality in alcoholism. *Q J Stud Alcohol, 12*:268-272, 1951.

Castelnuovo-Tedesco, P.: Ulcerative colitis in an adolescent boy subjected to a homosexual assault. *Psychosom Med, 24*:148-156, 1962.

Engel, G.: Studies of ulcerative colitis. *Am J Med, 19*:231-256, 1955.

Ericksen, C.: Perceptual defense as a function of unacceptable needs. *J Abnorm Soc Psychol, 46*:557-564, 1951.

Gibbins, R., and Walters, R.: Three preliminary studies of a psychoanalytic theory of alcohol addiction. *Q J Stud Alcohol, 21*:618-641, 1960.

Glick, B.: Homosexual panic. *J Nerv Ment Dis, 129*:20-29, 1959.

Grauer, D.: Homosexuality and the paranoid psychoses as related to the concept of narcissism. *Psychoanal Q, 24*:516-526, 1955.

Karon, B., and Roseberg, J.: The homosexual urges in schizophrenia. *Psychoanal Rev, 45*:50-56, 1958.

Klaf, F., and Davis, C.: Homosexuality and paranoid schizophrenia. *Am J Psychiatry, 116*-1070-1075, 1960.

Knight, R.: The relationship of latent homosexuality to the mechanism of paranoid delusions. *Bull Menninger Clin, 4*:149-159, 1940.

Lester, D.: On the relationship between paranoid delusions and homosexuality. *Arch Sex Behah,* in press.

Machover, S., Puzzo, F., Machover, K., and Plumeau, F.: Clinical and objective studies of personality variables in alcoholism. *Q J Stud Alcohol, 20*:528-542, 1959.

Marguis, D., Sinnett, E., and Winter, W.: A psychological study of peptic ulcer patients. *J Clin Psychol, 8*:266-272, 1952.

Monsour, J.: Migraine. *Psychoanal Q, 26*:476-493, 1957.

Norman, J.: Evidence and clinical signs of homosexuality in 100 unanalyzed cases of dementia praecox. *J Nerv Ment Dis, 107*:484-489, 1948.

Reitzell, J.: A comparsion study of hysterics, homosexuals, and alcoholics using content analysis of Rorschach responses. *Rorsch Res Exch, 13*:127-141, 1949.

Rosenfeld, H.: Remarks on the relation of male homosexuality to paranoia, paranoid anxiety and narcissism. *Int J Psychoanal, 30*:36-47, 1949.

Scott, M., and Lyman, S.: Paranoia, homosexuality and game theory. *J Health Soc Behav, 9*:179-187, 1968.

Vetter, H.: The prediction of Rorschach content from the psychoanalytic theory of obsessive-compulsive neurosis. *Diss Abstr, 15*:1437, 1955.

CHAPTER 13

PSYCHOLOGICAL CORRELATES OF HOMOSEXUALITY

A NUMBER OF STUDIES HAVE APPEARED that investigate some psychological trait in homosexuals or administer some psychological test, often without much of a theoretical rationale for doing so. The present chapter is a review of this research.

HOMOSEXUALS AND MARRIAGE

Imielinski (1969) found that the more homosexual a man was on the Kinsey scale, the more likely he was to be divorced and the shorter his heterosexual marriage had been. The reasons homosexual men gave for getting married included the desire to have children, attempts to control their homosexual behavior, emotional attachment to the female, desire for a homekeeper, and advice from a physician as part of a cure for homosexuality. Dank (1972) noted that homosexual men were raised in an environment which had an antihomosexual bias and that the men, although engaging in homosexual sexual activity, did not readily adopt a homosexual identity. They thought in terms of the heterosexual attitudes and goals of the society and hence often considered marriage (and often married).

HOMOSEXUALITY AND AGE

Weinberg (1970) administered a questionnaire to a wide variety of homosexuals, obtaining responses from over 3,500 (representing a return rate of only about 30 percent). Compared to the men aged twenty-six to forty-five, the older homosexuals were less likely to frequent gay bars, had less association with other homosexuals and more association with heterosexuals, were more likely to be living alone and less likely to be living with males, and engaged in less homosexual activity. The old and younger homosexuals did not differ in their reported loneliness or unhappiness. The older man had fewer worries about exposure, more self-acceptance, less interpersonal awkwardness, and less desire for psychiatric treatment. Weinberg found that the homosexuals under twenty-six years of age resembled the older homosexuals more than those aged twenty-six to forty-five.

Weinberg suggested that although the social isolation of the older homosexuals seemed at odds with their better personal adjustment the older homosexuals had come to terms with their lives and themselves.

However, it is by no means clear from this study whether these differences are a direct result of age or a result of the different eras in which the men of different ages grew up.

SEXUAL BEHAVIOR

Attitudes toward Females

Ramsay and Velzen (1968) devised a questionnaire to assess positive and negative attitudes to homosexual and heterosexual situations, and they reported that male homosexual students were not merely unresponsive or indifferent to heterosexual situations. Rather, they had a negative emotional reaction to heterosexual situations, much as the heterosexual students had a negative emotional reaction to homosexual situations.

Kuethe and Weingartner (1964) had homosexuals and heterosexual prisoners place cut-out figures of males and females on a board. The homosexuals put more distance between male and female figures and placed the male figures closer together than did the heterosexuals.

McConaghy (1970) explored the penile response to slides of nudes discussed in Chapter 20. He found that the volume of the penises of homosexuals increased to male nudes and decreased to female nudes, whereas the reverse was found for heterosexuals. The size of the increase in penile size to the preferred object (the positive response) was related to the size of the decrease to the nonpreferred object (the negative response) in the heterosexuals but not in the homosexuals. McConaghy suggested that the same process determines positive and negative unconditioned sexual responses in heterosexuals but not in homosexuals.

McConaghy then conditioned the sexual responses to neutral symbols and found for both groups that the size of the conditioned response (for both positive and negative responses) was correlated with the size of the unconditioned responses. For the positive responses, the conditioned response was smaller than the unconditioned response for both groups. For the negative responses, the conditioned and unconditioned responses were similar in size for the heterosexuals, but the conditioned response was larger than the unconditioned response for the homosexuals. The special nature of aversion to females was again highlighted by this study on homosexuals.

Aspects of Sexual Behavior

Bieber (1962) asked psychoanalysts to complete a detailed questionnaire about their homosexual and heterosexual male patients. In the manifest content of their dreams, the homosexuals had more homosexual imagery and the heterosexuals had more heterosexual imagery. There were no differences in incestuous content. The homosexuals did have heterosexual dreams and Bieber concluded that they did have the potential to be heterosexual. However, the homosexuals were more dissatisfied with their penises and had a greater aversion to female genital organs. The homosexuals showed an association between fearing the female genitals, fear of genital injury for themselves, and seeking partners with large penises. (Bieber found no correlates of being especially attracted to the buttocks of male partners.)

Manosevitz (1970) in nonclinical samples of male homosexuals and heterosexuals found no differences in fear of the female genitals, fear of disease or injury to their own genitals, or feelings about the size of their own genitals. More of the homosexuals had never been excited by females. The pattern of sexual history resembled that reported by other studies: the homosexuals had more homosexual experiences at all ages, had more total sexual activity, and had less heterosexual activity.

Fine (1961) noted that whereas male heterosexual patients usually developed homosexual wishes toward their psychoanalyst at some point during the analysis, male homosexual patients did not.

Athanasiou and Shaver (1970) compared male homosexuals

and a random sample from the respondents to a *Psychology Today* questionnaire about pornography. Those males who reported greater arousal to pornography were more likely to be homosexuals. The homosexuals appeared to be more sexually liberated and less romantic, and had their first sexual experience at an earlier age and more often with their first sexual partner only once. The response to pornography showed different patterns of correlations with sexual behaviors and social attitudes in the homosexual and the random sample.

Psychosexual Conflict

DeLuca (1967) compared male homosexual inductees with heterosexuals on the Blacky test and found only one difference in thirty variables examined. DeLuca concluded that there were no differences in psychosexual conflict between homosexuals and heterosexuals as assessed by the Blacky test.

APTITUDE AND INTERESTS

Interests

Ross and Mendelsohn (1958) reported on a sample of homosexuals seen at a college health service and reported that the homosexuals were less likely to be graduate students but more likely to be in applied arts than other students.

Haselkorn (1956) gave a battery of vocational tests to male Veterans Administration patients who were homosexuals, medical patients, or neuropsychiatric patients. The groups were compared on seventy-five different scales and only eight significant differences were found. Thus there appeared to be few vocational differences that distinguished the homosexuals. Haselkorn noted that the few differences that appeared were related to traditional male occupations rather than traditional female occupations. The only two scales for which the homosexuals differed from both control groups were "senior chartered public accountant" (the homosexuals appeared less interested) and author-journalist (the homosexuals appeared more interested).

Houston (1965) studied youthful offenders and compared the passive male homosexuals with nonhomosexual males on the California Picture Interest Inventory. The homosexuals had higher interest scores on the scales for interpersonal, computational, business, verbal, and time perspective and lower interest scores on the scales for natural, mechanical, and scientific. The two groups did not differ on the scale for esthetic.

Lewis and Schoenfeldt (1973) compared male homosexuals in a gay activist group with male freshmen. There were no differences in academic achievement, positive academic attitude, scientific interest, literary historical interest, social effectiveness, or emotional maturity. The homosexuals participated less in team sports and less in organized religious activities, were more verbally outspoken and independent, had lower math achievement and higher English achievement, and had a lower applied vocational orientation and a higher score on a scale for pseudointellect. The homosexuals were not all similar in their scores on the test battery, and Houston identified three distinctly different patterns.

O'Connor (1964) compared homosexuals with neurotics in the Air Force and found that the homosexuals liked robust sports less, had artistic hobbies more, and preferred clerical and nonmanual tasks more.

Green and Money (1966) studied twenty prepubertal boys who had effeminate mannerisms and behaviors (such as liking to dress as girls, wishing to be like girls, walking and talking like girls, and so on). The boys were seen in treatment, but homosexuality was not a presenting problem. Nine of the boys displayed an interest in the theater and in acting and seven utilized opportunities to play the female role in games. It may have been that the boys adopted the feminine role because they were good at role playing. Once they began to behave effeminately, they may have extended the feminine role, taking to dressing up and acting. Green and Money asked what might have triggered this path, and they concluded that it must be some personality trait. Green and Money saw the causes of homosexuality as environmental but allowed that a personality trait of having a talent for role playing might facilitate a homosexual response to environmental pressures. Green and Money concluded that the theater may not be merely a haven for homosexuals, but that role taking may be a part of the talent of effeminate boys who may eventually become homosexual.

Intelligence

Vilhotti (1958) compared postpubertal males in an institution for the retarded and found no differences in intelligence between the homosexual and nonhomosexual boys. In a comparison of youthful offenders, Houston (1965) found that passive male homosexuals had significantly lower intelligence test scores than nonhomosexual offenders.

Academic Performance

Ross and Mendelsohn (1958) reported on homosexuals seen at a college health service. The males did not differ from other patients in academic achievement, but the female homosexuals had better academic performance scores than other female patients.

Braaten and Darling (1965) compared overt male homosexuals, covert homosexuals (in whom homosexual impulses were manifest in dreams and fantasy but not in overt behavior), and heterosexual controls seen at a college counseling center. The overt and covert homosexuals did not differ in grades or artistic activities, but the homosexuals as a group performed better academically than the heterosexuals (though they did not differ in scholastic aptitude), and they engaged more in artistic activities. Compared to the covert homosexuals, the overt homosexuals were more likely to be in the schools of hotel management, architecture, and agriculture.

MALADJUSTMENT

The MMPI

Loney (1971) gave homosexual males in the community and heterosexual controls the MMPI and found that the F scale scores of the homosexuals were greater than those of the heterosexuals. Manosevitz (1971) compared nonclinical samples of homosexuals and heterosexuals and found the homosexuals to have high F, D, Pd, Mf, Pa, Pt, Sc, and Si scores and lower K scores. Cubitt and Gendreau (1972) compared homosexual and heterosexual prisoners and found the homosexuals to have higher Hs, D, Hy, Mf, and Pa scores (and to be older). Mosberg, et al. (1969) found no differences on the L scale between homosexuals and heterosexuals in the service.

Braaten and Darling (1965) compared males seen at a college counseling center and found the overt homosexuals differed from the covert homosexuals (in whom homosexual impulses were found only in dreams and fantasies) on only the Pd scale (the coverts had lower scores) and Si (the overts had lower scores). Compared to heterosexuals, only the *Mf* scale differentiated the groups with the homosexuals obtaining higher scores.

Doidge and Holtzman (1960) rated Air Force trainees for the degree of homosexuality and found that the homosexuals obtained higher F, Hy, Pd, Mf, PA, Pt, Sc, Hs, D, and Si scores. On a forced choice scale adopted from the Taylor Manifest Anxiety Scale, the homosexuals obtained higher scores. (They also had more food aversions and took longer in a word association test to respond to homosexual homonyms, but they did not differ in the identification of the sex of drawings of human figures.)

Oliver and Mosher (1968) compared homosexuals and heterosexuals in a reformatory. The heterosexuals were older, more educated, and better behaved than the homosexual insertors but did not differ from the homosexual insertees. There were no differences in age at first conviction, number of previous convictions, or months served. On the MMPI, the insertees had higher scores than the heterosexuals on Hs, Hy, Pd, Mf, and Pt. The insertors had higher scores on F, Hs, D, Hy, Pd, Pa, Pt, and Sc. The insertors and insertees did not differ on any scale.

Although the particular scales that differentiate homosexuals and heterosexuals differ from study to study, it is found consistently that homosexuals obtain higher scores. The data suggest greater maladjustment on the part of homosexuals.

The MMPI Mf Scale

Five studies have reported that homosexuals obtain higher *Mf* scores: Manosevitz (1971) with a community sample, Cubitt and Gendreau (1972) with a prisoner sample, Doidge and Holtzman (1960) with Air Force personnel, Oliver and Mosher (1968) with insertees in a reformatory, and Friberg (1967) with psychiatric patients. Two studies found no differences: Spencer (1959) with college psychiatric patients and Oliver and Mosher (1968) with insertors in a reformatory. (Cubitt and Gendreau found that *Mf* scores were not related to age or education.)

Cubitt and Gendreau (1972) found no differences in a prisoner sample on Panton's Hsx scale, while Friberg (1967) found that homosexuals got higher Hsx scores in a sample of psychiatric patients. Friberg found that Mf and Hsx scores were not associated and that the homosexuals obtained higher scores on both scales than psychiatric patients involved in other sexual deviations.

In general, it appears that homosexuals do obtain higher femininity scores than heterosexuals.

The 16PF

Evans (1970) compared male homosexuals and heterosexuals from the community on the 16PF and found differences on nine scales: the homosexuals were *less* emotionally stable, conscientious, and controlled and *more* tense, tender-minded, suspicious, imaginative, apprehensive, and self-sufficient. Evans felt that the homosexuals resembled normals more than they resembled anxiety neurotics, and he felt that the homosexual was only mildly neurotic at the most.

Cattell and Moroney (1962) found no differences in the profiles of uncharged and charged homosexual males. They felt that the profile of the homosexual resembled the profile of the neurotic more than the profiles of psychotics, psychopaths, or psychosomatic persons. It especially resembled the profile of the anxiety and obsessional neurotic. Compared to the neurotic profile, the homosexual profile was more extraverted and lower in guilt, suggesting that there was more acting out of the neurosis. As compared to nonsexual offenders, the homosexuals had lower emotional stability, higher suspiciousness, higher imagination, and higher tender-mindedness.

Cattell and Moroney concluded that sexual deviation was not the primary problem for homosexuals but rather a symptom chosen by a neurotic individual who had ego weakness (an unusual degree of regression), extraversion (and thus acts out), low superego strength (permitting nonconformity), and radicalization of outlook (leading to a bohemian life).

Cubitt and Gendreau (1972), using a prisoner sample, found differences on only three scales. The homosexuals had less emotional stability, were less experimenting, and were more shrewd.

Again, although differences are not consistent, the trends are for greater maladjustment or neurosis in the homosexual.

Gough's Adjective Checklist

Evans (1971) compared homosexuals and heterosexuals in the community on the Gough Adjective Checklist. The homosexuals checked more adjectives (suggesting that they had more drive and less repression). They scored as less defensive, less self-confident, less need for achievement, less dominant, less endurance, less need for order, more succorant, more need for abasement, and more counseling readiness. They checked more unfavorable adjectives but fewer personal adjectives. The groups did not differ on the number of favorable adjectives checked, self-control, lability, intraception, nurturance, affiliation, heterosexuality, exhibitionism, autonomy, aggression, change, and deference. On the masculine-feminine scale, the homosexuals scored as more feminine. Evans concluded that the homosexuals were more neurotic.

Other Tests

Hooker (1957) compared male homosexuals and heterosexuals in the community and found that judges found no differences in overall adjustment from their Rorschach protocols. The judges could not distinguish the homosexuals from the heterosexuals. Similarly, no differences in overall adjustment were found in the TAT protocols, although it was easy to distinguish the two groups from these protocols.

Grygier (1958) compared male neurotics on the Dynamic Personality Inventory. The homosexuals resembled the heterosexuals in oral aggression, verbally expressed aggression, unconventionality, interest in children, authoritarianism, adventurousness, interest in social activities, ego strength, acceptance of sexual impulses, oral dependence, and psychophysical drive. The homosexuals scored higher on passivity and need for comfort/support, feminine narcissism, and feminine identification and lower on masculine identification.

Thompson, et al. (1971) compared male and female homosexuals and heterosexuals in the community and found no differences in their rating of themselves on the Semantic Differential. On the Gough Adjective Checklist, the male homosexuals rated themselves as less defensive and less self-confident than the male heterosexuals, but the female homosexuals rated themselves as more self-confident than the female heterosexuals. More of the homosexuals had been in or were presently in psychotherapy than the heterosexuals, but this variable did not affect the results. Thompson, et al. suggested that the increased incidence of psychotherapy in the homosexuals was a reflection of family or social pressures rather than greater maladjustment.

DeLuca (1966) compared homosexual and heterosexual army inductees on the Rorschach. No one sign differentiated the groups, but the homosexuals did have significantly more homosexual signs in total. The groups did not differ in the use of primitive defenses (using poor form responses as the criterion) or creative potential (using Bruno Klopfer's scoring method). DeLuca concluded that the homosexuals showed more hostility and disgust toward female figures, more anxiety toward father figures, but did not differ in psychosexual inadequacy. DeLuca found no differences when he classified the homosexuals on the basis of their preferred sexual mode for gratification.

Using the Cornell Selectee Index, Darke and Geil (1948) found that homosexual prisoners were more neurotic than heterosexual prisoners. Among the homosexuals, the active oral homosexuals were the most neurotic and the active anal homosexuals least neurotic.

Braaten and Darling (1965) gave the Mooney Problem Checklist to males seen at a college counseling center. Covert homosexuals (whose homosexual impulses manifested themselves only in dreams and fantasies) had more problems in social relationships and fewer in adjustment to college work than the overt homosexuals. Compared to the heterosexuals, the homosexuals had more problems in social relationships, home and family, and courtship/sex/marriage, but fewer in college work.

Siegelman (1972) gave samples of homosexuals and heterosexuals in the community the Scheier and Cattell's Neuroticism Scale Questionnaire. For the total sample, the homosexuals were more tender-minded, more submissive, more anxious, and had a higher total score; there were no differences in depression. When he matched the groups for age and their responses to the Marlow-Crowne Social Desirability Scale, the same pattern of results was obtained. Siegelman compared respondents with low femininity scores and found only one difference: the homosexuals were more tender-minded than the heterosexuals.

Siegelman also administered parts of other scales, and in general the homosexuals were more goal-directed, more nurturant, more neurotic, and less well-adjusted. Siegelman also compared those homosexuals who belonged to a homosexual organization and those who did not and found those in the organization to be more depressed, more submissive, and to have a higher total score on the Neuroticism Scale Questionnaire.

Oliver and Mosher (1968) compared homosexual and heterosexual boys in a reformatory on the Mosher Forced-choice Guilt Inventory. The homosexuals and heterosexuals did not differ on hostility guilt, morality-conscience guilt, or sex guilt. The active and passive homosexuals differed only in that the passive homosexuals had more hostility guilt (that is, more guilt over aggressive behavior). Oliver and Mosher suggested that heterosexuals with high guilt tended to be anxious, introverted, inhibited, and sensitive; active homosexuals with high guilt tended to be apathetic and evasive, while the passive homosexuals with high guilt tended to have narrow interests and lack of sexual confidence. With increasing feminine attitudes, the heterosexuals and passive homosexuals, but not the active homosexuals, had more guilt.

Kendrick and Clarke (1967) compared male homosexual psychiatric patients with normal heterosexuals and found no differences on the Maudsley Personality Inventory on the Lie scale or the Extraversion scale. The homosexuals had higher neuroticism scores (predictably given the choice of a control group).

General Psychiatric Studies

Saghir, et al. (1970) compared male homosexuals and single male heterosexuals in the community and found that the homosexuals were more likely to be or have been in psychotherapy, more likely to abuse alcohol and other drugs (though not more likely to be addicts), more likely to have physical disabilities, and to have more parents psychiatrically ill. They were also slightly more likely to have attempted suicide and to have stronger sadistic and masochistic tendencies. Saghir, et al. concluded that the homosexuals were more disturbed than the heterosexuals.

Spencer (1959) found that male homosexual college students who were psychiatric patients had had more previous psychiatric illness than heterosexual psychiatric patients but did not differ in the familial incidence of psychiatric illness. The homosexual patients had attempted suicide more than the heterosexual psychiatric patients. O'Connor (1964) studied Air Force psychiatric patients and found no difference between homosexuals and heterosexuals in neurotic traits or family history of neurosis.

Diagnosis

Saghir, et al. (1970) found no differences in diagnosis between homosexuals and heterosexuals in the community. Ellis (1959) had psychotherapists evaluate homosexuals and heterosexuals in psychotherapy and found the homosexuals were judged more often to be psychotic and less often as neurotic.

Rubins (1968) saw the sexual perversion as a primary acting-out of impulses that neurotics repress. Sexual deviants, according to Rubins, have neurotic symptoms. The compulsive quality of the sexual behavior of sexual deviants also suggests neurosis. Rubins noted that disturbances occur in sexual deviants in nonsexual areas of functioning. Lamberd (1969) noted that homosexuality in some cases is a reflection of a phobia of females.

SELF-CONCEPT

Chang and Block (1960) studied a nonclinical sample of male homosexuals and heterosexuals and found no differences using an adjective checklist in the discrepancy between the self-concept and the ideal self-concept. The ego-ideals were virtually identical but the self-concepts differed somewhat. The homosexuals saw themselves as more affected, dependent, determined, personally charming, restless, and tactful.

Clark and Epstein (1969) gave a nonclinical sample of male homosexuals the Tennessee Self-Concept Rating Scale. Each subject was shown a sequence of faces, and he had to predict whether the next face would be male or female and smiling or angry. Homosexuals with a low self-concept expected angry faces more than homosexuals with a high self-concept (and especially for female faces). Also, over all subjects, females were expected more than males to have angry faces. Clark and Epstein argued that homosexuals with low self-concepts have a stronger expectation of negative reinforcement from females whereas homosexuals with a high self-concept resemble heterosexuals in this respect.

Dickey (1961) measured the self-concept of a nonclinical sample of male homosexuals using the self-ideal/self-discrepancy and an MMPI-type inventory of self-adequacy. Self-concept was not linked with any of the following: association primarily with homosexuals or heterosexuals, active participation in a homosexual organization, noticeable job conflict, disclosure or concealment of his homosexuality, or his objective assessment of his role conflicts. A higher self-concept was found in those who were satisfied with their jobs, perceived more desirable characteristics in the typical male heterosexual, and saw themselves as more similar to the typical male heterosexual. Differences were found on one measure of self-concept (but not on the other) for some variables: married homosexuals obtained higher adequacy scores, and those who both preferred to associate with male heterosexuals and did so had lower self-ideal/self-discrepancies. Dickey concluded that if the homosexual adopted society's attitudes with respect to masculine norms and was aware of his deviation, then he will have a more adequate self-concept.

Mosberg, et al. (1969) compared male homosexuals and heterosexuals in the armed forces and found significant differences in self-concept. The homosexuals had stronger feelings of physical and social inadequacy. Kendrick and Clarke (1967) compared homosexual psychiatric patients with normal heterosexuals (an inappropriate control group) and found differences on both the Semantic Differential and George Kelly's REP Grid in their self-concept. On the whole, the homosexuals had less favorable attitudes toward themselves, but they also had less favorable attitudes to other concepts, such as British justice, sex, and being normal.

OTHER VARIABLES

Curiosity

Schiffer (1970) gave male and female homosexuals and heterosexual college students a questionnaire to assess their general curiosity. The female homosexuals were significantly less curious than the other groups.

Creativity

Ellis (1959) compared homosexuals and heterosexuals in psychotherapy (matched for age, sex, and education) and found that their psychotherapists rated the heterosexuals as more creative. The homosexuals who in addition showed a sex-role inversion were judged to be the least creative. Holding diagnosis constant eliminated the significance, although a trend was still present.

Masculinity-Femininity

Thompson, et al. (1973) compared homosexuals and heterosexuals in the community and found no differences on the Franck Drawing Completion Test. The female homosexuals were more masculine than the female heterosexuals on a masculine-feminine adjective checklist whereas the male heterosexuals were more masculine than the male homosexuals.

Miscellaneous

Andress, et al. (1974) compared male homosexuals in an activist group with male students in introductory psychology courses on the Menninger Word Association Test and found no differences between the groups, either in the popularity of their responses or the commonality of their responses, although both groups differed significantly from the norms for the test.

SUMMARY

Two major trends stand out in these data. First, homosexuals do appear to resemble the opposite sex more in tests of masculinity-femininity. Second, homosexuals do seem to be less well-adjusted than heterosexuals. This latter finding is open to two interpretations. It may be that homosexuality is a behavior engaged in by those members of society who are less well-adjusted or who are psychologically disturbed. It may also be, however, that being a homosexual in a heterosexual society is the stress that makes for poorer adjustment. That is to say, if the societal prejudice and persecution of homosexuals was eliminated, then homosexuals might not differ in adjustment from heterosexuals. The methodology employed in the studies reviewed do not permit tests of these rival hypotheses.

REFERENCES

Andress, V., Franzini, L., and Linton, M.: A comparison of homosexual and heterosexual responses to the Menninger Word Association Test. *J Clin Psychol, 30*:205-207, 1974.

Athanasiou, R., and Shaver, P.: Correlates of response to pornography. *Proc Am Psychol Assoc, 5*:349-350, 1970.

Bieber, I.: *Homosexuality*. New York, Basic, 1962.

Braaten, L., and Darling, C.: Overt and covert homosexual problems among male college students. *Genet Psychol Monogr, 71*:269-310, 1965.

Cattell, R., and Moroney, J.: The use of the 16PF in distinguishing homosexuals, normals and general criminals. *J Consult Psychol, 26*:531-540, 1962.

Chang, J., and Block, J.: A study of identification in male homosexuals. *J Consult Psychol, 24*:307-310, 1960.

Clark, T., and Epstein, R.: Self-concept and expectancy for social reinforcement in noninstitutionalized male homosexuals. *Proc Am Psychol Assoc, 4*:575-576, 1969.

Cunitt, G., and Gendreau, P.: Assessing the diagnostic utility of MMPI and 16PF indices of homosexuality in a prison sample. *J Consult Clin Psychol, 39*:342, 1972.

Dank, B.: Why homosexuals marry women. *Med Aspects Hum Sex*, Aug., 1972, p. 14-24.

Darke, R., and Geil, G.: Homosexual activity. *J Nerv Ment Dis, 108*:217-240, 1948.

Deluca, J.: The structure of homosexuality. *J Proj Tech, 30*:187-191, 1966.

Deluca, J.: Performance of overt male homosexuals and controls on the Blacky Test. *J Clin Psychol, 23*:497, 1967.

Dickey, B.: Attitudes toward sex roles and feelings of adequacy in homosexual males. *J Consult Psychol, 25*:116-122, 1961.

Doidge, W., and Holtzman, W.: Implications of homosexuality among Air Force trainees. *J Consult Psychol, 24*:9-13, 1960.

Ellis, A.: Homosexuality and creativity. *J Clin Psychol, 15*:376-379, 1959.

Evans, R.: 16PF questionnaire scores of homosexual men. *J Consult Clin Psychol, 34*:212-215, 1970.

Evans, R.: Adjective checklist scores of homosexual men. *J Pers Assessment, 35*:344-349, 1971.

Fine, R.: A transference manifestation of male homosexuals. *Psychoanal Rev,* 48:116-120, 1961.

Friberg, R.: Measures of homosexuality. *J Consult Psychol,* 31:88-91, 1967.

Green, R., and Money, J.: Stage-acting, role-taking and effeminate impersonating during boyhood. *Arch Gen Psychiatry,* 15:535-538, 1966.

Grygier, T.: Homosexuality, neurosis, and "normality." *Br J Del,* 9:59-61, 1958.

Haselkorn, H.: The vocational interests of a group of male homosexuals. *J Counsel Psychol,* 3:8-11, 1956.

Hooker, E.: The adjustment of the male overt homosexual. *J Proj Tech,* 21:18-31, 1957.

Houston, L.: Vocational interest patterns of institutionalized youthful offenders as measured by a nonverbal battery. *J Clin Psychol,* 21:213-214, 1965.

Imielinski, K.: Homosexuality in males with particular reference to marriage. *Psychother Psychosom,* 17:126-132, 1969.

Kendrick, D., and Clarke, R.: Attitudinal differences between heterosexually and homosexually oriented males. *Br J Psychiatry,* 113:95-99, 1967.

Kuethe, J., and Weingartner, H.: Male-female schemata of homosexual and non-homosexual penitentiary inmates. *J Pers,* 32:23-31, 1964.

Lamberd, W.: The treatment of homosexuality as a mono-symptomatic phobia. *Am J Psychiatry,* 126:512-518, 1969.

Lewis, M., and Schoenfeldt, L.: Developmental-interest factors associated with homosexuality. *J Consult Clin Psychol,* 41:291-293, 1973.

Loney, J.: An MMPI measure of maladjustment in a sample of "normal" homosexual men. *J Clin Psychol,* 27:486-488, 1971.

Manosevitz, M.: Early sexual behavior in adult homosexual and heterosexual males. *J Abnorm Psychol,* 76:396-402, 1970.

Manosevitz, M.: Education and MMPI Mf scores in homosexual and heterosexual males. *J Consult Clin Psychol,* 36:395-399, 1971.

McConaghy, N.: Penile response conditioning and its relationship to aversion therapy in homosexuals. *Behav Res Ther,* 1:213-221, 1970.

Mosberg, L., Snortum, J., Gillespie, J., Marshall, J., and McLaughlin, J.: Family dynamics and homosexuality. *Psychol Rep,* 24:763-770, 1969.

O'Connor, P.: Aetiological factors in homosexuality as seen in Royal Air Force psychiatric practice. *Br J Psychiatry,* 110:381-391, 1964.

Oliver, W., and Mosher, D.: Psychopathy and guilt in heterosexual and subgroups of homosexual reformatory inmates. *J Abnorm Psychol,* 73:323-329, 1968.

Ramsay, R., and Velzen, V.: Behavior therapy for sexual perversions. *Behav Res Ther,* 6:233, 1968.

Ross, M., and Mendelsohn, F.: Homosexuality in college. *Arch Neurol Psychiatry,* 80:253-263, 1958.

Rubins, J.: The neurotic personality and certain sexual perversions. *Contemp Psychoanal,* 4:53-72, 1968.

Saghir, M., Robins, E., Walbran, B., and Gentry, K.: Homosexuality. *Am J Psychiatry,* 126:1079-1086, 1970.

Schiffer, D.: Relation of inhibition of curiosity to homosexuality. *Psychol Rep, 27*:771-776, 1970.
Siegelman, M.: Adjustment of male homosexuals and heterosexuals. *Arch Sex Behav, 2*:9-25, 1972.
Spencer, S.: Homosexuality among Oxford undergraduates. *J Ment Sci, 105*:393-405, 1959.
Thompson, N., McCandless, B., and Strickland, B.: Personal adjustment of male and female homosexuals and heterosexuals. *J Abnorm Psychol, 78*:237-240, 1971.
Thompson, N., Schwartz, D., McCandless, B., and Edwards, D.: Parent-child relationships and sexual identity in male and female homosexuals and heterosexuals. *J Consult Clin Psychol, 41*:120-127, 1973.
Vilhotti, A.: An investigation of the use of the DAP in the diagnosis of homosexuality in mentally deficient males. *Am J Ment Defic, 62*:708-711, 1958.
Weinberg, M.: The male homosexual. *Soc Prob, 17*:527-537, 1970.

CHAPTER 14

FEMALE HOMOSEXUALITY

INTEREST IN HOMOSEXUALS has focused chiefly on male homosexuals, but a number of studies devoted to female homosexuality have appeared, especially in recent years. Because the psychodynamics of female homosexuality may differ from those of male homosexuality, the literature on female homosexuality will be reviewed separately in this chapter.

PHYSIOLOGICAL STUDIES

Traditionally, it was believed that female homosexuals had a masculine physique. Henry and Galbraith (1934), for example, described the typical female homosexual as having firm adipose tissue, deficient fat on the shoulders and abdomen, firm muscles, excess hair on the chest, back, and legs, a masculine distribution of pubic hair, a small uterus, over-or underdeveloped labia, a small or a large clitoris, a tendency toward underdevelopment of the breasts, excess hair on the face, and a low pitched voice. Such a description seems rather fanciful.

Kenyon (1968a) compared large samples of female homosexuals and heterosexuals living in the community and found no differences in height or hip measurements. The lesbians had larger waists and busts and were heavier. The groups did not differ in their self-report of physical health, number of operations (although the lesbians had had more appendectomies and fewer gynecological operations), age of menarche, regularity of menses, dysmenorrhoea, amenorrhoea, menorrhagia, or the source from which they learned about menstruation. The lesbians resented their periods more but had less premenstrual tension. (The lesbians had more often chosen a female as a doctor.)

Kenyon compared the exclusive and nonexclusive lesbians and found no differences in the variables she studied except that the exclusive lesbians had begun menstruating later and had less premenstrual oedema.

Loraine, et al. (1970) studied a small sample of female homosexuals in the community and found the level of testosterone excretion high, the level of oestrone excretion low, their estradiol and estriol levels low, the luteinizing hormone level low, and the follicle stimulating hormone level low. (However, these abnormal levels were not found in every one in the sample.)

It is clear that physiological studies of lesbians have been rare. The two recent studies that have appeared need replication by other investigators before their results can be considered reliable, and in the case of the hormonal study, a larger sample is needed for reliable conclusions. (Loraine, et al. utilized only four lesbians.)

PSYCHOLOGICAL STUDIES OF FEMALE HOMOSEXUALS

Miller and Hannum (1963) compared female prisoners who engaged in homosexual behavior while in prison with those who did not and found no differences in their MMPI protocols. On the Kuder Preference Record, the homosexuals scored lower on *social service* and higher on *music*.

Wilson and Greene (1971) gave the Eysenck Personality Inventory to female homosexuals and heterosexuals living in the community. The lesbians were more educated, but there were no age differences. The groups did not differ on the lie or extraversion scales, but the homosexuals were less neurotic. On the Edwards Personal Preference Schedule, only three of the sixteen scales differentiated between the groups: the lesbians scored lower on heterosexuality, higher on endurance, and higher on dominance. On the California Psychological Inventory, there were differences on five of the eighteen scales: the lesbians had higher dominance, capacity for status, good impression, and intellectual efficiency and lower femininity. The groups did not differ in self-report of emotional stability, happiness, or desire to seek help for personal problems. Wilson and Greene concluded that the lesbians were psychologically healthier than the heterosexuals.

Kenyon (1968c) compared homosexuals and heterosexuals

in the community who did not differ in age or education. On the Eysenck Personality Inventory, there were no differences in extraversion, but the homosexuals obtained higher neuroticism scores. On the Cornell Medical Index, the lesbians scored higher on fourteen of the eighteen scales. Thus, Kenyon concluded that the lesbians were more neurotic than the heterosexuals. Kenyon (1968b) found no differences between exclusive and nonexclusive lesbians on these tests.

Giannell (1966) compared the scores of female homosexuals in the community with college student norms for the Edwards Personal Preference Schedule. Giannell has a theory that the criminal/deviant person has a personality characterized by high frustration, low internal inhibitions, low external inhibitions, poor contact with reality, high situational crime potential, and a high potential for satisfaction from the crime committed. In part, he predicted that lesbians should have a highly frustrated need to give and receive affection and high needs for aggression, independence, and noncomformity. On the Edwards Personal Preference Schedule, the lesbians scored higher than the norms on succorance and nurturance and lower on autonomy, aggression, deference, and heterosexuality (which Giannell saw as supporting his predictions). They also differed on achievement, affiliation, dominance, change, and endurance. He found that lesbians with no particular role identification did not differ from "butches" or "femmes." However, the butches differed from the femmes in having higher scores on achievement, exhibition, and dominance. Giannell also divided the lesbians on the basis of their scores on the heterosexuality scale and found several differences. The low scorers appeared to have a high need for achievement, autonomy, abasement, endurance, and aggression and a low need for deference, affiliation, change, and heterosexuality. The high scorers had a high need for deference, aggression, and heterosexuality and a low need for affiliation. Giannell noted that interviews with the lesbians confirmed the existence of all six of his predicted traits, which, given the phenomenon of experimenter bias, is hardly surprising.

Hopkins (1969) gave homosexuals and heterosexuals in the community Cattell's 16PF Test. There were differences on five scales. The lesbians were more reserved, detached, critical, and cool; more dominant, assertive, and progressive; more careless of practical matters; more bohemian and self-sufficient, and less tense and driven. On the second-order traits, there were no differences in anxiety or extraversion, but the lesbians were more independent and had more poise and alertness. There were no differences in the neurotic profile.

Hopkins (1970) looked for signs on the Rorschach that differentiated homosexuals and heterosexuals in the community. Only three of many signs examined were found to differentiate the groups: the lesbians gave more responses, less often chose card VII as the most liked, and more often gave Wheeler's sign number 10 (seeing a depreciated female on card VII).

Armon (1960) gave the Draw-A-Person Test to homosexuals and heterosexuals in the community and found no differences in the sex of the first-drawn person. On the Rorschach, the groups did not differ on responses intended to assess dependency orientation, reactions of fear or anger toward the masculine role, and confusion and conflict about their sex role or rejection of female identification. The homosexuals were judged to perceive women with more hostility (their Rorschach images of females were more frightening or aggressive) suggesting to Armon that their homosexuality was a defense against hostility, fear, and guilt felt toward other women. The attitude of the lesbians toward men was more disparaging but not more hostile-fearful. In addition, the homosexuals had more limitations in personal-social orientation (their color reactivity was less, suggesting to Armon a reduced affective output and less emotional gratification in relation to women). There were no differences in an index of pathological thinking. Judges were not able to distinguish the groups from examination of either the Draw-A-Person or the Rorschach protocols.

Hopkins (1970) was not able to replicate these differences in her study, nor a difference reported by Fromm and Elonen (1951) which concerned depreciation of humans in general.

Thompson, et al. (1971) studied homosexuals and heterosexuals in the community who were similar in age and education. The homosexuals had had psychotherapy more often and were less likely to be married. On the Gough and Heilbrun Adjective Checklists, the homosexuals did not differ in the use of defensive or personal adjectives, but they did check more adjectives and had more self-confidence. On the evaluative scales of the Semantic Differential, there were no differences in the rating of "self." The experience of psychotherapy did not affect these results. The homosexuals did not, therefore, appear to be more disturbed, and Thompson, et al. felt that the increased use of psychotherapy by the homosexuals was a reflection of social and familial pressures.

Siegelman (1972) compared homosexuals and heterosexuals in the community who were similar in their education, the education of their fathers and mothers, and sibling position. The homosexuals were older, however. They were given the Scheier and Cattell Neuroticism Scale Questionnaire and a number of additional scales. On the Marlow-Crowne Social Desirability Scale, the homosexuals showed less of a tendency to give the socially desirable response. The groups did not differ in tender-mindedness, depression, anxiety, trust, alienation, sense of self, dependency, nurturance, or neuroticism. The homosexuals were less submissive, more goal directed, and more self-accepting. They had a lower total score on the Neuroticism Scale Questionnaire.

Overall, therefore, there is no evidence from psychological studies that female homosexuals differ from female heterosexuals. On the dimension of neuroticism, for example, the results conflict: some studies find lesbians to be less neurotic (Wilson and Greene, 1971), others find them to be more neurotic (Kenyon, 1968c), while others find no differences (Hopkins, 1969; Armon, 1960; Siegelman, 1972). These studies are relatively superior to studies of other groups reviewed in this book. The subjects have all been living in the community rather than in jail or under psychiatric treatment, the sample sizes have been large, and the psychological tests given, on the whole, are valid.

PSYCHIATRIC STUDIES OF FEMALE HOMOSEXUALS

There have been three large psychiatric studies of female homosexuals. In the first, Kaye, et al. (1967) surveyed psychoanalysts for cases of female homosexuals in psychoanalysis. They found that cases were much rarer than found in a similar survey for male homosexuals conducted by Bieber (1962). Kaye, et al. compared a sample of the female homosexuals (of whom about half were actually bisexual) with a sample of female heterosexual patients in psychoanalysis. The data came from questionnaires completed by the psychoanalysts about their patients.

There were few differences in the parental relationships (alcoholism, open demonstrations of affection, or the sexual relationship), but there was a tendency for the mothers of the lesbians to regard the father as inferior and for the mothers to be more dominant. There were no differences in the sibling position of the two groups.

There were no differences in the affection of the mothers for their daughters (being the mother's favorite,) or the sex of the mother's favorite child. The homosexuals did feel more accepted by their mothers, who had a tendency to be more seductive. The homosexuals saw their mothers as more genuine. The mothers of the homosexuals tended to discourage feminine traits from developing in their daughters. The homosexuals were babied more and were less afraid that their behavior would anger their mothers or lose their mothers' love. There were no differences in the frequency of postpartum psychoses or homosexuality in the mothers.

The fathers of the homosexuals were more puritanical, and the homosexuals were more afraid of their fathers. The fathers of the homosexuals were more possessive, disapproved more of the boy and girl friends of their daughters, attempted to ally the daughter against the mother more, showed undue concern about the daughter's physical health, and babied the daughter more. The homosexual daughters felt exploited more to satisfy their fathers' own needs. Their fathers reacted more negatively to displays of emotion between daughter and mother and discouraged the feminine traits in their daughters. The picture was of a close-binding father. Kaye, et al. described the father of the homosexual daughter as a superficially feared and puritanical man, covertly manifesting an inverted Oedipal striving toward his daughter, overly possessive, and attempting to discourage his daughter's development as a female.

In their relationship to their siblings, the homosexual patients did not differ from the heterosexual patients.

The two groups did not differ in their masturbatory pattern or history or in the onset of heterosexual activity. The first homosexual experience was later for the female homosexual patients than for the male homosexual patients in the study of Bieber, (1962), and bisexuality was more common in the female homosexuals than in the male homosexuals. The first homosexual partners of the female homosexuals were only slightly older than the patients, and the patients had not been seduced into homosexuality by older, experienced females.

The two groups did not differ in orgasmic experience or difficulties or in penis envy. The homosexuals appeared to have more fear of and aversion to the penis, scrotum, and semen. They had been punished and threatened more for sex play with boys (but not for sex play with girls). There were no differences in the manifest dream content dealing with heterosexual behavior. The homosexuals did dream more about homosexual behavior. There were no differences in the frequency of dreams with incestuous content or pregnancy, but the homosexuals did have a greater conscious fear of pregnancy and a greater preference for the active role in sexual behavior.

Kaye, et al. concluded that there was a significant heterosexual drive in the homosexuals, but that the increased anxiety, fear, and threats centered around heterosexual activity inhibited the heterosexual development.

The homosexuals had displayed more masculine behavior as children: they fought more, played with guns, played with boys' toys more and girls' toys less, disliked dolls, disliked playing house, and saw themselves as tomboys. During adolescence and puberty, the homosexuals had more crushes on women (but did not differ in their crushes on men). They did not differ in menstrual abnormalities. Kaye, et al. concluded that the homosexuals avoided feminine activities and the female role.

The homosexuals tended toward alliances with older women and tended to identify their lovers with family members. The lover was seen as female and maternal. Kaye, et al. felt that the homosexuals were moving away from their Oedipally-tinged father in their choice of a lover. The homosexuals were more hostile toward and contemptuous of homosexual men which

Kaye, et al. saw as a projection of their feelings about themselves and their fathers. Kaye, et al. felt that there was a tendency for the homosexuals to be more psychotic.

Saghir, et al. (1970) compared homosexual and heterosexual females in the community. The groups did not differ in their experience of psychiatric treatment or in their psychiatric diagnosis. The homosexuals had attempted suicide more, had more alcohol problems, and used more nonprescription drug use. More of the homosexuals were judged to be psychiatrically disturbed. The homosexuals were also more likely to have dropped out of college.

Saghir, et al. (1969) compared the homosexual females to a sample of homosexual males in the community. The males had masturbated more and at an earlier age. During adolescence, the females had had more heterosexual experience, but in adulthood the males had had more. More of the females had experienced heterosexual intercourse. The males had had homosexual experiences at an earlier age and more often during adolescence. In adulthood, there were no differences. The males had had more homosexual partners and fewer long-term affairs. Saghir, et al. felt that the female homosexuals were more psychiatrically disturbed than the males since they were more often depressed, had made more suicide attempts, used drugs more, and received a psychiatric diagnosis more often.

Kenyon (1968d) compared homosexual and heterosexual females in the community and found no differences in age, education, number of siblings, sex of siblings, sibling position, experience of boarding school, mother's age, father's age, death of father, parental social class, or which parent was the dominant one. The lesbians were less often married, of a higher social class, had a more unstable work record, more often went to college, were less likely to have a religious affiliation, were more often members of the armed forces or police, and belonged less to women's clubs.

The lesbians reported worse relationships with both parents, a higher incidence of mother's deaths, fewer happily married parents, more divorced and separated parents, and a greater incidence of psychiatric treatment for their mothers. (Other relatives did not differ in the frequency of psychiatric care.)

The lesbians were more likely to have been adopted, had unhappier childhoods, and had had more nervous breakdowns, although they had the same number of neurotic traits as children.

The lesbians had families that were less accepting of sex with a greater incidence of homosexuality in the relatives and parents who more often wanted a son rather than a daughter. Early homosexual seduction was rare but more common for the lesbians (8 percent versus 0 percent). The lesbians had been frightened by males more often. The lesbians were less fond of babies, obtained less pleasure from heterosexual intercourse (if they had experienced it), were less at ease with males, masturbated more, felt less feminine, and cross-dressed more.

Kenyon (1968b) compared the exclusive homosexuals with the nonexclusive ones. There were few differences. The same variables were examined as those discussed above. The exclusive homosexuals less often went to boarding school, more often had brothers, had fewer nervous breakdowns, experienced less heterosexual behavior and enjoyed it less, had experienced homosexual feelings and behavior at an earlier age, had had more homosexual partners, preferred older partners, and felt less guilt over being homosexual. Kenyon concluded that the exclusive homosexuals were better adjusted.

THE PARENTS OF FEMALE HOMOSEXUALS

The studies reviewed above touch upon aspects of the parents of female homosexuals. In addition, two more detailed studies have been conducted upon this topic.

Bene (1965) compared homosexuals and heterosexuals in the community who were similar in age, social class, parental age, and the sex of their siblings. On a sixty-eight-item questionnaire, only four items distinguished the mothers whereas twenty-four distinguished between the fathers. The homosexuals were more hostile and less affectionate toward both parents. More of the lesbians reported fear-invoking behavior from their fathers. The lesbians judged their fathers to be less competent. Fewer of the homosexuals wanted to model themselves after either parent. The homosexuals reported that the parents wanted a son rather than a daughter.

Thompson, et al. (1973) found similar results. Female homosexuals (like male homosexuals) perceived themselves as less similar to either parent as compared to heterosexuals and saw themselves as less similar to people of their biological sex. The female homosexuals did not see themselves as more similar to one parent than the other. Thompson, et al. concluded that the female homosexuals were alienated.

On an adjective checklist, the female homosexuals rated themselves more often on masculine traits. On a parent-child interaction questionnaire the female homosexuals reported that they were tomboys as children, that they had experienced maternal rejection and father overacceptance, and the female homosexuals rejected their father more than the heterosexuals had. The pattern for the female homosexuals was almost diametrically opposite to the pattern found for male homosexuals.

SUMMARY

The studies on female homosexuals are in general very sound methodologically and have produced some consistent results. On the whole, female homosexuals do not appear to be any more psychologically disturbed than female heterosexuals. They do appear to be more alienated and to have come from unhappier homes. The female homosexuals have felt little affection for either parent, but in comparison to heterosexuals, the daughter-father relationship seems most disturbed. The results are not completely consistent, probably because female homosexuals are a heterogenous group, and the studies may well differ in the constitution of their samples.

In this connection, it is worth noting that no useful classification of female homosexuals has been proposed. Most investigators group all homosexuals together for purposes of study.* Finally, another omission is of interest. There have been no studies of the children born to homosexual mothers, although Lidz and Lidz (1969) presented a case of a schizophrenic female whose mother had homosexual tendencies.

---

*Keiser and Schaffer (1949) classified homosexual female adolescents into three kinds: aggressive fighting masculine girls, outwardly passive girls, and completely maladjusted girls who had refused the feminine role from infancy onwards.

REFERENCES

Armon, V.: Some personality variables in overt female homosexuality. *J Proj Tech, 24*:292-309, 1960.
Bene, E.: On the genesis of female homosexuality. *Br J Psychiatry, 111*:815-821, 1965.
Bieber, I.: *Homosexuality.* New York, Basic, 1962.
Fromm, E., and Elonen, A.: The use of projective techniques in the study of a case of female homosexuality. *J Proj Tech, 15*:185-230, 1951.
Giannell, A.: Giannell's criminosynthesis theory applied to female homosexuality. *J Psychol, 64*:213-232, 1966.
Henry, G., and Galbraith, H.: Constitutional factors in homosexuals. *Am J Psychiatry, 13*:1249-1270, 1934.
Hopkins, J.: The lesbian personality. *Br J Psychiatry, 115*:1433-1436, 1969.
Hopkins, J.: Lesbian signs on the Rorschach. *Br J Proj Psychol Pers Stud, 15*:7-14, 1970.
Kaye, H., Berl, S., Clare, J., Eleston, M., Gershwin, B., Gershwin, P., Kogan, L., Torda, C., and Wilber, C.: Homosexuality in women. *Arch Gen Psychiatry, 17*:626-634, 1967.
Keiser, S., and Schaffer, D.: Environmental factors in homosexuality in adolescent girls. *Psychoanal Rev, 36*:283-295, 1949.
Kenyon, F.: Physique and physical health of female homosexuals. *J Neurol Neurosurg Psychiatry, 31*:487-489, 1968a.
Kenyon, F.: Studies in female homosexuality. *Acta Psychiatr Scand, 44*:224-237, 1968b.
Kenyon, F.: Studies in female homosexuality. *J Consult Clin Psychol, 32*:510-513, 1968c.
Kenyon, F.: Studies in female homosexuality. *Br J Psychiatry, 114*:1337-1350, 1968d.
Lidz, R., and Lidz, T.: Homosexual tendencies in mothers of schizophrenic women. *J Nerv Ment Dis, 149*:229-235, 1969.
Loraine, J., Ismail, A., Adamopoulos, D., and Dore, G.: Endocrine function in male and female homosexuals. *Br Med J, 4*:406-409, 1970.
Miller, W., and Hannum, T.: Characteristics of homosexuality involving incarcerated females. *J Consult Psychol, 27*:277, 1963.
Saghir, M., Robins, E., and Walbran, B.: Homosexuality. *Arch Gen Psychiatry, 21*:219-229, 1969.
Saghir, M., Robins, E., Walbran, B., and Gentry, K.: Homosexuality. *Am J Psychiatry, 127*:147-154, 1970.
Siegelman, M.: Adjustment of homosexual and heterosexual women. *Br J Psychiatry, 120*:447-481, 1972.
Thompson, N., McCandless, B., and Strickland, B.: Personal adjustment of male and female homosexuals and heterosexuals. *J Abnorm Psychol, 78*:237-240, 1971.
Thompson, N., Schwartz, D., McCandless, B., and Edwards, D.: Parent-child relationships and sexual identity in male and female homosexuals and heterosexuals. *J Consult Clin Psychol, 41*:120-127, 1973.

Wilson, M., and Greene, R.: Personality characteristics of female homosexuals. *Psychol Rep. 28*:407-412, 1971.

SECTION III
OTHER DEVIATIONS OF OBJECT

CHAPTER 15

INCEST

DEFINING THE PHENOMENA

INCESTUOUS BEHAVIOR PRIMARILY INVOLVES SEXUAL INTERCOURSE between a father and his daughter, a mother and her son, or a brother and his sister. However, the legal and cultural definitions of incest often extend beyond these three instances. For example, in Ohio incest is defined as adultery or fornication between persons of nearer kin by affinity than cousins. Thus incest may be committed by a stepfather and stepdaughter, an uncle and a niece by marriage, and a sister of the defendant's wife and the defendant. Excluded from this definition are the following: a husband and his wife's brother's wife and a father and his adopted daughter.

It is not relevant to the present purpose to survey different societal definitions of what constitutes incest. However, as Goody (1956) has noted, what anthropologists sometimes call incest for a particular society would be labelled as mere adultery in our society. Because of the variation in the definition of incest, different workers often use the term "incest" to refer to different behaviors.

FREQUENCIES OF OCCURRENCE

Incest is commonly held to be rare. Weinberg (1955) reported that the incidence of prosecuted incest participants in the United States is one-to-two cases per million per year. Prohibitions against incest are believed to be universal. Murdock (1949) surveyed 250 societies and found that no society permitted father/daughter, mother/son, or brother/sister intercourse or marriage.

Murdock missed some important societies, however. Slotkin (1947) has documented a lack of incest regulations and even a

This chapter is reprinted with permission from D. Lester, "Incest," *The Journal of Sex Research*, vol. 8 (1972). pp 268-285.

positive advocacy of next-of-kin marriage in old Iran. This was true for both rulers and commoners. Middleton (1962) noted that inbreeding was characteristic of all classes in Ancient Egypt. In the United States Schroeder (1915) felt that Mormons sanctioned almost all types of incest, although some psychologists dispute his opinions.* Many states outlawed first cousin marriages only recently.

Gebhard, et al. (1965) carried out a survey in the United States and were able to document that 3.9 percent of the average population had experienced incest and that 13.1 percent of a prison population had.

From the literature on incest, it seems that father-daughter incest is most common (e.g., Rhinehart, 1961). However, the data of Gebhard, et al. indicated that brother/sister incest is about five times as common as father/daughter incest. Mother/son incest is the rarest of the three. Moore (1964) found that brother/sister incest was five times more common than father/daughter incest and eleven times more common than mother/son incest in the creation myths of societies.

Freud argued that incest wishes are universal among human children. Lindzey (1967) tried to support Freud's assertion that man has strong and pervasive incestuous impulses with the following evidence. (1) The existence of a universal incest taboo, together with the strong emotions aroused by its violations, suggests strong incest impulses that require societal regulation. Although it has been shown that the taboo is not universal, it is certainly present in most societies. (2) Incest themes are common in the myths of primitive societies, the dreams of modern man, and literature. (3) The incidence of incestuous behavior is high in modern societies as indicated above. (4) Lindzey argued that mate selection is determined by homogamous need matching rather than complementary need matching and cited research to support this contention (Tharp, 1963). Furthermore, he noted that social choice is powerfully affected by physical and geographical proximity. Lindzey argued that these two factors made mate selection from within the nuclear family a high frequency choice unless regulated by society.

---

*Personal communication from Dr. James Deese.

"INCEST" IN LOWER ANIMALS

Work on inbreeding in lower animals may be informative with respect to human regulation of sexuality. Aberle, et al. (1963) suggested that inbreeding was rare in long-lived, large, slow-maturing, more intelligent animals since inbreeding depression (from genetic causes) would be more devastating in such animals. A different mechanism may work to prevent inbreeding in smaller animals. In animals where there are many offspring, frequent litters, and early sexual maturity, the number of possible sexual partners is increased relative to animals which produce few young and become sexually mature late in life. The probability that a mate will be chosen from among kin varies inversely with the number of possible choices. Thus, the short-lived, fast-maturing animals are statistically less likely to inbreed. Species which have long-lasting spouse pairs (such as the Canada goose) also show little inbreeding. The tendency toward outbreeding is facilitated by the parent's expelling the young when they reach sexual maturity.

Sade (1968) noted that mother/son incest was rare in free-ranging rhesus monkeys since (1) males often leave the group containing their mother, (2) higher-ranking males inhibit the mating behavior of lower-ranking males, and (3) young males are often of lower dominance than their mothers. Copulation between mother and son was observed only when the male became dominant over the mother. Thus, sociopsychological factors may also act to discourage inbreeding.

Segner (1968) reared male rats with their sisters and then allowed them to mate either with their sisters or with unrelated females. She found that males allowed to mate with their sisters showed less sexual behavior than those allowed to mate with unrelated females. Thus, familiarity through rearing appeared to dull sexual attraction. A study by Leziak (1965) confirmed these results, and data from Leziak (1964) and Krazanowska (1964) implicated the role of olfactory cues in this phenomenon.

The results of inbreeding are generally thought to reduce the biological fitness of the offspring since inbreeding increases the likelihood that recessive alleles will affect the organism and inherited deleterious conditions are more often recessive than dominant (e.g. Lindzey, 1967). However, McClearn (1967) has pointed out that general statements about inbreeding depression are true only for the average level of a stock composed of many lines. The behavior of any one line after inbreeding is to a large extent unpredictable.

THE RESULTS OF HUMAN INCEST

The Resulting Offspring

In view of the widespread distaste for incestuous sexual relations, it is important to ask whether such behavior actually has undesirable results. Recent reviews of studies of the effects of consanguinity on morbidity and mortality (Morton, 1961; Schull and Neel, 1965) have concluded that inbreeding does have a deleterious effect on humans. Adams and Neel (1967) compared the offspring of brother/sister and father/daughter incest with control offspring and found a greater incidence of major defects and early death in the incestuous offspring. Roberts (1967) reported an association between the degree of inbreeding and the frequency and severity of mental retardation among the inhabitants of Tristan da Cunha.

Schull and Neel (1965) reported on data from Japan comparing the offspring of marriages between cousins with those from nonconsanguineous marriages. The offspring of cousins were significantly worse in school performance, neuromuscular tests, WISC scores, physical dimensions, and age when they talked. They did not differ in skeletal measurements, dental tests, school attendance, or blood pressure. Inbreeding also had a significant effect on mortality and morbidity. Schull and Neel noted that the differences, though significant, were small.

However, inbreeding depression is not always found. Hartzog* has studied the Hutterites in Northern America and, although inbreeding has been common in these groups, their health is better than that of control groups.

Psychological Effects on the Incest Participants

There has been virtually no research on the effects of incestuous wishes or behavior on the participants. The effects of the experience on the child in parent/child incest have been thought to be deleterious (Kaufman, et al. 1954) but some workers have argued that negative effects can be minimal

*Personal communication from Dr. Sandra Hartzog.

(Yorukoglu and Kemph, 1966). The age at which the experience occurs has been hypothesized to be a crucial factor, with greater psychological harm to postadolescent children than to preadolescent children (Sloan and Karpinski, 1942). The anxiety and guilt of the parents have also been suggested as relevant variables (Barry and Johnson, 1958). Rascovsky and Rascovsky (1950) argued that overt incest could be less harmful to the personality than repressed incestuous desires.

Lidz, et al. (1965) noted that incest experiences were occasionally traumatic factors in the lives of schizophrenics, but there has been no counting of the exact frequency of occurence in these and comparison patients. Lidz, et al. suggested that a continuation of incestuous impulses into late adolescene and adulthood could be a focal issue in the patient's faulty ego structure (rather than an etiological factor). This state of affairs may occur when parents fail to repress their own incestuous desires and fail to facilitate the repression of incestuous desires in the children. This leads to panic and a fear of being overwhelmed in the children. The children cannot regress into a dependent state since this brings them nearer to the seductive parent. They therefore regress to a very primitive state and withdraw.

McCord, et al. (1962) followed up a group of normal and sexually deviant boys. Those deviants judged to be sexually anxious and repressed sexually to the point of phobia were found to have come from families where experiences of incest and illegitimacy were more common. McCord, et al. did not present data separating the experiences of incest and illegitimacy.

THE KINDS OF PEOPLE WHO COMMIT INCEST

Bias In The Research

Extensive bias is present in the research carried out on the participants in incest. First, the majority of subjects who come to the attention of researchers are those brought to court as a result of the incest behavior. This increases the apparent incidence in families from the lower social classes and the likelihood of incest being noted in disorganized, unstable families since these variables increase the chances that the incest will be reported and legal action instituted.

A second source of bias is that many cases of incest in the

literature are in families—some of whose members are in therapy. This increases the likelihood that the participants will be seen as psychologically disturbed. These biases are apparent in that most cases of incest reported are instances of father/daughter incest whereas brother/sister incest is much more common.

A third source of bias is that families are examined after the incest has been reported and legal or therapeutic action taken. These actions may have a profound effect on the family. Gligor (1967) did not find incestuous families disorganized or unstable as Weinberg (1955) did, and Gligor felt that Weinberg's data were a reflection of the disorganization brought about by the legal prosecution of Weinberg's fathers. It is clear from the case reports that prosecution of the father followed by jailing or detention in a psychiatric hospital for many years has a profound effect on the daughters. Usually the daughters are not allowed to see their fathers during this period, a separation that may be especially traumatic since commonly father/daughter incest is protracted rather than episodic. The guilt, sexual acting-out, and other behavior problems found in the daughters invariably commence after the discovery of the incest and the break-up of the home.

In addition, methodological problems are frequent in the research. Often control groups are not employed in the research design. Occasionally, some subjects are excluded (for reasons of low intelligence or too great a psychological disturbance) and so those tested may not be representative of incest participants. Occasionally, the results of the study are different for different racial or ethnic groups, and so the generality of the findings is suspect.

There have been no sound studies on mother/son or brother/sister incest. Thus, the following review of research deals solely with father/daughter incest.

Father/Daughter Incest

The conclusions of the many papers dealing with father/daughter incest by means of a case study approach have been summarized by Machotka, et al. (1967, pp. 99-100).

1) Although the incest-prone father may be influenced by loss of wife through death, separation, or divorce, father-daughter incest usually

occurs in an unbroken home and begins following sexual estrangement between husband and wife; the liasons are protracted, not episodic.

2) The liason is made possible and later perpetuated by the collusion of several members; father-daughter incest typically results from the mother pushing the daughter into adult responsibility; the mother is dependent and infantile and reverses the mother-daughter role with her daughter, thus assuming with her daughter the relationship she would have wished to have with her own rejecting mother. The mother generally feels worthless as mother and woman; sometimes she encourages father/daughter intimacy directly; her collusion is made possible for her by her very strong denial of the incestuous relation; in effect she is the cornerstone in the pathological family system.

3) The daughter sees the mother as cruel, unjust, and depriving; the daughter's incest with her father is therefore very importantly the daughter's revenge against the mother; the meaning of the incest for her is pre-genital, seeming to have the purpose of receiving some sort of parental interest.

Kaufman, et al. (1954) noted that the paternal grandfather had frequently deserted the family, and the mother's ties to the maternal grandmother were intense. The maternal grandmother was described as a stern, demanding, controlling, cold woman who focused her hostility felt toward the maternal grandfather onto the mother.

The Father

Martin (1960) compared men jailed for incest with their daughters to men jailed for sexual crimes against minors and for nonsexual crimes, eliminating those of low intelligence and severe mental disturbance. The incest offenders showed a greater amount of psychosexual disturbance as assessed by the Blacky Test (Blum, 1950); they were more orally dependent, had a higher castration anxiety, and a greater likelihood of unresolved Oedipal conflict. The groups did not differ in their responses to TAT cards scored to measure resentment toward authority, contempt, and hostility toward women; the sexual availability of their wives; their own ability to compete; and the perception of adolescent females as sexually available. Martin felt that the tests used may have been inadequate measures of the variables and, furthermore, that the fact that all subjects were in prison may have affected his results. For example, all subjects saw their wives as sexually unavailable, which was true.

Gebhard, et al. (1965) extended the research of Alfred Kinsey to a study of sexual offenders, including incest offenders who were compared with other kinds of sex offenders, other prisoners, and the average population. The incest offender against children (ages zero to eleven) had a poor relationship with his parents and came from an unhappy unstable home. He engaged in much premarital sex, chiefly with girls. He was typically ineffectual, nonaggressive, dependent, drank heavily, worked sporadically, and was preoccupied with sex. He liked mouth-genital contact, variety in coital positions, lengthy foreplay, extramarital coitus, and frequent masturbation after marriage. Incest offenders against minors (aged twelve to fifteen) were too diverse and nondescript for Gebhard, et al. to describe. On the whole, sex was not too important for them. Alcohol played a part in precipitating the act.

Incest offenders against adults (aged sixteen +) came from large families with many sisters. The relationship with the parents was good, and there was little premarital sexual activity. They were quite moral and concerned with public opinion and preferred sex with prostitutes than with their fiances. After marriage, they were restrained sexually but fertile. In their middle thirties they began to take an interest in mouth-genital contact and extramarital sex. They were less often criminals or alcoholics and were the most opposed to homosexuality. In sum, they were conservative, moralistic, restrained, religiously devout, traditional, and uneducated. Their impulse control was poor, and they came from families where morality was stressed publicly but breached privately.

Frosch and Bromberg (1939) published data on the demographic and personal history of different kinds of sex offenders. Analysis of these data* indicates that the incest offenders resemble most closely the pedophiliacs and least closely those men accused of statutory rape. These kinds of comparisons extended to an examination of psychological variables would be of interest.

Ellis and Brancale (1956) compared incest offenders with other sex offenders and found no differences in psychological disturbance, recidivism, intelligence, emotional deprivation

---

*D. Lester, "The Incestuous Father as a Pedophiliac," unpublished paper, 1972.

during the childhood, or basic hostility. The incest offenders were less likely to be sexually inhibited, were more emotionally immature, and were more likely to have been drunk at the time of the offense.

Weinberg (1955) hypothesized that there were three kinds of incestuous fathers. The *endogamic* father confines his sexual objects to family members and resorts to incest with a daughter or sister because he does not cultivate and does not crave social or sexual contacts with women outside of the family. Some incestuous fathers are *indiscriminately promiscuous.* These men are often psychopathic. A third kind are *pedophiles* and are retarded psychosexually and socially immature.

The Daughter

Myerhoff (1963) had probation officers rate the families of delinquent girls with and without experience of incest for over 100 characteristics and found differences for only fourteen variables. Some differences reflected greater instability and incompatibility in the incestuous families. The other differences centered around the mothers. The mothers in the incestuous families had lower self-esteem, were more lax, were more distant from the daughter (yet saw her as a confidante), were more promiscuous, and were more apt to drink heavily. In view of the small number of differences, Myerhoff concluded that the incest families were not extremely deviant.

Using the semantic differential, Myerhoff found that the two groups of girls did not differ in their ratings of "father" as compared to other concepts. However, the mothers of the incestuous girls were perceived as less worthy role models and the value of femininity was minimized. The incestuous girls also had lower self-esteem.

The mothers of the incestuous girls were described by their daughters on the absolute ratings of the semantic differential as more strong, kind, beautiful, friendly, and soft than the mothers of the nonincestuous girls. Myerhoff felt that this could reflect the operation of defense mechanisms of denial, rationalization, and overcompensation. It might also reflect the expression of desired rather than perceived characteristics. The girls did not differ in the absolute ratings of their fathers. Myerhoff concluded that the mothers were the crucial figures in incestuous families.

Weiss (1955) investigated the role of the girl in initiating and maintaining the relationship. In incest with fathers, brothers, and uncles the girls took an active role in about 60 percent of the instances. In incest with stepfathers and stepbrothers, the girls took an active role in about 100 percent of the instances.

The Mother

Gligor (1967) compared families where the father was charged with incest with the daughter to families where the daughter was charged with nonincestuous heterosexual offenses. Here data indicated that the incestuous fathers were more deviant (promiscuous, history of drinking, previous charges, etc.) than the fathers of delinquent girls and that the delinquent girls were more deviant than the incestuous daughters.

The mothers of incestuous daughters were more often stepmothers, were younger, more promiscuous, and had more children than the mothers of delinquent daughters. The incest mothers tended to be more lax and indifferent toward their daughters (though the daughters did not feel less loved). Their reaction toward the offense was more often indifference or ambivalence. The mothers of the incestuous girls were less likely to be pregnant at the initiation of the offense than the mothers of delinquent girls. This does not support the notion that the sexual unavailability of the mother provokes the father's incest behavior. The homes of both groups were equally stable.

Gligor analyzed her data separately for whites and blacks. The results above were for whites. There were too few blacks in the sample for significant differences to appear. It should also be noted here that Gligor's statistical tests were incorrectly carried out.

THE ORIGIN OF THE INCEST TABOO

How did incestuous behavior come to be forbidden not only by law but by taboo? At least seven major theories of the taboo's origin have been proposed.

The Genetic Theory

The genetic theory states that there are biological results from inbreeding that makes survival of the population less likely. Inbreeding does appear to have deleterious consequences for the offspring (see above). Lindzey noted that he could find no examples of inbreeding resulting in the accentuation of an advantageous characteristic. He argued that inbred populations might be superior in one characteristic, but overall they would be less fit and able to survive. The data mentioned above from the Hutterites refutes this argument.

A second objection to the theory is that primitive man could not have been aware of the relationship between incest and inferior offspring. Segner (1968) noted that many primitive societies were aware of the relationship. However, natural selection could operate regardless of the awareness of the society about the relationship between incest and inferior offspring.

The Indifference Theory

Westermarck (1894) postulated an innate sexual repulsion among all kin while Freud (1949) postulated a universal sexual attraction between kin. Fox (1962) resolved these contradictory positions by postulating the following. Close interaction as siblings leads to aversion after puberty; this should lead to low levels of anxiety about incest in a society and therefore only mild sanctions against it. Separation as siblings leads to desire and temptation after puberty. This will lead to high levels of anxiety over incest in the society and strong sanctions against it.

Wolf (1966, 1970) noted that the marriages in Taiwan where the bride is raised from childhood with the groom are much more unstable than conventional marriages. Talmon (1964) noted that sabras raised together in Israeli Kibbutzim rarely, if ever, marry or have sexual intercourse with one another.

Sex appears to be aversive with those with whom one was raised. Why? Fox felt that learning played the major role here. Contact between family members, at least one of whom is sexually immature, results in sexual excitement which cannot be satisfied, which in turn leads to frustration and anger, the evocation of competing responses, and a consequent dulling of sexual desire toward the stimulating other. Wolf argued that socialization involves inhibition of impulses (sexual, aggressive, etc.) toward family members. Furthermore, socialization involves punishment and pain, and children socialized together associate each other with this experience. Sexual behavior is rare in situations where one has experienced pain (Beach, 1951). Clearly, however, the incest taboos extend to those who were not raised in close association with one another.

The indifference theory is not pertinent to the origin of the taboo against incest, since sexual repulsion between kin would not require the support of a taboo (Aberle, et al., 1963). The indifference theory is more pertinent to the behavior of incest per se. Although it does explain some phenomena of incestuous behavior, the frequency of incestuous relationships suggests that the indifference aroused by group rearing can easily be overcome.

Role Strain Theory

Coult (1963) noted that in many societies sexual intercourse was allowed between relatives who were forbidden to marry. Relatives allowed to marry were always allowed to have sexual intercourse. Since exogamy rules are broader in scope than incest rules, they can be used to account for incest rules.

Coult argued that exogamy rules serve to prevent confusion of multiple kin roles. Some relatives of a child have defined roles with respect to that child. If such a relative married that child, then the relative will have two roles: the former role and that of spouse. This will create role strain. Exogamy facilitates adaptation to new family roles by providing a neutral person with respect to whom the person can form the new role. It preserves the structure of role differentiation and eliminates role strain. Weich (1968) felt that referring to family members by their role ("mother," "sister," etc.) was a way of defending against incest desires.

This theory can easily explain why particular secondary relatives may be covered by the incest rules of a particular society. For example, in patrilineal societies, the patrilineal relatives have defined roles and the incest taboos extend to patrilineal relatives (Murdock, 1949). A similar pattern is observed in matrilineal and bilineal societies.

Family Cohesiveness Theory

Seligman (1932) argued that any kind of family conflict is disruptive and that sexual jealousy between kin is most disruptive. Thus, incest taboos serve to consolidate the family as a cooperative unit, promote the efficiency of its societal services, and strengthen the society as a whole by eliminating this source of conflict. However, Aberle, et al. (1963) noted that sharing of spouses does occur in some societies. Sisters may share a husband or father and son share a wife. However, no society permits sharing of a husband by mother and daughter, a situation which might involve more conflict than the above examples.

Socialization Theory

Parsons (1954) argued that erotic gratification of the child was an indispensible instrument of the socialization process. The parent socializes the child by making use of the child's erotic needs. Unrestricted gratification however, would stand in the way of the maturation of the child's personality and the efficient functioning of society. The institution of the family provides the organized setting for positive utilization of erotic factors while the incest taboo prevents its getting out of hand. The incest taboo is universal because it regulates the universal erotic component of socialization. This theory is clearly better able to explain parent/child incest taboos than other incest taboos.

Survival Theory

Slater (1959) argued that incest was virtually impossible for early primitive man since there was a dearth of appropriate partners. By the time a child reached sexual maturity, his parents were probably dead. Siblings were rarely available since few survived to maturity and those that did were quickly paired off. If an elder sibling were available, by the time the younger sibling was sexually mature the elder sibling would have wasted part of his or her fertile period. The pair would thus have less time to produce offspring than exogamous pairs, and their line would either die out or be forced into exogamy. This would be true for parent/child marriage also.

Slater argued, therefore, that exogamy was inevitable. This led to cooperative bonds between families and institutionalization of these practices so that, when survival was easier and incest might have been possible, the customs were too entrenched to change. The incest taboos were instituted to maintain the societal customs that had developed.

Culturalogical Theory

White (1948) argued that man could not have survived without cooperation between families and between tribes. The incest taboo guaranteed the exchange of women between groups and helped to ensure such cooperation. Seligman (1950) noted, however, that if society did not require that spouses be virgins at marriage, there would be no need for an incest taboo. Premarital sexual intercourse between family members would not prevent alliances between families.

Comments

The papers reviewed above have several shortcomings. (1) A major problem is the implication that there is only one topic here. In fact there are at least five: the occurrence of incest in different societies, the existence of a taboo in different societies, the emotional reaction to incest, the sanctions against incest in different societies, and the extension of the incest taboo outside the nuclear family. (2) A second major problem is the implication that the variables are dichotomous. The frequency of incest in different societies, the severity of sanctions, and so on vary continuously across different societies. This dichotomous thinking (incest occurs or it does not) leads to the implication that the behaviors are universal, that every society has, for example, an incest taboo. Rather each society has a different kind of taboo enforced with different degrees of rigor. (3) Thirdly, these many facets of incest behavior may not be independent. (4) Finally, it is time to accept that there is not just one correct theory, as many authors imply. Each theory may contribute a part to the total explanation as is discussed below.

DISCUSSION

Several facts have emerged from this review. First, it seems valid to conclude that the offspring of incestuous breeding are somewhat more likely to be biologically impaired than the offspring of nonincestuous breeding. A second conclusion is that previous investigators of incest behavior have erred in estimating the frequency of incest behavior. In 1949, Murdock could argue that incest taboos were present in every society that he studied, yet since then a lack of incest taboos has been documented in Ancient Iran and Ancient Egypt, to give but two examples. Whereas investigators have cited criminal prosecutions for incest of one case per million, data from Gebhard, et al. (1965) indicate that 4 percent of Americans have had incest experiences.

The research into incestuous behavior is quite inadequate in some respects. The majority of reports study father/daughter incest which is not the most common form of incestuous behavior. The studies are often methodologically weak. Furthermore, the bias that incestuous behavior is the behavior of psychologically disturbed individuals is prevalent. This bias is found in those concerned with the legal aspects of incest. It is regrettable that the bias is also found in social science researchers. Incest behavior can take place without any special psychological harm to the participants and without disrupting the family (Yorukoglu and Kemph, 1966). It is clear that in many cases of father/daughter incest, incarceration of the father in a jail or a psychiatric hospital serves to increase the psychological distress of the family. This is especially true for the daughter, who in such situations must deal with the guilt over providing evidence against her father and with the loss of a loved parent.

Apart from these areas of bias, there are several omissions. It is clear that incest participants are a heterogeneous group of people. As yet there is no adequate way to categorize the kinds of individuals involved. Bagley (1969) identified five types of father offender: *functional,* in which incest played a role in the stability and pattern of family interactions; *accidental* or *disorganized,* in which the incest took place impulsively under stress in disorganized living; *pathological,* in which the participant is mentally retarded or psychologically disturbed; *object fixation,* in which the incest offender has a stable psychological fixation upon particular forms of sexual gratification; and a *residual category*. The adequacy of this particular taxonomy has not yet been tested. However, without a taxonomy progress in understanding the incest participant will be slow. The data of Gebhard, et al, (1965) indicate, for example, that the age of the daughter in father/daughter incest is associated with the psychological characteristics and the behavior of the father. Perhaps this kind of factor needs to be incorporated into an adequate taxonomy.

A striking feature of the research reviewed above is that the incest participants did not on the whole differ greatly from control groups. They were not more severely disturbed, for example, or more sadistic. This finding of few differences is all the more remarkable since these studies were of the small proportion of incestuous acts that come to the knowledge of the legal profession. The majority of incestuous acts do not result in public exposure or prosecution, and the differences between these participants and a comparison population may be quite small and so require very sensitive psychological tests in order to explore the psychodynamics involved.

Theorization about incest and the incest taboo has produced ideas with some explanatory power, although no single theory deals adequately with all the issues. Let us first consider the relevance of the theories to the incest taboo. Greaves (1966) noted that the genetic and indifference theories make a taboo unnecessary. The only reasons Greaves could advance for the origin of the taboo came from a statement by Wolf (1966) that people are repelled by transgressions of what they themselves would not feel comfortable doing. To protect their sensibilities, they institute a taboo. If incestuous tendencies are present in all of us, then incestuous behavior in others and in our kin presents us with stimuli that are threatening to us. The taboo serves to keep the anxiety, aroused through stimulation of our repressed desires, to a minimum. Greaves felt that the culturalogical theory and the indifference theory could act to maintain the taboo once it was originated.

How do the theories cope with the behavior of incest? The genetic, survival, and indifference theories adequately explain the infrequency of incest behavior in societies. The culturalogical, family cohesiveness, and socialization theories could act to maintain the infrequency of the behavior in societies.

Another issue that must be dealt with is the question of the extent to which incest taboos have extended beyond the nuclear family. Only one theory, Coult's role strain theory, is applicable here. Goody (1956) is the only theorist to attend to the issue of the emotional reaction of the society to transgressions of the incest taboo. He argued, with examples, that brother/sister incest is viewed with horror in societies where descent moves through the female members of the clan, as in the matrilineal Ashanti. In the patrilineal Tallensi, on the other hand, brother/ sister incest is merely a disreputable offense. The importance of the females in the Ashanti, the sisters, suggests that Coult's role strain theory is applicable to this phenomenon. The sisters have important roles in determining descent and, therefore, role strain would be high for them if they were to become a wife of their brother.

With regard to the different frequencies of occurrence of the different pairings in incest, only the indifference theory could account for the greater frequency of father/daughter incest over mother/son incest. The tie between mother and son is closer than that between father and daughter, and learned aversion will be greater.

REFERENCES

Aberle, D., Bronfenbrenner, U., Hess, E., Miller, D., Schneider, D., and Spuhler, J.: The incest taboo and the mating patterns of animals. *Am Anthropol, 65*:253-265, 1963.

Adams, M.S., and Neel, J.V.: Children of incest. *Pediatrics, 40*:55-62, 1967.

Bagley, C.: Incest behavior and incest taboo. *Soc Prob, 16*:505-519, 1969.

Barry, M.J., and Johnson, A.: The incest barrier. *Psychoanal Q, 27*:485-500, 1958.

Beach, F.A.: Instinctive behavior. In Stevens, S.S. (Ed.): *Handbook of Experimental Psychology.* New York, Wiley, 1951, pp. 387-434.

Blum, G.S.: *The Blacky Pictures.* New York, Psychological Corporation, 1950.

Coult, A.D.: Causality and cross-sex prohibitions. *Am Anthropol, 65*:266-277, 1963.

Ellis, A., and Brancale, R.: *The Psychology of Sex Offenders.* Springfield, Thomas, 1956.

Fox, J.R.: Sibling incest. *Br J Sociol, 13*:128-150, 1962.

Freud, S.: *An Outline of Psychoanalysis.* New York, Norton, 1949.

Frosch, J., and Bromberg, W.: The sex offender. *Am J Orthopsychiatry, 9*:761-766, 1939.

Gebhard, P.H., Gagnon, J.H., Pomeroy, W.B., and Christenson, C.V.: *Sex Offenders.* New York, Har-Row, 1965.

Gligor, A.M.: Incest and sexual delinquency. *Diss Abstr, 27B*:3671, 1967.

Goody, J.: A comparative approach to incest and adultery. *Br J Sociol,* 7:286-305, 1956.
Greaves, T.: Explaining incest rules. *Cornell J Soc Rel,* 1:39-50, 1966.
Kaufman, I., Peck, A.L., and Tagiuri, C.K.: The family constellation and overt incestuous relations between father and daughter. *Am J Orthopsychiatry,* 24:266-279, 1954.
Krazanowska, H.: Studies on heterosis. Cited in Segner (1968).
Leziak, K.: The influence exerted by olfactory agents on the course of the sexual cycle in female mice. *Genet Pol,* 5:363-369, 1964.
Leziak, K.: Influence of external and genetic factors on the amount of inbreeding. *Genet Pol,* 6:177-196, 1965.
Lidz, T., Fleck, S., and Cornelison, A.R.: *Schizophrenia and the Family.* New York, International Universities Press, 1965.
Lindzey, G.: Some remarks concerning incest, the incest taboo, and psychoanalytic theory. *Am Psychol,* 22:1051-1059, 1967.
Machotka, P., Pittman, F.S., and Flomenhaft, K.: Incest as a family affair. *Family Process,* 6:98-116, 1967.
Martin, J.O.: A psychological investigation of convicted incest offenders by means of projective techniques. *Diss Abstr,* 21:241, 1960.
McClearn, G.: Gene, generality, and behavior research. In Hirsch, J. (Ed.): *Behavior Genetic Analysis.* New York, McGraw, 1967, pp. 307-321.
McCord, W., McCord, J., and Verden, P.: Family relationships and sexual deviance in lower class adolescents. *Int J Soc Psychiatry,* 8:165-179, 1962.
Middleton, R.: Brother-sister and father-daughter marriage in ancient Egypt. *Am Sociol Rev,* 27:603-611, 1962.
Moore, S.: Descent and symbolic filiation. *Am Anthropol,* 66:1308-1321, 1964.
Morton, N.E.: Morbidity of children from consanguinous marriages. In Steinberg, A.G. (Ed.): *Progress in Medical Genetics.* New York, Grune, 1961, 1, 261-291.
Murdock, G.P.: *Social Structure.* New York, Macmillan, 1949.
Myerhoff, B.G.: Incest in myth and fact. Master's thesis, University of Chicago, 1963.
Parsons, T.: The incest taboo in relation to social structure and the socialization of the child. *Br J Sociol,* 5:101-117, 1954.
Rascovsky, M., and Rascovsky, A.: On consummated incest. *Int J Psychoanal,* 31:42-47, 1950.
Rhinehart, J.W.: Genesis of overt incest. *Comp Psychiatry,* 2:338-349, 1961.
Roberts, D.F.: Incest, inbreeding, and mental abilities. *Br Med J,* 4:336-337, 1967.
Sade, D.S.: Inhibition of son-mother mating among free-ranging rhesus monkeys. *Sci Psychoanal,* 12:18-38, 1968.
Schroeder, T.: Incest in Mormonism. *Am J Urol Sexol,* 11:409-416, 1915.
Schull, W.J., and Neel, J.V.: *The Effects of Inbreeding on Japanese Children.* New York, Har-Row, 1965.
Segner, L.L.: Two studies of the incest taboo. *Diss Abstr,* 29B:796, 1968.
Seligman, B.Z.: The incest barrier. *Br J Psychol,* 22:250-276, 1932.

Seligman, B.Z.: The problem of incest and exogamy. *Am Anthropol,* 52:305-316, 1950.

Slater, M.K.: Ecological factors in the origin of incest. *Am Anthropol,* 61:1042-1059, 1959.

Sloane, P., and Karpinski, E.: Effects of incest on participants. *Am J Orthopsychiatry,* 12:666-673, 1942.

Slotkin, J.S.: On a possible lack of incest regulations in old Iran. *Am Anthropol,* 49:612-617, 1947.

Tharp, R.G.: Psychological patterning in marriage. *Psychol Bull,* 60:97-117, 1963.

Weich, M.J.: The terms "mother" and "father" as a defence against incest. *J Am Psychoanal Assoc,* 16:783-791, 1968.

Weinberg, S.K.: *Incest Behavior.* New York, Citadel, 1955.

Weiss, J., Rogers, E., Darwin, M.R., and Dutton, C.E.: A study of girl sex victims. *Psychiatr Q,* 29:1-27, 1955.

Westermarck, E.: *The History of Human Marriage.* London, Macmillan, 1894.

White, L.A.: The definition and prohibition of incest. *Am Anthropol,* 50:416-435, 1948.

Wolf, A.P.: Childhood association, sexual attraction, and the incest taboo. *Am Anthropol,* 68:883-898, 1966.

Wolf, A.P.: Childhood association and sexual attraction. *Am Anthropol,* 72:503-515, 1970.

Yorukoglu, A., and Kemph, J.P.: Children not severely damaged by incest with a parent. *J Am Acad Child Psychiatry,* 5:111-124, 1966.

CHAPTER 16

PEDOPHILIA

PEDOPHILES ARE THOSE WHO HAVE CHOSEN CHILDREN AS OBJECTS FOR SEXUAL GRATIFICATION. Samples of pedophiles often include incest offenders; for example, Frisbie (1959) reported that 27 percent of a sample of heterosexual pedophiles were incest offenders.

There have been few adequate categorizations of pedophiles proposed. Bromberg (1965) distinguished between pansexuals (who were gratified by any sexual object and who tended toward attraction for boys) and the sexually neurotic (who tend to be attracted toward girls). A distinction is usually made between heterosexual and homosexual pedophiles, and a number of differences between these two kinds of pedophiles have been reported. Fitch (1962) classified pedophiles as immature, frustrated, sociopathic, pathological (retarded, psychotics, etc.), and miscellaneous. Homosexual pedophiles were more often judged to be immature and sociopathic whereas heterosexual pedophiles were more often judged to be frustrated and pathological.

CHARACTERISTICS OF PEDOPHILIA

Mohr, et al. (1962) found heterosexual and homosexual pedophiles to be very different. The victims of the heterosexual pedophiles, for example, were quite young (aged six to twelve with a peak at ten and eleven) while the homosexual pedophiles chose victims from all ages. This age difference in victims has been reported in other studies (Frisbie, 1959).

In heterosexual pedophilia, the act usually involved fondling and exhibiting the genitals (and sometimes seemed to be an extension of exhibitionistic behavior). Homosexual pedophiles more often tried to reach orgasm via fellatio, masturbation, and anal intercourse. Orgasm was sought by 6 percent of the heterosexual pedophiles and 50 percent of the homosexual pedophiles. The heterosexual offenses occurred primarily in the home of the pedophile or the victim. This was less often true for the homosexual pedophile who tended more to seek out the victim and set up a rendezvous. The heterosexual pedophile often had a close relationship to the victim whereas the homosexual pedophile was less often related to the victim. For both kinds of pedophiles, the victim was rarely an absolute stranger.

Other deviations were rare in the pedophiles: a few of the heterosexual pedophiles had been exhibitionists and a few of the homosexual pedophiles had been labelled as homosexuals.

The age distribution of the pedophiles was trimodal.

   1. The adolescent pedophile was usually psychosexually and psychosocially retarded and had had no sexual experience with adults and did not desire it.

   2. The middle-aged pedophile (in his mid to late thirties) was characterized by regression. He had severe marital and social maladjustment, and alcohol played a significant role in his behavior. Actual or quasi-incestuous wishes were common, and he quite often assumed a parental role toward the victim.

   3. The old age pedophile (mid to late fifties) was a lonely, impotent man. His social and psychological state was usually much sounder and he was less likely to be a recivist. However, some of this group were chronic pedophiles.

The intelligence distribution of the pedophiles was average with no differences between the homosexual pedophiles and the heterosexual pedophiles. However, like the exhibitionists studied by Mohr, et al. (1962), their educational attainment was poorer than average (again with no differences between the heterosexual and the homosexual pedophiles). About one third of the pedophiles had been in the armed services. The pedophiles had more social interests than the exhibitionists, especially in youth groups such as the scouts (which perhaps reflects their sexual interests).

The heterosexual pedophile had a vague concept of his father and his description of the father was undifferentiated and impersonal. The homosexual pedophile saw his father as distant but was more likely to express positive affect and to express a wish for his father's affection.

The heterosexual pedophile described his mother in terms related to his dependency needs (describing her as either supportive or rather cold) while the homosexual pedophile had a very positive relationship with his mother.

There were no differences in birth order, family size, or the male/female sex ratio of the siblings. Heterosexual pedophiles tended to talk more of their sisters whereas homosexual pedophiles talked more of their brothers (which is consistent with their sexual orientation).

Most of the young heterosexual pedophiles over twenty years of age were or had been married, whereas only about a half of the homosexual pedophiles were or had been married. The pedophiles tended to marry later than the exhibitionists studied by Mohr, et al. The middle-aged heterosexual pedophiles had a poor marital adjustment (separation, disintegration due to alcohol, promiscuity by the wife, and conflict). The middle-aged homosexual pedophiles had loose relationships with a quiet wife who was often frigid. The old age heterosexual pedophiles either had a dependency marriage to a rich wife or a lack of personal and sexual attraction in an outwardly stable marriage. The old age homosexual pedophiles were rarely married.

The pedophiles complained more about their physical health than the exhibitionists, but in actuality were as healthy. Diagnoses of neurosis or psychosis were rare. The recividism rate was 13 percent after three years. The recividism rate was three times higher for the homosexual pedophiles than for the heterosexual pedophiles. Similarly, Frisbie (1965) reported that homosexual pedophiles were twice as likely to repeat as compared to heterosexual pedophiles. Pedophiles who were recidivists were less often married, were younger and better educated, and more often had a foreign born mother than a foreign born father. They did not differ in religion, occupation, or whether a migrant or not.

McCaghy (1968) compared pedophiles who denied or excused their acts (for example, by blaming alcohol) with those who accepted their guilt. When asked what the motives of other pedophiles were, the deniers more often gave derogatory attributions, and both the deniers and excusers recommended more punitive measures for pedophiles. McCaghy saw the deniers and excusers as disavowing their deviancy in order to sustain their identity as normal.

Fitch (1962) compared heterosexual and homosexual pedophiles and found no differences in age, age at first offense, and intelligence. The heterosexual pedophiles had fewer convictions for sex offenses, were more often laborers, were less often single, had less recidivism, and more often were incestuous offenders.

Toobert, et al. (1959) compared pedophiles with general offenders. The modal pedophile was white, near his fortieth year, married, educated only through grammar school, a first offender, from a broken home, and admitted his guilt. The MMPI profile of the pedophiles was elevated over the profile for general offenders on the *Mf* and *Pa* scales. An examination of the items differentiating the pedophiles from other offenders showed the pedophile to be sexually dissatisfied, with strong religious interests, feelings of inadequcy in his interpersonal relations, sensitive to the evaluations of others, and with a good deal of guilt.

Nedoman, et al. (1971) compared homosexual pedophiles, heterosexual pedophiles with victims aged zero to twelve, and heterosexual pedophiles with victims aged twelve to fifteen. The groups did not differ in their adolescent heterosexual experiences. The homosexual pedophiles masturbated at an earlier age than the heterosexual pedophiles and more often; the heterosexual pedophiles against teenagers masturbated latest and least often. The homosexual pedophiles also masturbated more as adults, while the heterosexual pedophiles against teenagers had the most heterosexual experience as adults. The sexual activity of the homosexual pedophiles and heterosexual pedophiles against children was higher than normal, while that of the heterosexual pedophiles against teenagers was normal. The homosexual pedophiles had the most pedophilic contacts and the heterosexual pedophiles against teenagers the least. Manual sexual contact was used most by the homosexual pedophiles, coital contact by the heterosexual pedophiles against teenagers, oral contact most by the homosexual pedophiles and the heterosexual pedophiles against children, and having the child masturbate the man was used most by the homosexual pedophiles.

Shoor, et al. (1966) noted, in agreement with other reports that, although the intelligence scores of pedophiles were quite variable, the educational achievement of the men was below capacity.

PSYCHOLOGICAL STUDIES OF PEDOPHILES

Freund (1967) measured sexual arousal by noting changes in penis size and explored the reactions of pedophiles to slides. Heterosexual pedophiles preferred female children over female adults but preferred any female over any male. The homosexual pedophiles preferred male children over male adults but preferred female children over adult males. Thus, sex of object was more important to the heterosexual pedophile while age was more important to the homosexual pedophile. The homosexual pedophiles differed in this respect from the homosexuals who preferred teenage males and adult males, but who preferred any male over any female.

Hammer (1954a, 1954b, 1955) carried out a study on rapists, pedophiles, and nonsexual offenders in prison using the House-Tree-Person Test. Rapists, heterosexual pedophiles, and homosexual pedophiles showed no differences in the sex of the first drawn person. The trees of the rapists were older than the trees of the heterosexual pedophiles (no data were given on the homosexual pedophiles), and the female figure drawn was older than the male figure drawn for the heterosexual pedophiles but not for the rapists. Hammer interpreted these differences as indicating that the psychosexual age of the heterosexual pedophiles (as assessed by the age of the tree) was less than that of the rapists and that the heterosexual pedophiles were characterized by feelings of inferiority or maternalization of sex figures, rendering them forbidden (as assessed by the relative ages of the male and female figures drawn). Fewer of the rapists described their tree as dead, more of the heterosexual pedophiles so described their trees, while even more of the homosexual pedophiles did so. This was felt by Hammer to reflect greater psychopathology with increasingly inappropriate sexual object choice.

In a Rorschach study, Hammer and Jacks (1955) studied movement responses to Card III. The homosexual and heterosexual pedophiles responded similarly, giving fewer extensor movement responses than the rapists (supposedly indicating less assertiveness) and less often gave no movement responses (supposedly indicating less hostility and a less dehumanizing approach toward people). The groups did not differ in flexor responses (supposedly a reflection of dependency and lack of assertiveness) or blocked movement responses (supposedly indicating indecisiveness).

Pascal and Herzberg (1952) compared offenders who had committed acts of rape, homosexuality, heterosexual pedophilia, and nonsexual offenses. The subjects were administered the Rorschach test and two measures were found to differentiate the groups: rejecting a card and whether a genital organ was seen in a statistically unusual place on a card. The more deviant the choice of sexual object, the more deviant the responding to the Rorschach using these criteria. That is to say, the pedophiles and homosexuals more often met the criteria than the rapists and nonsexual offenders.

Fisher (1969) examined the Edwards Personal Preference Schedule scores of heterosexual pedophiles, and Fisher and Howell (1970) looked at the scores of homosexual pedophiles. Control scores came from studies by other investigators. The homosexual pedophiles scored lower than the heterosexual pedophiles on *order* and *endurance* and higher on *heterosexuality*, but did not differ on the other thirteen scales. Compared to the norms for males, both groups of pedophiles differed on about half of the scales. Both groups of pedophiles scored lower on *aggression* and *autonomy* and higher on *intraception* and *abasement*. The homosexual pedophiles scored lower on *achievement* and *order* and higher on *nurturance* and *heterosexuality* (perhaps they were faking normality), while the heterosexual pedophiles scored lower on *change* and higher on *endurance* and *deference*.

Cowen and Stricker (1963) reported that pedophiles (and alcoholics) rated the social desirability of adjectives less extremely than schizophrenics, hospital controls, and normals. The ratings of the pedophiles differed considerably from those of normals, differed moderately from those of schizophrenics and hospital controls, and differed only a little from those of the alcoholics. Stricker (1964, 1967) reported a similar avoidance of extreme ratings for a task which involved rating ink blots and the Blacky pictures on the Semantic Differential scales. On the Blacky pictures, the pedophiles were inconsistent in their ratings of cards 1 and 2, which Stricker felt reflected oral problems. Overall, Stricker concluded that pedophiles were responding guardedly, trying to reveal little, and he felt that they were infantile and feminine in their response patterns.

A number of clinical studies of pedophiles have appeared, and Kurland (1960) noted the following traits were stressed by the authors: early infantile deprivation, fear of maternal separation, a great deal of sibling rivalry and hostility, inability to directly express aggression, some degree of grandiosity, one or more episodes of depersonalization, a clinical diagnosis of schizophrenia, and being a loner. Pedophiles were rarely found to be old men with senile or chronic brain syndromes. They were usually passive, immature persons, without the courage to attempt sexual relations with mature females.

THE SEXUAL HISTORY OF PEDOPHILES

Gebhard, et al. (1965) divided pedophiles by the sex and the age of the victim and by the amount of aggression used. The aggressors against children were on the whole intellectually retarded and came from broken and unhappy homes. As teenagers they had poor relationships with females, and they came to rely on prostitutes. They had numerous unstable marriages. The heterosexual offenders against children were older men who had difficulty delaying gratification due to personality defects or mental retardation. They rushed into marriage, masturbated often even after marriage, and utilized prostitutes and children who were strangers as sexual partners. They were often moral and conservative and sexually restrained with their wives. With the child victims, they rarely attempted intercourse and were on the whole nonviolent men.

The homosexual offenders against children came from broken homes and had poor relationships with their parents. They had a good deal of homosexual experience around the time of puberty. Almost a third had been sexually approached by older men. As adults, they masturbated often and had a low frequency of heterosexual activity. They were sexually flexible as to the age, gender, or species of their sexual partner.

The aggressors versus minors came from broken homes where there was much parental friction. They were generally delinquent and were irresponsible, aggressive, amoral, with an inability to delay gratification. They were active sexually and sought novelty and variation in their sex. They often rushed into unstable marriages. The heterosexual offenders versus minors were a healthy group who had had good relationships with their parents. They were unimaginative, uneducated, and lower class. They were free and easy with other people's property. The offense was usually their first conviction. Often their offense was an error of judgment.

The homosexual offenders versus minors had had a bad relationship with their fathers and a poor one with their mothers. They socialized well as children and were involved in a good deal of prepubertal sex play, often homosexual, and with frequent oral and anal activity. After puberty, their homosexual orientation grew and few married. They were on the whole homosexual men who were retreating from the adult homosexual competition, or who had made an error of judgment in choosing a partner.

On the whole, the younger the victim the greater the pedophilic tendencies of the man, the more force used the more delinquent and amoral the man, and the choice of male children reflected the homosexual orientation of the man.

Gebhard and Gagnon (1964) reported on a group of pedophiles (mainly heterosexual) who had used children under the age of five. (The offenders against children discussed above used children aged zero to twelve.) Compared to other sexual offenders, they did not differ in the incidence of broken homes, their present relationship with their parents, homosexual experiences with adult males, sexual play as children, physical or speech defects, or the number of their children. They were more often devout Protestants, and in unskilled occupations. They were not senile. Over half had had homosexual experiences as adolescents, which was more than the other sexual offenders, and about a quarter had used animals for sexual gratification. They did not differ in experience of fellatio by females, anal intercourse with adult females, or marital conflict. They engaged more in cunnilingus. They were less educated, had lower intelligence scores, and were more often feeble-minded. The majority were sober at the time of the act and repeated their pedophilic acts. There was often a lack of affect when they talked about their pedophilic actions.

Glueck (1956) studied sexual offenders and found that the pedophiles had been more feminine in childhood, had less heterosexual interest and behavior, had more postintercourse anxiety and sexual difficulties such as premature ejaculation, more early fears related to sex, and a less adequate self-image with respect to sex. The sexual difficulties of the pedophiles accounted for their reduced likelihood of marrying. Their parents' attitudes toward sex were not remarkable.

CAUSES OF PEDOPHILIA

Very few studies have looked at the causes of pedophilia. Weiss, et al. (1955) noted the role of the child. In a sample of female victims, they found that 60 percent had participated in the initiation of the act. The participant girls were older, more often knew the male, and more often had vaginal intercourse with the offender.

Freund, et al. (1972) studied the penile responses of normal males to slides and found that they responded more to females than to males. The age of the male in the slide had no effect on penile volume changes whereas the age of the female in the slide did: the males responded more to the older females. The response to slides of males was no greater than that to landscapes, whereas the response to young females was greater than that to landscapes. Freund, et al. argued, therefore, that normal males generalize their sexual interest to younger females. If no suitable female partner is available, then they may under some circumstances turn to younger partners without being pedophiles.

Karpman (1950) reported a case of a pedophile which seemed to result from his fear of pubic hair. This etiology is probably quite rare.

PSYCHOANALYTIC VIEWS

Psychoanalysts have not devoted much thought to the pedophile. Cassity (1927) distinguished two kinds of pedophiles. In one kind, the behavior develops because of severe weaning trauma with a subsequent paucity of maternal warmth, sustenance, and stimulation. This creates hostility toward maternal figures which in later life is displaced onto small female children. The second kind has identified with the mother figure and apparently acts out the role of the mother and treats the child as a projection of himself as he was in childhood. Hirning (1947) felt that mature women represented the maternal figure and an incestuous object for the pedophile, while the small child represented himself as he would prefer to be, a small child again.

SUMMARY

Available data on the pedophile indicate that he is perhaps the most deviant of all the sexual offenders, and this is especially true of the homosexual pedophile. In the studies conducted, the pedophiles differ from normal controls more than any other group of sex offenders. However, psychopathology is not very common in pedophiles, and neuroses and psychoses are only infrequently reported. Pedophilia is a term that covers a broad array of offenses. The more aggressive the offender, the more likely he is to resemble delinquents and criminals in general. The older the child victim, the healthier the offender is found to be, so that offenders (who use no violence) against minors (those aged twelve to sixteen) appear reasonably healthy. The younger the victims, the more the offender fits the pattern of the true pedophile, that it to say a person who is sexually attracted more by young children than by adults. Many studies of pedophiles include incest offenders as pedophiles, and it would be useful in future studies to separate the two groups.

REFERENCES

Bromberg, W.: Sex offense as a disguise. *Correct Psychiatry, 11*:293-298, 1965.
Cassity, J.: Psychological considerations of pedophilia. *Psychoanal Rev, 14*:189-199, 1927.
Cowen, E., and Stricker, G.: The social desirability of trait descriptive terms. *J Soc Psychol, 59*:307-315, 1963.
Fisher, G.: Psychological needs of heterosexual pedophiles. *Dis Nerv Syst, 30*:419-421, 1969.
Fisher, G., and Howell, L.: Psychological needs of homosexual pedophiles. *Dis Nerv Syst, 31*:623-625, 1970.
Fitch, J.: Men convicted of sexual offenses against children. *Br J Criminol, 3*:18-37, 1962.
Freund, K.: Erotic preference in pedophilia. *Behav Res Ther, 5*:339-348, 1967.
Freund, K., McKnight, C., Langevin, R., and Cibiri, S.: The female child as a surrogate object. *Arch Sex Behav, 2*:119-133, 1972.
Frisbie, L.: Treated sex offenders and what they did. *Ment Hyg, 43*:263-267, 1959.
Frisbie, L.: Treated sex offenders who reverted to sexually deviant behavior. *Fed Prob, 29*:52-57, 1965.
Gebhard, P., and Gagnon, J.: Male sex offenders against very young children. *Am J Psychiatry, 121*:576-579, 1964.
Gebhard, P., Gagnon, J., Pomeroy, W., and Christenson, C.: *Sex Offenders.* New York, Har-Row, 1965.
Glueck, B.: Psychodynamic patterns in the homosexual sex offender. *Am J Psychiatry, 112*:584-590, 1956.
Hammer, E.: A comparison of H-T-P's of rapists and pedophiles. *J Proj Tech, 18*:346-354, 1954a.
Hammer, E.: Relationship between diagnosis of psychosexual pathology and the sex of the first drawn person. *J Clin Psychol, 10*:168-170, 1954b.
Hammer, E.: A comparison of H-T-P's of rapists and pedophiles. *J Clin Psychol, 11*:67-69, 1955.
Hammer, E., and Jacks, I.: A study of Rorschach flexor and extensor human movement responses. *J Clin Psychol, 11*:63-67, 1955.
Hirning, L.: The sex offender in custody. In Lindner, R. and Seliger, R. (Eds.): *Handbook of Correctional Psychology.* New York: Philosophical Library, 1947, pp. 233-256.
Karpman, B.: A case of pedophilia (legally rape) cured by psychoanalysis. *Psychoanal Rev, 37*:235-276, 1950.
Kurland, M.: Pedophilia erotica. *J Nerv Ment Dis, 131*:394-403, 1960.
McCaghy, C.: Drinking and deviance disavowal. *Soc Prob, 16*:43-49, 1968.
Mohr, J., Turner, R., and Ball, R.: Exhibitionism and pedophilia. *Correct Psychiatry, 8*:172-186, 1962.
Nedoman, K., Mellan, J., and Pondelickova, J.: Sex behavior and its development in pedophilic men. *Arch Sex Behav, 1*:267-271, 1971.
Pascal, G., and Herzberg, F.: The detection of deviant sexual practice from the Rorschach. *J Proj Tech, 16*:366-373, 1952.

Shoor, M., Speed, M., and Bartelt, C.: Syndrome of the adolescent child molester. *Am J Psychiatry, 122*:783-789, 1966.
Stricker, G.: Stimulus properties of the Rorschach to a sample of pedophiles. *J Proj Tech, 28*:241-244, 1964.
Stricker, G.: Stimulus properties of the Blacky to a sample of pedophiles. *J Gen Psychol, 77*:35-39, 1967.
Toobert, S., Bartelme, K., and Jones, E.: Some factors related to pedophilia. *Int J Soc Psychiatry, 4*:272-279, 1959.
Weiss, J., Rogers, E., Darwin, M., and Dutton, C.: A study of girl sex victims. *Psychiatr Q, 29*:1-27, 1955.

_____ CHAPTER 17 _____

FETISHISM

FETISHISM IS A STATE IN WHICH A PERSON IS SEXUALLY AROUSED by an object other than a person or an animal. The object can vary widely. It may be an object with obvious connotations of another person, such as underwear or hair, or apparently unconnected, such as baby carriages or vinyl sheets. The fetish can be an object of a *particular* person. Wulff (1946) described a sixteen-month old boy who demanded his mother's stockings.

The concept of the fetish has been extended by some writers to considerable lengths. Some see the male homosexual as having a penis or even a foreskin fetish (Khan, 1965). Others see the attachment of the small child to objects such as dolls and blankets (called transitional objects by Winnicott [1953]) as a fetishism. However, Winnicott (1953) felt that transitional objects were potentially the mother's breast or phallus (see the section on psychoanalytic views later) and so *illusions*. They are universal and nonpathological. Fetish objects are transitional objects that persist into adulthood and which are linked *delusionally* with the mother's breast or phallus.

Buxbaum (1960) viewed hair-pulling in children as related to fetishism and to the attachment of children to transitional objects. Grant (1953) noted that the practice of foot-binding in ancient China and the sexual arousal occasioned by viewing bound feet in the society were similar to a fetish.

Grant (1949) discussed the phenomenon of "amorous fixation" in which a person may become attracted to particular features of the person with whom he is in love. Grant suggested that this kind of attraction (which is often nonsexual in nature) is analagous to sexual fetishism. The fetishism remains normal as long as the integral parts of the attractive person are involved and as long as the emotion engendered by the fetish extends to the entire personality of its owner. In a similar vein, Romm (1949) noted that for normal people the sexual object chosen must usually possesses certain qualities, such as a particular stature, hair color, shape, and so on. The supposed fixation of American men on the female breast is sometimes viewed as a fetishism.

Such a broadening of the concept points to the continuity of fetishism with so-called normal behaviors, but it would appear to lessen its value as a useful category for research purposes.

CHARACTERISTICS OF FETISHISM

The fetishist usually masturbates with the fetish but occasionally a fetishist may not masturbate at all or he may have an ejaculation without masturbating. Socarides (1960) noted the following characteristics of fetishism.

1. Fetishes are most commonly feet, shoes, corsets, and underwear. Very often the objects are closely related to skin and especially to odiferous skin.

2. Many cases exist of minor fetishism which involves a fetishistic ritual, such as observation of the female in a particular state of undress as a necessary preliminary stimulus to intercourse.

3. Fetishistic support may sometimes be necessary for homosexual or heterosexual intercourse.

4. Fetishism is rare in females. It may appear in women with masculine tendencies and fantasies of possessing a penis. (Socarides considered behaviors such as kleptomania, rituals in preparation for masturbation and intercourse, or the use of lucky charms as fetishistic behavior, and these behaviors are frequently found in females. However, these behaviors cannot be conceptualized as fitting a narrow definition of fetishism.)

5. The fetish usually appears in adolescence.

6. Socarides claimed that fetishism was nearly always associated with other sexual deviations, a claim which is at the moment undocumented.

7. The fetish must be durable (to reduce fears of annihilation), inanimate (so as to be nonretaliatory), immobile (to counteract the anxieties that stem from sensations of changing size and shape of the body), and able to remain intact outside of the body (to stabilize the sense of one's own body).

CHARACTERISTICS OF THE FETISHIST

There have been no research studies of fetishists. The

following speculations are based upon clinical studies. Romm (1949) hypothesized that the quantity of sexual activity was reduced in the fetishist. Some fetishists can have sexual intercourse occasionally without the fetish but such acts are forced, often incomplete, and accompanied by fetishistic fantasies. Romm felt that most fetishists were passive with admixtures of aggression and sadism (since the fetishist depreciates his mate by his displaced interest). The behavior is often compulsive. In fact much sexual behavior may be viewed as compulsive and, although the fetishist may have a reduced rate of sexual intercourse, his masturbatory rate may be quite high. However, the notion that the fetishist has a below average level of sexual activity is quite widespread (for example, Abraham, 1948).

Payne (1939) speculated that fetishists were depressed, paranoid, with inhibitions and self-destructive tendencies. Nagler (1957) felt that the majority of fetishists would be diagnosed as borderline psychotics. Romm (1949) felt that fetishists were orally dependent and passive and prone to the utilization of fantasy (since they symbolized and substituted rather than acted-out their desires).

Nagler felt that fetishists, in common with homosexuals and transvestites, had neither a fear of castration nor a fear of women, but rather a fear of the male social role in all its entirety in the face of an overwhelming sense of inadequacy and a low self-esteem. Nagler felt that this might stem from maternal overprotectiveness and oversolicitousness brought on by illness in the fetishist as a child and rejection by an overwhelmingly masculine father who demands that the boy meets impossible goals.

THE DEVELOPMENT OF FETISHISM

Epstein (1960) reviewed clinical studies of fetishists and found that the fetishist is usually described as reserved and nonassertive. He displays little warmth, emotion, or spontaneity. He shows obsessive-compulsive traits, passivity, and dependency. Fantasy life is strong and centered primarily around the fetish. Sexual fears are strong and the fetishist avoids sexual intercourse and romantic attachments. He has marked fears of bodily mutilation which can be expressed as phobic or hypochondriacal symptoms.

The attachment to the mother was often close. Often sexuality was precocious, primarily involving self-stimulation. Sadistic behavior was frequently present in childhood but this disappeared usually by adolescence, remaining only in the fantasies.

The close mother-son tie (with possible maternal seductiveness) with a possibly impressionable and responsive child encouraged the child's wish to possess the mother (both orally and manually). This was thwarted by the physical impossibility of doing so and by maternal rejecting behavior. The child then turned to an object that had an associative link with the mother as a substitute. The fetish could be fondled, mouthed, and served to reduce motor tension and fears of desertion.

The desire to possess the mother made the Oedipal conflict especially threatening and led to strong castration anxiety. The tension is reduced by withdrawing from the actual conflict and focusing desires upon the fetish. Adolescence leads to a renewed increase in castration anxiety, and preoccupation with the fetish increases. The fetish object serves both to symbolize the mother and the fetishist's wish to possess and be possessed by the mother.

Weissman (1957) speculated that the married fetishist suffers a rise in his fetishist tendencies when he feels neglected or rejected by his wife (the rejection may be real or fantasied) or when he becomes angry at her.

Grant (1954) developed a conditioning theory of fetishism. The child, at the moment of his first sexual excitement, has his attention caught by a detail of the situation. This detail somehow registers vividly upon his imagination and by this accidental contingency acquires the power to evoke sexual excitement by itself. The sexual arousal that has been originally elicited by the genital zones is now displaced to the fetish as a result of the accidental conditioning. Grant raised the possibility that the learning may be gradual for some fetishists rather than one-trial learning. Some of the learning may appear in retrospect to be one-trial learning, but the fetishist may forget many incidents related to the learning situation.

Grant noted that this simple theory did not explain many of the characteristics of fetishism: (1) the fetishist was often indifferent to primary sexual characteristics and often found them aversive, (2) fetishism was rare, (3) fetishism was more common in men than in women, (4) the needs of the fetishist might be extremely specific (cf. imprinting), (5) the fetish possessed an extraordinary power of erotic arousal, and (6) the relative frequency of particular fetish objects was not correlated with their frequency of presence in sexual situations (for example, plastic raincoats). Some of these difficulties are explained by the learning etiology proposed by McGuire, et al. (1965) for sexual deviations in general and discussed in Chapter 21.

In support of a learning etiology, Rachman and Hodgson (1968) have shown how fetishistic behavior may be induced (and extinguished) in a heterosexual male through simple techniques of classical conditioning. However, it must be noted that learning theorists tend to think, illogically, that if a behavior can be treated through conditioning techniques and created in adults through conditioning techniques, then this proves that the behavior was learned in childhood by conditioning techniques.

FETISHISM AND BRAIN DAMAGE

Epstein (1960) argued that some of the behaviors of fetishists resemble the symptoms of temporal lobe dysfunction. These symptoms include epileptic seizures, episodic symptoms (including disturbances in perception, affect, and motor and visceral function which appear suddenly and involuntarily), and acute psychotic states of brief duration. Epstein reviewed case studies of fetishists and claimed that they displayed many of these behaviors.

Furthermore, Epstein felt that behaviors of fetishists could be classified into two kinds: those due to a state of increased organismic excitability and those representing attempts to maintain organismic control. For example, the increased organismic excitability was shown by the marked responsiveness of the genitals and alimentary tract to symbolic and physical stimuli (for example, the great ease and frequency of ejaculation and sexual arousal to feeling states ordinarily nonerotic such as fear), sleep disturbances with unusually vivid dreams (especially with multilation themes), and episodic behavior ranging from the relatively uncomplex through epileptic states and culminating in acute psychotic reactions (for example, sudden transitory feelings of fear, depression apparently unrelated to current thought content, an imperative urge to perform certain motor functions, and occasional forced thinking).

The defenses that develop to deal with these behaviors include compulsions, obsessive thought processes, and a facade of emotional reserve. Epstein saw the masochistic fantasies (especially those of being bound) as symbolizing the fetishist's struggle to inhibit his impulses. The fetish object seems to serve both kinds of behaviors: it excites yet facilitates control.

Epstein's hypothesis is clearly quite speculative. He has advanced no physiological evidence to directly point to temporal lobe dysfunction in fetishists.

PSYCHOANALYTIC VIEWS

Freud's view of fetishism is that the male child values his penis and assumes that females have a penis also. When he learns eventually that females do not possess a penis, he concludes that they originally do have one but that they have had it removed. This realization has two effects: it arouses the child's castration anxiety and it makes him seek a symbol for the (once) revered and (now) missed female penis. The fetish is a symbol for the female's (most often the mother's) penis and a token of his triumph over the threat of castration. The fetish both denies and asseverates the fact of castration. The fetish prevents the fetishist from becoming a homosexual by endowing females with an attribute that makes them acceptable as sexual objects. (The implication here seems to be that fetishists are latent homosexuals.)

The fetish enables gratification of incestuous desires (since it symbolizes the mother's penis) and spares the fetishist from castration/punishment by the vengeful father. The fetishist's inability to accept the fact that women have no penis makes the female genitalia aversive and this also arouses his castration anxiety anew while at the same time the fetish may enable him to have heterosexual coitus—an ambivalent situation.

Freud felt that the choice of a fetish object lay in the last impression received by the child prior to the trauma of seeing the penisless female genitals. Freud admitted that it was not possible to explain why castration anxiety results in homosexuality in some males and fetishism in others. Fetishism is, after all, merely one possible solution to castration anxiety. Katan (1964) noted that while the fetishist is denying the absence of a penis in the female, the homosexual accepts the absence and concentrates his interest on finding the male phallus.

Socarides (1960) argued that the development of fetishism may be linked with nuclear conflicts occurring in the pre-Oedipal phase, for example, the unresolved wish in the male to have a child which stems from pre-Oedipal mother fixation and a lifelong primary female identification. If this is so, then it is possible that fetishism may have no etiological connection with phallic or genital sexuality.

One issue that psychoanalysts have speculated upon is the symbolism of the fetish. Some see it as symbolic of the vagina (for example, Balint, 1935)—it is often used a receptacle for semen during masturbation. Others see it as a symbol for feces or the uterus. Wulff (1946) felt, like Freud, that the fetish was a substitute for the mother's missing penis, but Wulff also saw it as a symbol for the mother's breast and body in some fetishists.

Transvestism is often seen by psychoanalysts as similar to fetishism, since both may involve overevaluation of female clothing. The transvestite, however, has to wear the clothes while the fetishist may be content with merely manipulating the fetish. Glover (1933) saw fetishism as similar to phobias, and he called certain phobic states "negative fetishistic phenomena."

SUMMARY

The concept of fetishism has been considerably broadened by those who have studied the topic, but his broadening is probably deleterious for research. Research would be more likely to be successful if a narrow definition were used, since then the subjects of the study would be more homogeneous. However, virtually no research study on fetishism has appeared. Psychoanalytic case studies stress the castration anxiety of fetishists and speculate upon the symbolism involved in the choice of the fetish. Learning theorists have proposed a conditioning etiology for fetishism involving chance associations initially between the eventual fetish and sexual arousal.

REFERENCES

Abraham, K.: Remarks on the psychoanalysis of a case of foot and corset fetishism. In Abraham, K. (Ed.): *Selected Papers on Psychoanalysis.* London, Hogarth, 1948.

Balint, M.: A contribution on fetishism. *Int J Psychoanal, 16*:481-483, 1935.

Buxbaum, E.: Hairpulling and fetishism. *Psychoanal Stud Child, 15*:243-260, 1960.

Epstein, A.W.: Fetishism. *J Nerv Ment Dis, 130*:107-119, 1960.

Glover, E.: The relation of perversion-formation to the development of reality sense. *Int J Psychoanal, 14*:486-503, 1933.

Grant, V.W.: A fetishistic theory of amorous fixation. *J Soc Psychol, 30*:17-37, 1949.

Grant, V.W.: A case study of fetishism. *J Abnorm Soc Psychol, 48*:142-149, 1953.

Grant, V.W.: A problem in sex pathology. *Am J Psychiatry, 110*:589-593, 1954.

Katan, M.: Fetishism, splitting of the ego, and denial. *Int J Psychoanal, 49*:237-245, 1964.

Khan, M.: Foreskin fetishism and its relation to ego pathology in a male homosexual. *Int J Psychoanal, 46*:64-80, 1965.

McGuire, R., Carlisle, J., and Young, B.: Sexual deviations as conditioned behavior. *Behav Res Ther, 2*:185-190, 1965.

Nagler, S.H.: Fetishism. *Psychiatr Q, 31*:713-741, 1957.

Payne, S.M.: Some observations of the ego development of the fetishist. *Int J Psychoanal, 20*:161-170, 1939.

Rachman, S., and Hodgson, R.J.: Experiementally-induced "sexual fetishism." *Psychol Rec, 18*:25-27, 1968.

Romm, M.E.: Some dynamics in fetishism. *Psychoanal Q, 18*:137-153, 1949.

Socarides, C.W.: The development of a fetishistic perversion. *J Am Psychoanal Assoc, 8*:281-311, 1960.

Weissman, P.: Some aspects of sexual activity in a fetishist. *Psychoanal Q, 26*:494-507, 1957.

Winnicott, D.W.: Transitional objects and transitional phenomena. *Int J Psychoanal, 34*:89-93, 1953.

Wulff, M.: Fetishism and object choice in early childhood. *Psychoanal Q, 15*:450-471, 1946.

SECTION IV
OTHER SEXUAL DEVIATIONS

CHAPTER 18

TRANSVESTISM

TRANSVESTISM IS A SEXUAL DEVIATION CHARACTERIZED by a desire to wear the clothes of the opposite sex and (less often) a wish to be looked upon and to be socially accepted as a member of the opposite sex. (In contrast, transexuals also desire to undergo an operation to convert anatomically to the opposite sex.)

In its mildest form, transvestism is confined to the desire to wear clothes of the opposite sex. The person may either wear an item like underpants of the opposite sex permanently or he may confine his cross-dressing to the privacy of his own home when he may attire himself completely in clothes of the opposite sex. In its stronger forms, transvestism becomes an irrestible urge, resembling an obsessive-compulsive neurosis. Some transvestites, when psychologically disturbed in addition, may have delusions of menstruation (or psychosomatic disorders such as rectal bleeding that resemble menstruation). Some transvestites desire to have children and may delusionally believe themselves to be pregnant.

Stoller (1971) has noted that the term transvestite is applied to various behaviors by different investigators.

    1. There is fetishistic cross-dressing in which one garment (or more than one) is worn to generate genital excitement. This behavior is unreported in females and occurs primarily in heterosexual males who are not effeminate. The penis is a source of pleasure to these males, and they consider themselves to be males.

    2. In transexualism the behavior is not fetishistic and there is no sexual excitement. The males are feminine but not effeminate. They tend to act as passive homosexuals and to hate their own penises. They are not generally psychotic.

    3. Some effeminate homosexuals cross-dress. They do not become sexually excited by cross-dressing. They are not feminine, but they are effeminate. They are homosexual and enjoy their penises.

    4. Some cross-dressers are overt, borderline, and latent psychotics

and the behavior results from their psychosis. Lukianowicz (1962) reported cases in which cross-dressing occurred only during psychotic episodes.

5. Some cross-dressing may be biologically induced, perhaps either through biochemical inbalances (such as congenital hypogonadism) or through brain damage (such as temporal lobe disease).

6. Some persons cross-dress casually, as at costume parties.

7. Some cross-dressers do not fall into these categories and may be designated as mixed types.

Stoller noted that transvestites can be categorized on five variables: fetishism, erotic pleasure in the penis, object choice, sense of maleness, and feminine behavior. It is clear from this that transvestites may constitute a varied group.

CHARACTERISTICS OF TRANSVESTITES

Prince and Bentler (1972) surveyed over 1000 readers of a magazine for transvestites, with a return rate of approximately 40 percent. The men varied widely in education, occupation, income, and religion. Physical and sociological variables appeared to be unrelated to the other variables studied.

Some 64 percent were married, and a further 14 percent separated, divorced, or widowed. Some 89 percent of the sample considered themselves heterosexual and only 1 percent homosexual. Only 12 percent considered themselves to be a woman trapped inside a male's body (transexual) and only 12 percent considered themselves only to have a sexual fetish for feminine attire; the remaining 69 percent considered themselves as males who have a feminine side seeking expression. Some 78 percent considered themselves to be a different personality when cross-dressed. Some 5 percent were taking female sex hormones while 50 percent would like to do so. Some 14 percent would like a sex change operation and a further 34 percent would have had one when they were younger. Those respondents with indications of transexualism did not differ from the other respondents on the other psychological or sociological variables.

The respondents appeared to be upwardly mobile compared to their fathers. Some 50 percent were firstborn with only 26 percent second born. (In contrast to this, Taylor and McLachlan [1962] in a sample of only ten transvestites found 50 percent to be youngest borns.) Broken homes were rare, occurring in only

18 percent of the respondents' families. Some 72 percent felt that their fathers provided a good masculine image for his sons and 51 percent felt that the father was the dominant parent.

Some 83 percent of the respondents were treated as boys as far as they could remember. Only 4 percent were treated as girls because the mother wanted a girl, and only 4 percent were made to wear dresses as a punishment. On the other hand, 54 percent of the respondents had their first transvestic experience before the age of ten.

Some 20 percent of the wives were unaware of their husbands' transvestic behavior and those that were aware varied widely in their acceptance of the cross-dressing. A number of the males liked to wear female attire during sexual intercourse, with nightgowns being the most popular item. Prince and Bentler estimated that 18 percent had appeared cross-dressed in public and that a further 16 percent had probably appeared in public.

Some 72 percent of the sample planned to expand their transvestic behavior as compared to only one percent who planned to restrict it. However, 69 percent of the sample had at one time or another tried to discontinue the activity.

Sado-masochistic tendencies were infrequent among the respondents.

PSYCHOLOGICAL STUDIES OF TRANSVESTITES

Bentler and Prince (1969) recruited a sample of transvestites from the readership of a transvestite magazine and gave them (and a control group) the Personality Research Form (Jackson, 1967). A discriminant function analysis showed that the two groups differed. In general, the transvestites appeared to be more controlled in their impulse expression, more inhibited in their interpersonal relationships, less involved with others, and more independent.

In a second study, Bentler and Prince (1970) gave the same subjects an MMPI-type personality questionnaire and found no differences between the two groups on a variety of scales (including such variables as cynicism, depression, familial discord, headache proneness, health concern, hostility, hypochondriasis, impulsivity, irritability, lying, neurotic disorganization, psychotic tendencies, rebelliousness, sadism, shallow affect, socially deviant attitudes, and somatic complaints).

In a third study, Bentler, et al. (1970) gave the Holtzman Ink Blot Test to a small sample of male transvestites in the community and compared the scores of the men to published norms for the test. The transvestites had a higher level of general intellectual responses, responded to form rather than to color, had a high body preoccupation, had pathological thought processes, but had no differences in perceptual differentiation.

These studies suffer from three defects: the use of no (or a poorly chosen) control group, the use of relatively poorly validated psychological tests, and the use of speculative interpretations of projective test responses. On the whole, the differences seem few and those that were found may well be unreliable and nonvalid.

Money and Wang (1966, 1967) compared a mixed group of transvestites and transexuals with males who had Klinefelter's syndrome, boys who were precociously pubertal, and effeminate juveniles. On the Draw-A-Person Test, the transvestites and transexuals (like the males with Klinefelter's syndrome and the effeminate juveniles) drew the male figure first less often than the precocially pubertal boys. The quality of the drawings by the transvestites and transexuals was better than those by the other groups. Money and Epstein (1967) found no differences between the overall verbal and nonverbal intelligence of a mixed group of transvestites and transexuals. The verbal comprehension scores of the male transvestites and transexuals, the female transvestites and transexuals, and the effeminate prepubertal boys were higher than the perceptual organization scores and the arithmetic and digit-span scores. Money and Epstein interpreted these differences to conclude that male transvestites and transexuals resembled normal females in their performance on intelligence tests. However, the sample sizes in the study were small and the statistical analysis of the data was poor. In addition, the fact that the female transvestites and transexuals resembled the male transvestites and transexuals argues against their conclusion. The data for the female transvestites should have resembled the results for normal males. Money and Epstein compared their data with norms for the tests used rather than using a matched comparison group, which is less than ideal. Finally, the failure to distinguish between transvestites and transexuals implies that Money believes that these two kinds of individuals are similar, a belief which is presently without foundation.

CLINICAL STUDIES OF TRANSVESTITES

Lukianowicz (1959a) has summarized a number of clinical studies of transvestism. A number of adverse psychological experiences in childhood have been proposed as etiological factors, including parental rejection of the child because of his unwanted sex which leads to feelings of inferiority and insecurity, to an unhealthy precocious preoccupation with problems of femininity and masculinity, to a confusion regarding his own sexual identity, and finally to transvestism.

In addition, some transvestites develop a hostile sadomasochistic attitude toward their own genitalia which leads to a desire to hide the genitals under the clothes of the opposite sex or to have them removed.*

Other experiences proposed include the dressing of children in the garb appropriate to the opposite sex, using cross-dressing as a punishment (primarily for males since only for them is it humiliating), the favoring of little girls in the family group, close visual contact with a female (usually a mother or a sister) leading to "primary identification" (a process which implies the existence of exhibitionistic behavior on the part of the female), and a reversal of parental roles in the family leading to identification with the same-sex parent.

Psychoanalytic writers view transvestism as an attempt to overcome castration anxiety by creating an imaginary phallic woman and subsequently identifying with her. Again, psychoanalytic writers see exhibitionistic behavior by an important female figure in childhood (primarily the mother) as an important precipitator of this state of affairs.

Psychoanalysts have often claimed that the sexual drive in transvestites is weak, but there is little documented evidence that this is so. Transvestites may be asexual, onanistic, homosexual, heterosexual, or bisexual. Randell (1959) found that the majority of male transvestites (and transexuals) were heterosexual whereas the majority of female transvestites (and transexuals) were homosexual. (The males were more often married but there

---

*Yazmajian (1966) has presented a case in which he felt that cryptorchism was a precipitating factor for a male transvestite.

were no differences in social class.) Clinicians have noted the occurrence of other sexual deviations in conjunction with transvestism, such as homosexuality, fetishism, exhibitionism, and narcissistic and masochistic traits, but again reliable data on this are presently unavailable.

Transvestites sometimes claim that they have always desired to be of the opposite sex. However, although transvestic behavior is observed in children, there are presently no longitudinal studies of these children. Thus, we are forced to rely on retrospective reports by adult transvestites of their childhood feelings—reports which are open to distortion.

Most writers assert that transvestism is primarily a male behavior. However, societal attitudes toward the arrest of the sexual deviant and societal toleration of cross-dressing may account for this. For example, females are allowed to wear trousers in our society, whereas only Scotsman wear kilts.

Lukianowicz (1959b) reviewed cases of persons who were both transvestites and psychotics. He noted that, although nonpsychotic transvestites showed transvestic behavior early in their lives, the psychotic transvestites did not. The psychosis seems to break down the defenses in a "latent" transvestite (though see Ch. 10 for a criticism of the concept of "latency"). The manic transvestites were all French and were overtly homosexual. The Anglo-Saxon and German cases were mostly schizophrenic and showed only latent homosexual traits. There were more male cases of psychotic transvestites than female cases and, in accordance with data from nonpsychotic transvestites, more of the female psychotic transvestites were homosexual.

Taylor and McLachlan (1964) examined a small sample of male transvestites and claimed to find a family pattern in which the opposite sex parent was dominant, in which there was a weak or absent same sex parent to act as an appropriate role model, and in which the transvestites were treated as girls from an early age.

Stoller (1967) studied the women associated with transvestites (their wives and mothers) and described three kinds: (1) the malicious male haters (primarily the mothers) who initiate the boy in cross-dressing, (2) the succorers (mainly wives) who support cross-dressing tendencies sympathetically once they come to know a transvestite, and (3) the symbiotes (mainly mothers) who are often homosexual or indifferent to sex. These latter females are hostile to males (except their sons with whom they have a close attachment). They tend to feminize their sons.

Female transvestism is viewed as less serious than male transvestism by psychoanalysts. It is regarded as the displacement of penis envy to envy of masculine appearance. The wearing of male clothes creates the illusion for others that she does possess a penis. As has been noted, female transvestites are primarily homosexual. Lukianowicz (1959a) has suggested that this may be the result of female transvestites' being less psychologically stable and thus less inhibited in the free expression of their homosexual desires (which is in contradiction to the view that transvestism is less psychopathologically serious in females. Alternatively, female transvestism is seen as a screen for homosexuality. It is also possible that societal punishment for male homosexuality is greater than that for female homosexuality and so males tend to be more inhibited in their expression of homosexuality.

TRANSVESTISM AND BRAIN DAMAGE

Several investigators have reported cases of transvestism occurring in males with EEG abnormalities (especially in the temporal lobe) (for example, Epstein, 1961) and following cerebral concussion, relievable by anticonvulsant medication (Walinder, 1965).

TRANSVESTISM, HANGING, AND ACCIDENTAL DEATH

A phenomenon has been reported in males whereby they obtain sexual satisfaction from partial strangulation by means of hanging (Resnick, 1972). Often these males cross-dress prior to the strangulation. Occasionally, they are unable to free themselves and die accidentally. (Their deaths are sometimes judged to be suicidal.) No research studies have been conducted on this phenomenon, but Resnick has reviewed the psychodynamic formulations that have been proposed.

TRANSVESTISM, GENES, AND HORMONES

Housden (1965) reviewed cases of transvestites in the literature and found that of thirty-six cases, four were judged to have feminine physiques, one was judged to have a feminine body hair distribution, and one was judged to have feminine facial hair distribution. Two were judged to have abnormal endocrine function, although none had gynocomastia or abnormal sexual organs. In these cases it is difficult to rule out self-administered hormone therapy.

Similarly, Taylor and McLachlan (1964) found no gonadal or endocrine abnormalities in a sample of transvestites that they examined. All were chromosomally male. Randell (1959) and Barr and Hobbs (1954) found the chromosomal structure of their male transvestites to be normal.

Thus, there is little evidence for genetic or hormonal abnormalities in transvestites.

THE TRANSVESTITE CAREER

Buckner (1970) described the typical transvestite as male, married, with children, and exclusively heterosexual. He dresses privately at home and tends to be fairly passive and secretive about his behavior. Buckner viewed transvestites as quite different from homosexuals who like to cross-dress. Although transvestism can occur in combination with other sexual deviations, it can occur in a pure form.

Buckner attempted to trace the typical development of the pure male heterosexual transvestite. First, Buckner acknowledged that there may be a biological condition or predisposition, perhaps leading to passivity, a low sexual drive, and a weak aggressive drive. The passivity and lack of social drive could easily be learned, however. In any event, biological conditions are not necessary precursors. There is no evidence for a biological etiology, of course.

Secondly, the boy comes to associate some article of clothing with sexual gratification between the ages of five and fourteen, usually through masturbation. The boy may also act out roles in fantasy that he will not expect to experience in later life (such as that of the female role). The boy may notice a trait which he shares with the female members of his family, and cross-dressing may reinforce this. He may value his mother, and his feminization may be encouraged by her.

Third, he begins to perceive heterosexual difficulties which may stem from his low sexual drive or a lack of a stable sense of self-esteem. This may be made worse by his being a perfectionist, by his having an exaggerated notion of the requirements of masculinity, by his involvement in roles too dominant for comfortable performance, or by his having an exaggerated fear of heterosexual failure, failure at sports, occupation, or marriage. Up to this point, the transvestite's development resembles that of the homosexual.

Fourth, homosexual outlets must be blocked. This can occur through his socialized aversion to homosexuality or through lack of an opportunity to learn behavior appropriate to homosexuals. Thus blocked heterosexually and homosexually, he regresses to his earlier pattern of gratification, masturbating with female apparel. At this point he resembles the fetishist.

Fifth, he elaborates the masturbation fantasies into the development of a feminine self. The regression to autoeroticism may result in an increase in sexual energy which he uses to complicate his gratificatory object. He may come to feel that he is a transvestite and learn what is appropriate to this role. Also his drive toward completion or perfection may accelerate this process.

Finally, the gratification becomes fixated in the pattern of transvestic behavior. The combination of autoerotic regression, elaboration of the fetishistic interest into cross-dressing, and the possible development of a feminine personality permits a synthetic dyad to be created within the individual, allowing narcissistic and dyadic regression. The transvestite can play out culturally prescribed heterosexual role patterns by giving himself gifts of clothing, by *becoming* a nurturant wife after a hard day at the office (rather than coming home to a nurturant wife), and so on. Some transvestites talk of their two aspects in a way that is suggestive of dissociation, with conscious awareness of what they are doing, however. As one male transvestite put it, "She belongs to me." They don't want to renounce their transvestism, just as happily married couples don't want to get divorced.

He may marry because he still has the ideal of the successfully functioning male heterosexual adult. But he often finds that his actual marriage is not as satisfying for tension release as his internal marriage.

Many transvestites try to keep their transvestism a secret from their wives while others inform their wives (or are discovered). Some wives are cooperative (and occasionally are enthusiastic). In other marriages, the wife goes along because of her dependence upon her husband. In some marriages, the wife does try to stop her husband's transvestic behavior but this often leads to divorce for the wife can rarely replace the internalized "wife."

SUMMARY

Transvestism is a term that covers a variety of behaviors. In its pure form, it refers to behavior in which a person gains pleasure (not necessarily genital pleasure) from dressing in clothes of the opposite sex. Transvestism can easily be confused with transexualism, fetishism, and homosexuality, and this may account for the belief (currently untested) that transvestism is often associated with other sexual deviations. There are few studies describing the personality of the transvestite and no studies of the development of transvestites. There are, however, clinical speculations concerning the kinds of childhood experiences that lead to transvestic behavior, focusing primarily upon identification with the opposite sex parent and early experience (under coercion or for play) of cross-dressing.

REFERENCES

Barr, M., and Hobbs, G.: Chromosomal sex in transvestites. *Lancet, 1*:1109, 1954.

Bentler, P., and Prince, C.: Personality characteristics of male transvestites. *J Abnorm Psychol, 74*:140-143, 1969.

Bentler, P., and Prince, C.: Psychiatric symtomatology in transvestites. *J Clin Psychol, 26*:434-435, 1970.

Bentler, P., Sherman, R., and Prince, C.: Personality characteristics of male transvestites. *J Clin Psychol, 26*:287-291, 1970.

Buckner, H.: The transvestic career path. *Psychiatry, 33*:381-389, 1970.

Epstein, A.: Relationship of fetishism and transvestism to brain and particularly to temporal lobe dysfunction. *J Nerv Ment Dis, 133*:247-253, 1961.

Housden, J.: An examination of the biologic etiology of transvestism. *Int J Soc Psychiatry, 11*:301-305, 1965.

Jackson, D.N.: *Manual for the Personality Research Form.* Goshen, Research Psychologists Press, 1967.

Lukianowicz, N.: Survey of various aspects of transvestism in the light of our present knowledge. *J Nerv Ment Dis, 128*:36-64, 1959a.

Lukianowicz, N.: Transvestism and psychosis. *Psychiatr Neurol, 138*:64-78, 1959b.

Lukianowicz, N.: Transvestite episodes in acute schizophrenia. *Psychiatr Q, 36*:44-54, 1962.

Money, J., and Epstein, R.: Verbal aptitude and prepubertal effeminacy. *Trans NY Acad Sci, 29*:448-454, 1967.

Money, J., and Wang, C.: Human figure drawings. *J Nerv Ment Dis, 143*:157-162, 1966.

Money, J., and Wang, C.: Human figure drawings. *J Nerv Ment Dis, 144*:55-58, 1967.

Prince, V., and Bentler, P.: Survey of 504 cases of transvestism. *Psychol Rep, 31*:903-917, 1972.

Randell, J.: Transvestism and transexualism. *Br Med J, 2*:1448-1452, 1959.

Resnick, H.: Erotized repetitive hangings. *Am J Psychother, 26*:4-21, 1972.

Stoller, R.: Transvestites' women. *Am J Psychiatry, 124*:333-339, 1967.

Stoller, R.: The term "transvestism." *Arch Gen Psychiatc, 24*:230-237, 1971.

Taylor, A., and McLachlan, D.: Clinical and psychological observations on transvestism, *N Z Med J, 61*:495-506, 1962.

Taylor, A., and McLachlan, D.: Transvestism and psychosexual identification. *N Z Med J, 63*:369-372, 1964.

Walinder, J.: Transvestism. *Int J Neuropsychiatry, 1*:567-573, 1965.

Yazmajian, R.: The testes and body-image formation in transvestism. *Jr Am Psychoanal Assoc, 14*:304-312, 1966.

CHAPTER 19

TRANSEXUALISM

THE SYNDROME OF TRANSEXUALISM is characterized by the desire of the person to undergo a transformation by surgical and hormonal means to the opposite sex. In general, the transexual appears to possess a complete identification with the opposite gender role. The transexual has the interests, attitudes, behaviors, style of dress, and sexual object choice of the opposite sex and strives to approximate the anatomy of the opposite sex.

CHARACTERISTICS OF MALE TRANSEXUALS

Pauly (1965) reviewed one hundred cases of male transexuals reported in the literature and was able to draw the following conclusions.

There are few data that support the notion of a genetic or organic etiology. Biological variables are within normal limits in most cases, but there are exceptions. Five cases had gonadal underdevelopment. Pauly noted that the presence of normal androgen levels and 17-ketosteroid urinary levels in adult males does not rule out prenatal or postnatal hormonal imbalance.

The sex chromatins appeared to be normal when examined, with the exception of one case who had Klinefelter's syndrome (XXY). There was one case of concordance for transexualism in male monozygotic twins.

(Benjamin [1964b] claimed to find hypogonadism as assessed by morphological measurements, low excretion rates of 17-ketosteroids, and genital size in some 31 percent of transexuals. However, their androgen-estrogen levels in the urine were normal. Only 7 percent had the onset of transexualism at puberty; the rest had a prepubertal onset.)

In 13 percent of the cases, Pauly found that the individual had been encouraged to identify with the feminine gender role.

The parents designated the child as male, but subtly (and sometimes not subtly) encouraged him to identify with the feminine role. Eventually, however, the parents tried to discourage the feminine traits in their sons, but the majority of sons (some (87%) continued to reject the masculine role in opposition to parental and societal wishes.

Pauly found that the intrafamily dynamics were varied and no clear pattern emerged. However, there was a tendency for the mother of the male transexual to be perceived by her son as ideal and the mother-son relationship was often excessively close. The father was usually seen as aloof and ineffectual at best, and punitive and brutal at worst. The father seemed to be distant and rejecting, providing no model for masculine identification.

From both the reports of the parents and the transexual, it seems that the symptoms appeared early in the child's life, and the boy's desire for the female role led to rejection by peers and consequent isolation and unhappiness. (Pauly noted, however, that transexuals are poor historians, prone to lying, distortion, and repression.) By the age of five, two thirds of the men felt as though they belonged to the female sex, and the parents confirmed this. Before puberty many of the boys dressed as females, acted and played like girls, and were embarrassed to undress in front of boys. These trends became stronger after puberty.

Cross-dressing often occurs in preschool days and causes further rejection by male peers. A cycle of teasing and humiliation, which causes isolation and further rejection of the masculine role which in turn causes further ridicule, is easily set up. The isolation leads to poor interpersonal skills and a schizoid or inadequate personality often results. In adolescene and early adulthood, psychopathic acting out is common (occurring in about a third of the men). From latency on, the fantasy of being a female grows and provides escape from the painful reality of life.

Overt homosexuality begins in adolescence and the majority of transexuals prefer male partners. However, they abhor homosexuality and deny that their behavior is homosexual. They see themselves as females and choose heterosexual males as partners. Their sexual drive is low and gratification comes from passivity and playing the female role. They abhor their genitals and try to hide or remove them. A few homosexuals do seek removal of their genitals as a way to rationalze their homosexuality, but Pauly saw such men as pseudotransexuals.

The transexual eventually develops a fixed role and then the desire to obtain surgery becomes the important goal for him. He may become convinced that he really is a woman. Monthly cramps and rectal bleeding may be reported and be interpreted as menstruation. Shrinkage of the genitals, enlargement of the breasts, and skin and hair changes are reported. These can take on the quality of somatic delusions. Some transexuals, however, take estrogens surreptitiously to produce these changes. In an extreme form, these symptoms may resemble paranoidal states, especially if the transexual's feminine identity is challenged. Nineteen percent of the cases were judged to be psychotic and 20 percent were hospitalized. Decompensation and failure of the defenses often occurred, resulting in depression (in 38% of the cases), suicide threats (in 35%), suicide attempts (in 17%), and nongenital self-mutilation (in 18%). However, Pauly stressed that transexuals should not be judged psychotic or deluded simply on the basis of their transexualism. Although some authors consider this symptom as *prima facie* evidence for diagnosis as psychotic, such a judgment is foolish. Apart from this one symptom, the majority of transexuals function adequately and do not resemble psychotics.

A recent report by Pauly (1968) confirms the conclusions of his earlier report. Regarding biological factors, Pauly found reports of the association of transexuality with estrogen secreting tumors of the testis or adrenal gland. He found four cases of Klinefelter's syndrome and transexualism occurring together, but it is difficult to know with what to compare this incidence figure. Recent reports also claim to find a high incidence of abnormal EEGs in transexuals and transvestites (28%), but again a comparison group is crucial here in order to interpret the figure.

Since transexualism seems to manifest its symptoms very early in the child's development, there has been much recent interest in effeminate boys (e.g. Green, 1968). However, although transexuals have shown gender conflicts as children, it is by no means clear whether (and what proportion of) effeminate boys develop into transexuals (or other sexual deviants). Thus, the relevance of these studies on effeminate boys is not clear at the present time. So far no follow-up studies of the boys have appeared, but since the behavior is seen as a "problem" by Green and his associates, requiring treatment, the treatment given will affect the meaningfulness of the follow-up studies.

CHARACTERISTICS OF FEMALE TRANSEXUALS

Some authors feel that female transexuals are a mixed group. For example, Christodorescu (1971) suggested that there were four kinds.

   1. Homosexuals and transvestites for whom a sex change operation would remove guilt.
   2. Psychotics with delusions of bodily ambiguities.
   3. Hysterical exhibitionists who are drawn by the publicity.
   4. Intersexuals who are raised as one sex but whose somatic ambiguity leads them to identify with the opposite sex. (There is no evidence that such "intersexed" individuals exist.)

Other writers, such as Stoller (1972) describe a syndrome very similar in its characteristics to male transexualism.

According to Stoller, the female transexual is unequivocally assigned as a female at birth. As early as age three or four, the child begins to show masculine interests and behavior. This development of a masculine identity continues until by the age of seven or eight she has invented a male name for herself and may even talk of having a future surgical operation to change her body. There is no episode of feminine development which has been thwarted. She may pass as a man in young adulthood and soon thereafter will seek the surgical operation.

The female transexual is attracted to feminine females. She denies that she is a homosexual and she will avoid lesbians.

On the basis of thirteen cases that he had seen, Stoller concluded that five factors characterized the development of the female transexual. (1) As an infant, the baby girl did not seem beautiful, graceful, or feminine to her parents. (2) She was not cuddly and habitually pushed away from people. (3) The mother was feminine, who after the birth was emotionally withdrawn from the child, usually through depression. This withdrawal might occur later during the child's development also. (4) The father was masculine who was absent in two areas: he did not support his wife during her emotional withdrawals, and he did not encourage his daughter's femininity. (5) The result of this was that the daughter was forced into the role of the succoring husband to her mother. The parents encouraged her masculinity, and she herself took to her new role to mitigate her own loneliness.

Stroller felt that female transexualism was a less sharply delineated syndrome as compared to male transexualism and that it had a more variable etiology. Female transexualism appears to look more "homosexual." Stroller suggested that this may be because male transexualism arises through identification with the mother, a nonconflictual learning process, whereas female transexualism is a defense against trauma. Since Stoller views homosexuality as a defense against trauma, it follows that female transexualism will resemble female homosexuality more than male transexualism will resemble male homosexuality. Of course, Stoller's views are without empirical support.

PSYCHOLOGICAL STUDIES OF TRANSEXUALS

Demographic Variables

There seem to be more male transexuals than female transexuals, judging from letters to clinics requesting operations (Walinder, 1968) and from the total number of operations performed (Pauly, 1968).

Akesson and Walinder (1969) compared transexuals with controls and found that they did not differ in the population density of the area in which they dwelt as adolescents. However, by age thirty, the transexuals lived in more densely populated locales. The transexuals moved their domicile more.

Sexual Behavior

Hamburger (1953) examined letters from transexuals requesting surgery and noted that the males were more often married than the females. The number of offspring appeared to be low and the females appeared to be homosexual more often than the males. Some of the males appeared to be transvestites, also, but these males were older and more likely to be heterosexual.

Hoopes, et al. (1968) examined a series of persons requesting surgery and found both heterosexual and homosexual orientations in the sample. The female transexuals were less likely to be married. Many of the transexuals reported cross-dressing. (Of males who spontaneously mentioned cross-dressing, some 80% had cross-dressed). The transexuals reported greater gender identity problems with increasing age.

Meyer, et al. (1971) found that about 25 percent of persons seeking surgery denied cross-dressing. Of those who did cross-dress, the females did so more persistently. The females in this study were less often married and more often cohabiting with someone of the same sex.

Hoenig, et al. (1970) studied a sample of persons seeking surgery and reported that most were single and that most of the rest were divorced or separated. About a quarter were currently cohabiting with someone of the same sex. An early onset of symptoms was reported by the transexuals. Most had cross-dressed or had transexual desires by the age of ten, and the desire was well-established in most by the age of twenty. The fantasies of the females were exclusively homosexual while 18 percent of the males had heterosexual fantasies. The incidence of abnormal home backgrounds (30%) was felt to be average. Although the educational level of the transexuals was average, their work adjustment was poor.

Pomeroy (1967) reported that a sample of male transexuals that he studied were religious and regular churchgoers in their youth. The transexuals tended to be socially isolated from other children during their childhood. Their level of masturbation was on the low side, but there was much homosexual activity. About half of the sample was exclusively homosexual. They tended to be rigidly moral, but to have an active fantasy life which was compulsive and irreversible. They were not fetishistic, but cross-dressing and assuming the female role tended to produce feelings of relief.

Doorbar (1967) examined a sample of male transexuals and found that their siblings were often homosexual. The transexuals, however, generally rejected homosexuality. They tended to have feelings of disgust toward their own bodies and to draw the female figure first in the House-Tree-Person Test.

Masculinity-Femininity

Money and Primrose (1968) studied fourteen male transexuals. They obtained high scores on the M-F scale of the Guilford-Zimmerman Temperament Survey. They reported being seen as "sissies" by their peers as children, having negative feelings toward their penises, and preferring the insertee role in homosexual relations. The three who were married did report infrequent sexual intercourse with their wives. Much of their erotic imagery was of themselves as females, and they obtained pleasure from giving sexual satisfaction to their partners. The men did not report phantom penises after surgery, which Money and Primrose took to indicate a prior decathexis of the penis. (Other investigators have reported the occurrence of phantom penises in transexuals after surgery.) The men did not report maternal fantasies or childbearing fantasies. Although most of them wanted to adopt children, they were not felt to possess female maternal desires.

Money and Primrose noted that there was a dissociative quality in the ability of the male transexual to disengage his genital functioning while engaging his feminine imagery during sexual relations. One of the men went into a trance-like state when changing from his female to his male personality, similar to cases of multiple personality.

Acccording to Money and Primrose, these men differed from women in their lack of maternal attitudes and their threshold of erotic arousal to visual imagery.

Money and Brennan (1968) studied six female transexuals and found that they obtained masculine scores on the M-F scale of the Guilford-Zimmerman Temperament Survey. All were judged to be tomboys as children. Their genital-erotic functioning was more like that of the typical female than the typical male. The majority had had homosexual experiences. In their erotic imagery, they saw themselves as males. They showed less fetishistic attachment to male clothing than the typical male transvestite or transexual. None reported breast phantoms after surgery. Money and Brennan felt that the women did not show maternal urges and were, in fact, aversive to maternal behavior. Dissociative phenomena were less common than in male transexuals.

Verbal Behavior And Intelligence

Money and Block (1971) compared the speech characteristics of male transexuals to published norms. They did not talk more than normal, but they were found to be less evaluative in their speech. They used negation, qualification, retraction, and explanation more. They tended to talk more freely about intimate sexual and erotic matters. Money and Block suggested that the reduced evaluation implied a poorly developed superego or a dissociative facility for changing the premises ("yes, but not me"). The (nonsignificant) increased amount of talking was seen as suggestive of the involvement of the temporal lobe in the etiology (since this lobe of the cortex is supposedly involved in the control of both speech and sexuality).

Money and Brennan (1969) studied seven female transexuals who were above average intelligence and whose verbal and nonverbal intelligence test scores were similar. Their achievement was commensurate with their intelligence, but their emotional conflict over their sexual role had delayed their academic achievement for some of them. Their verbal skills were typically female. Money and Brennan suggested that a high verbal ability in childhood may facilitate the development of false assumptions about somatic sexual differentiation. If the family environment is pathological, this may lead to an error in gender identity. However, Money and Brennan failed to show that female transexuals do have an abnormally high verbal intelligence or that their verbal skills do develop abnormally early.

Doorbar (1967) found the intelligence of a sample of male transexuals to be above average.

Birth Order

Benjamin (1964a) noted that some thirty of a group of 125 transexuals were only children, a proportion that seems high but which, without a control group, is impossible to interpret.

Preferred Parent

Meyer, et al. (1971) found that males seeking surgery preferred their mothers while females seeking surgery preferred their fathers.

Psychiatric Disturbance

Data from Pauly's review of male transexualism relevant to the incidence of psychiatric disturbance was reported above. Hoopes, et al. (1968) found that 4 percent of those requesting a sex change operation spontaneously reported attempting suicide, not an overly high proportion. Hoenig, et al. (1970) found that almost half of a group of persons seeking surgery had criminal records with a third of these for nonsexual offenses. Prostitution was more common in the males than in the females. Some 70 percent of the sample were judged to be psychiatrically disturbed.

Worden and Marsh (1955) studied five male transexuals and found them to be well-adjusted, but with a strong need for recognition, conflicts over sex, and marked by urgency and impulsiveness. They were judged to have a memory disturbance but this might have been due to poor motivation in the testing.

There are a number of writers (e.g. Meerloo, 1967) who are ready to diagnose all transexuals as neurotic or psychotic, but it is clear that there has not yet been an adequate study which has endeavored to assess the psychiatric status of a group of transexuals and a control group.

THE ETIOLOGY OF TRANSEXUALISM

Freund, et al. (1974a) found no differences in experience of loss of either the mother or the father between male transexuals and male homosexuals. However, the homosexuals had experienced more loss than male heterosexuals. Similarly, the transexuals and homosexuals did not differ in closeness to their mothers or fathers, but the homosexuals were closer to their mothers and less close to their fathers than the heterosexuals.

Freund, et al. (1974b) asked transexuals whether the sight of their own body excited them, and their penile responses to pictures of themselves were also recorded. Their verbal and penile responses to pictures of themselves nude and dressed in female attire was less than to pictures of other males. Thus, there was no evidence for narcissism in transexuals. Masochistic desires were almost absent in the transexuals and relatively rare in homosexual controls. In response to a questionnaire, the transexuals indicated that their major preference was to possess morphologically female genitalia rather than mere ablation of their male genitalia. (Some 92% wanted most of all to possess female genitalia.) Only 8 percent of the transexuals felt satisfied by wearing female clothes under their male attire and only 10 percent found female garments sexually attractive. The transexuals, therefore, did not appear to transvestic or fetishistic.

None of the transexuals preferred homosexual partners, whereas 73 percent of the homosexuals preferred homosexual partners. None of the transexuals wanted the sex change operation merely to please other males. Although this was a motive for some, it existed also with the motive of pleasing themselves.

In penile responses to male and female nudes of various ages, the transexuals and homosexuals gave very similar responses, save for the transexuals' being less aroused by pubescent males.

The transexuals had had less heterosexual experience than the homosexual males, and, of those transexuals who had had heterosexual intercourse, 78 percent had imagined a sex reversal during the act.* None of the homosexuals had ever imagined that they were females during heterosexual intercourse, although all had imagined that their partner was a male.

Freund, et al. concluded that the following etiological theories of transexualism could be ruled out: narcissism, masochism, transvestism, and aversion to one's own penis.

Freund, et al. also developed a female gender identity measure (using a questionnaire). Scores on this scale were not related to heterosexual experience or masochistic desires in the homosexuals, but those homosexuals with high scores were more likely to prefer heterosexual partners and to have an earlier onset of homosexual development. (Incidentally, the earlier onset of homosexual experiences was only weakly associated with less heterosexual experience.) The female gender identity measure discriminated between the transexuals and heterosexual pretty well, misclassifying only 10 percent of the transexuals.

CONCLUSIONS

There has clearly been interest in transexuals. A number of correlates of the syndrome have been suggested and a number of biogenic and psychogenic antecedents have been explored. However, two things stand out in this research.

First, few studies have employed a control group. Oc-

---
*The groups did not differ in the rate of onset of homosexual experiences.

casionally male and female transexuals are compared, but rarely has a nontransexual group been employed. Thus, the validity of most of the conclusions reviewed above is to be doubted until the findings are replicated using methodologically adequate research designs.

Second, most of the authors make much of the difference between transexuals and homosexuals. Transexuals do not see themselves as homosexuals, we are told. They choose heterosexual partners. The skeptic might wonder about the particular defenses of denial and rationalization used by the transexual and especially about the heterosexuality of those individuals who consent to cohabit and have sexual relations with transexuals. The feeling is that many of the writers are letting themselves be persuaded by the transexuals' conceptualizations. Certainly, until some research appears comparing both transexuals *and* homosexuals with heterosexual controls, the difference between transexuals and homosexuals must be judged less apparent than the transexual would have us believe.

REFERENCES

Akesson, H., and Walinder, J.: Transexualism. *Br J Psychiat, 115*:593-594, 1969.

Benjamin, H.: Clinical aspects to transexualism in the male and female. *Am J Psychother, 18*:458-469, 1964a.

Benjamin, H.: Nature and management of transexualism. *Pac Med Surg, 72*:105-111, 1964b.

Christodorescu, D.: Female transexualism. *Psychiatr-Clin, 4*:40-45, 1971.

Doorbar, R.: Psychological testing of transexuals. *Trans NY Acad Sci, 29*:455-462, 1967.

Freund, K., Langevin, R., Zajac, Y., Steiner, B., and Zajac, A.: Parent-child relations in transexual and nontransexual homosexual males. *Br J Psychiatry, 124*:22-23, 1974a.

Freund, K., Langevin, R., Zajac, Y., Steiner, B., and Zajac, A.: The transexual syndrome in homosexual males. *J Nerv Ment Dis, 158*:145-153, 1974b.

Green, R.: Childhood cross-gender identification. *J Nerv Ment Dis, 147*:500-509, 1968.

Hamburger, C.: The desire for change of sex as shown by personal letters from 465 men and women. *Acta Endocrinol, 14*:361-375, 1953.

Hoenig, J., Kenna, J., and Youd, A.: A follow-up study of transexuals. *Psychiatr-Clin, 3*:85-100, 1970.

Hoopes, J., Knorr, N., and Wolf, S.: Transexualism. *J Nerv Ment Dis, 147*:510-516, 1968.

Meerloo, J.: Change of sex and collaboration with the psychosis. *Am J Psychiatr, 124*:263-264, 1967.

Meyer, J., Knorr, N., and Blumer, D.: Characterization of a self-designated transexual population. *Arch Sex Behav, 1*:219-230, 1971.

Money, J., and Block, D.: Speech, sexuality, and the temporal lobe. *J Sex Res, 7*:35-41, 1971.

Money, J., and Brennan, J.: Sexual dimorphism in the psychology of female transexuals. *J Nerv Ment Dis, 147*:487-499, 1968.

Money, J., and Brennan, J.: Achievement versus failure. *J Learn Dis, 2*:76-81, 1969.

Money, J., and Primrose, C.: Sexual dimorphism and dissociation in the psychology of male transexuals. *J Nerv Ment Dis, 147*:472-486, 1968.

Pauly, I.: Male psychosexual inversion. *Arch Gen Psychiatr, 13*:172-179, 1965.

Pauly, I.: The current status of the change of sex operation. *J Nerv Ment Dis, 147*:460-471, 1968.

Pomeroy, W.: A report on the sexual history of 25 transexuals. *Trans NY Acad Sci, 29*:444-447, 1967.

Stoller, R.: Etiological factors in female transexualism. *Arch Sex Behav, 2*:47-64, 1972.

Walinder, J.: Transexualism. *Acta Psychiatr Scand*, Suppl 203, 1968, pp. 255-257.

Worden, F., and Marsh, J.: Psychological factors in men seeking sex transformation. *JAMA, 157*:1292-1298, 1955.

SECTION V
GENERAL STUDIES OF SEXUAL DEVIATION

CHAPTER 20

THE DETECTION OF THE SEXUALLY DEVIANT

MUCH RESEARCH HAS BEEN CONDUCTED ON WAYS OF DETECTING THE INDIVIDUAL WHO IS SEXUALLY DEVIANT not by observing his sexual behavior, but by administering psychological tests. Often the aim is to determine the presence and kind of sexual deviation without letting the person know what is being assessed.

PROJECTIVE TESTS

The Rorschach Test

Wheeler (1949) tested the validity of a number of Rorschach signs of homosexuality that had been suggested by other writers and, subsequently, a number of investigators have explored the use of Wheeler's signs. Goldfried (1966) reviewed the research and concluded that six of the twenty signs were unquestionably poor, six were probably valid, and eight were still of ambiguous validity. Goldfried noted that no studies of the stability of the subjects' scores over time had yet been conducted. The research reviewed by Goldfried indicated that delusional psychotics typically gave more of the signs than nondelusional psychotics (see Ch. 13), that obsessive-compulsive neurotics gave more than undifferentiated neurotics, and that peptic ulcer patients gave more than other psychosomatic patients.

It is by no means clear whether the signs are equally good in measuring unconscious homosexual tendencies and overt homosexual behavior. (Wheeler's study used primarily repressed and suppressed homosexuals while later research has used overt homosexuals.) Goldfried also noted that no studies had been conducted to see whether the signs measure general sexual disturbance or deviance rather than homosexuality in particular.

Chapman and Chapman (1969) studied a couple of Wheeler's

signs that were valid and a couple that were invalid, and they found that, when asked, clinicians often reported the invalid signs to be indicators of homosexuality. (It should be noted that Chapman and Chapman differed from Goldfried in which signs were considered to be valid and invalid.) Chapman and Chapman also reported that the invalid signs had more connotative associations with homosexuality than the valid signs and that, in contrived data with no associations between homosexuality and the signs, students tended to "rediscover" the invalid signs (that is to say, using nonquantitative judgments and impressions, the students judged the invalid signs to be associated with homosexuality). As indicated above, this study is marred only by the injudicious choice of signs, given Goldfried's excellent review.

Schafer (1954) has also suggested a number of signs that should be indicative of homosexuality, and both Hooker (1958) and Anderson and Seitz (1969) have reported success in using these signs to differentiate homosexuals from heterosexuals. Raychaudhuri and Mukerji (1971) found Schafer's signs to be better than Wheeler's signs for distinguishing homosexuals from patients with sex role disturbances and from heterosexuals. However, neither set of signs distinguished the active homosexuals from the passive homosexuals.

Hooker (1958), Guertin and Tremboth (1953), and Nitsche, et al. (1956) have explored the validity of signs other than those proposed by Wheeler and Schafer, all without success. Coates (1962) investigated three signs and utilized a variety of dependent variables, including success in treatment, the mode of sexual gratification, and whether the homosexual had ever "loved" a partner. The signs seemed to be of limited use, though the study was poorly reported.

The Thematic Apperception Test (TAT)

Lindzey, et al. (1958) compared the TAT protocols of overt male student homosexuals and heterosexuals and found nine of twenty proposed signs to differentiate the groups. They then followed twenty students for two years and correlated these nine signs with reports by the students of their heterosexual needs and judged ratings of the students' homosexual tendencies. The signs were of little use in predicting either of these variables. Lindzey (1965) found that clinical judgments by psychologists were better than the nine signs in differentiating the protocols of homosexual students from those of heterosexual students. In a replication study using prisoners, Lindzey found that only one of the nine signs differentiated the homosexual from the heterosexual prisoners. Again, clinical judgments by psychologists were more accurate than the TAT signs. Lindzey concluded that the TAT was of little use in detecting homosexuality.

Davids, et al. (1956) studied ten possible TAT signs and found that homosexuals (at a student counseling center) gave more of the signs than normals and neurotics. The number of TAT signs correlated with the number of Wheeler's signs for the homosexual students but not for the normal and neurotic students.

The Szondi Test

David and Rabinowitz (1952) compared overt homosexuals and epileptics for signs on the Szondi Test proposed by Deri and Szondi as indicative of homosexuality. Only three of the nine signs differentiated the groups, and David and Rabinowitz concluded that the Szondi Test would be of limited use in identifying homosexuals.

The Draw-A-Person (DAP) Test

Several studies have examined the sex of the first drawn person. Mainord (1953), for example, reported that indeed males tended to draw a male first (93%) whereas females tended to draw the female figure first (57%). Brown and Tolor (1957) have noted that this difference in the tendency is contrary to the data of Kinsey and his associates in reporting a greater incidence of homosexuality in the male than in females, if the tendency to draw the opposite sex person first is a measure of homosexuality.

However, there appears to be no evidence that homosexuals do draw the opposite sex figure first. Barker, et al. (1953) found no differences between homosexual and heterosexual soldiers; Vilhotti (1958) found no differences between homosexual and heterosexual retarded males; Fisher (1968) found no differences between sex offenders and other prisoners; Fisher (1959) found no differences between general sexual deviants and neuropsychiatric patients; Jensen, et al. (1971) found no differences between sex offenders and nonsexual offenders; and Sipprelle and Swensen (1956) found no differences between homosexual and heterosexual male and female students.

Whitaker (1961) claimed to find the predicted effect among psychiatric patients when comparing homosexuals and heterosexuals and when comparing effeminate and noneffeminate men. Fraas (1970) found an almost significant effect using a sample of criminally insane males but his sample sizes were very small. Levy (1950) also claimed to find differences between a small sample of homosexuals and a sample of adults (sex not specified).

Thus, on the whole it would appear that the sex of the first drawn person is not a valid indicator of homosexual tendencies.

Wanderer (1969) found that clinicians were not able to differentiate between homosexuals, schizophrenics, neurotics, and normals from a free examination of DAP protocols. (Retarded persons were identified better than chance.)

Geil (1944) rated the male figure drawn for signs of effeminancy and found that the male figures of homosexual prisoners were significantly more effeminate than those of heterosexuals. This was confirmed in a second study by Darke and Geil (1948), who also reported that feminine features and absurd distortions were most common in active oral and passive anal homosexuals. On the other hand, Barker, et al. (1953) failed to find feminine features in the male figures drawn by homosexual and heterosexual soldiers.

Barker, et al. (1953) reported that homosexual soldiers gave more hostile comments regarding the female figure, had significantly greater distortions of the female figure, and had a greater delay in identifying the same-sex figure, tending to be more evasive and guarded.

Houston (1965) studied youthful offenders and found that the passive male homosexuals drew a female first more often than the nonhomosexual youths. Pustel, et al. (1971) compared the active and passive homosexuals in dyads formed between retarded males. They claimed to find feminine qualities in the drawings of males of both active and passive males, but more so in the drawings of the passive males.

Jensen, et al. (1971) found no differences between sex offenders and nonsexual offenders in the quality of the drawings, the nudity of the figures, or the drawing of figures of indeterminate sex. Grams and Rindler (1958) examined the validity of fifteen signs suggested by Machover as indicative of homosexuality using a sample of training-school boys, but reported that the signs were of no use in differentiating the homosexual from the heterosexual boys.

Cutter (1956) rated sexual differentiation from the DAP protocols and found no differences between homosexual pedophiles, rapists, and exhibitionists. Furthermore, those who accepted their deviant behavior did not differ from those who denied it or attributed the behavior to the victim or to alcohol. The sexual deviants did not differ, in addition, from psychiatric technicians.

The Draw-A-Person Test seems, therefore, to be of little use in differentiating homosexuals and other sexual deviants from heterosexual males.

NONPROJECTIVE TESTS

The MMPI

Panton (1960) derived a twenty-two-item scale from the MMPI that differentiated homosexual and heterosexual prisoners. Krippner (1964) confirmed the validity of the scale using homosexual and heterosexual college students in psychotherapy. Krippner noted that the scores on the scale were not related to the number of MMPI scales on which the subjects had scored more than seventy. Singer (1970), however, failed to validate the scale using psychiatric patients.

Marsh, et al. (1955) derived a scale from the MMPI to assess general sexual deviation by comparing the MMPI protocols of males committed to a state hospital for sex offenses and college students. This procedure is clearly inappropriate since the scale will surely also assess the severity of psychiatric disturbance. Marsh, et al. claimed that pedophiles obtained the highest scores among the sex offenders but gave no data to support the claim. They found no differences in scores between sex offenders, psychotics, and neurotics. They claimed, again without data, that paranoid schizophrenics obtained lower scores than catatonic and hebephrenic schizophrenics. Yamahiro and Griffith (1960) compared homosexual offenders with addicts in a federal hospital and found no differences in their scores on the scale.

Hartman (1967) found no differences between sociopaths in a psychiatric hospital who were sexual deviants and those who were not. Wattron (1958) compared sex offenders with other offenders and found no differences. Peek and Storms (1956) felt that the scale did not usefully differentiate between sex offenders in a psychiatric hospital, psychiatric patients, and psychiatric aides. However, their data indicate that the sex offenders did get the highest scores while the psychiatric aides obtained the lowest scores. Scores on the sex deviation scale correlated highly with the standard MMPI scales, suggesting that the scale is really a measure of general psychopathology.

Panton (1958) compared sexual offenders who performed aggressive acts, sexual offenders who performed deviant acts (not clearly defined), and nonsexual offenders on the standard MMPI scales. Differences between the groups were small, and Panton felt that the scores reflected a general prison profile. Carroll and Fuller (1971) compared violent, nonviolent, and sexual offenders on the MMPI and found that the sexual offenders did not differ from the nonviolent offenders. The violent offenders had higher scores on many of the MMPI scales and, controlling for age, the differences were significant for the *F, Sc,* and *Ma* scales. Hartman (1967) compared psychiatric patients diagnosed as sociopaths with sexual deviation with those diagnosed as antisocial reactions with alcoholism on a number of MMPI derived scales (amorality, social alienation, impulsivity, hostility, personal and emotional sensitivity, ego strength, responsibility, manifest anxiety, and emotional immaturity) and found no differences.

Dean and Richardson (1964) compared overt male student homosexuals in the community with heterosexual students and found differences on only the *Pd, Mf, Sc,* and *Ma* scales. Dean and Richardson judged the profiles to be in the normal range for both groups except for the *Mf* score. They concluded that neither group was seriously psychologically disturbed. Zucker and Manosevitz (1966) identified three profiles from the data of Dean and Richardson. The *Mf-Ma* were judged to have a good adjustment (24% of the homosexual subjects) and the *Mf-Sc* to have a marginal adjustment (17% of the subjects), while the *Mf-D* were judged to have concerns about their homosexuality (15% of the subjects). In response, Dean and

Richardson (1966) obtained data from a new sample of homosexuals living in the community and found no differences between the homosexual samples for the proportions having the three MMPI profiles. The original group of homosexuals did not differ from the heterosexuals in their MMPI profiles, but the second sample did. Dean and Richardson felt that this latter difference was due to the second group of homosexuals being less educated than the other groups. Dean and Richardson concluded that, when education is controlled for, homosexuals and heterosexuals living in the community do not differ in MMPI scores or profiles.

The Sex Inventory

Cowden and Pacht (1969) gave the sex inventory (Haupt and Allen, 1966) to sexual offenders and to a random sample of prisoners. The sex offenders did not differ on the scales of sex drive, neurotic conflict, repression of sex, sex-role confidence, or promiscuity, but they did obtain higher scores on the scale of sex maladjustment, loss of sex controls, and homosexuality. These differences were not affected by defensiveness as assessed by the validity scales of the MMPI (Cowden and Morse, 1970).

Comparing deviated and nondeviated sexual offenders, Cowden and Pacht found the deviated offenders to have more sex drive, more sex maladjustment, less repression of sex, more loss of sexual controls, more homosexuality, and more promiscuity. There were no differences in neurotic conflict or sex-role conflict.

Haupt and Allen (1966) administered the sex inventory to a variety of offenders. Compared to other offenders, the sex offenders had a moderately high level of sex drive and interests, the highest level of conscious frustration and maladjustment centered around the manner of sexual expression, and the next to the highest level of neurotic problems and symptoms. Their homosexual tendencies were high, and they were less masculine than college students. Heterosexual and homosexual offenders differed only on the homosexual scale and loss of sex control (with the homosexuals scoring lower on this latter scale).

Thorne and Haupt (1966) have also reported on this inventory. They found, for example, that rapists were conservative in their sex attitudes, with frustration and conflict over the expression of their sexual needs. Homosexuals in jail, on the other hand, had liberal sex attitudes but were frustrated and in conflict over their admitted sexual deviance.

Vocabulary

Slater and Slater (1947) devised two sets of words familiar to males and to females respectively. Male homosexual psychiatric patients knew more of the masculine words and more of the feminine words than normal males. Slater and Slater argued that the greater number of masculine words known indicated greater intellectual ability in the homosexuals. Holding the number of masculine words known constant, the homosexuals still knew more of the feminine words. (The scores of the homosexuals were also more variable.) Clarke (1965) argued that Slater and Slater should have matched their subjects for age, intelligence, and social class. He conducted a study in which he did match for these variables and found no differences in the knowledge of feminine words, but the homosexuals knew fewer masculine words.

The technique, therefore, remains of dubious validity at the present time.

Assessment of Sex Preference

Feldman, et al. (1966) devised a questionnaire to assess homosexual interest by asking subjects to rate the concepts "men" and "women" for six qualities (such as attractive and boring). The subjects are forced to choose between pairs of items such as "Men are sexually to me (1) quite boring (2) very interesting" and "Women are sexually to me (1) quite beautiful (2) very beautiful." Marks and Sartorius (1967) have devised a similar questionnaire. It is by no means clear whether these methods are more accurate in assessing homosexual preference than less cumbersome methods.

Masculine-Feminine Scores

Several studies have looked at whether homosexuals score less masculine than heterosexuals on masculine-feminine scales. Krippner (1964) compared college students reporting homosexuals' problems and those reporting none and found that the homosexuals obtained more feminine scores on the MMPI *Mf* scale.* He also noted that the higher *Mf* scores were associated with a greater amount of psychopathology on the other scales of the MMPI.

Dean and Richardson (1964) found that homosexual students living in the community obtained higher *Mf* scores than heterosexual students. Burton (1947) found that homosexual delinquents obtained higher *Mf* scores than other delinquents, with rapists obtaining intermediate scores.

Aaronson and Grumpelt (1961) compared homosexual and heterosexual psychiatric patients and found that the homosexual patients obtained higher scores on the *Mf* scale, but the rank of the *Mf* scale in the total profile was lower. Aaronson and Grumpelt derived a composite masculine-feminine index from the *Hy, Pa, Hs,* and *Pt* scales but found no differences between the groups. Aaronson and Grumpelt noted that although the homosexuals were more feminine on the average, a subset existed that obtained high masculine scores.

Singer (1970) found that the *Mf* scale did not differentiate overt homosexuals from those with homosexual concerns, but did differentiate both of these groups from heterosexuals. (Aaronson's [1959] *Mf* index, however, failed to differentiate between the three groups.)

In contrast to these findings, Fraas (1970), using small samples of the criminally insane, found no differences between the homosexuals and the heterosexuals on the *Mf* scale of the MMPI or on the *Fe* scale of the California Psychological Inventory. Walker (1941) used the Terman-Miles M-F Test and found no differences between active and passive homosexuals (although his data presentation is poor and difficult to interpret). He reported that homosexuals did not differ from other sexual offenders, but the sexual offenders were more feminine than robbers and less feminine than murderers (though again his data presentation was poor).

On the whole the evidence favors a difference between male homosexuals and male heterosexuals on tests of masculinity-femininity.

---

*The Mf scale of the MMPI was derived using a small sample of male homosexuals (Hathaway, 1956).

BEHAVIORAL TESTS

Pupil Size

Hess, et al. (1965) compared the pupil size of male homosexuals and heterosexuals to slides of male and female nudes. They reported that the pupil size of the homosexuals was smaller for male nudes whereas the pupil size of the heterosexuals was smaller for the female nudes. Scott, et al. (1967) tried to replicate this finding using homosexual and heterosexual prisoners and found no differences.

Galvanic Skin Response

Solyom and Beck (1967) showed a small number of slides to males with fetish preferences and found that the amplitude of the galvanic skin response to the fetish object was greater than that for other objects. There were differences also in the latency of the galvanic skin response and the recovery time.

Penile Volume

Freund (1967) introduced what has become a popular measure. He found that the penile volume of subjects varied when watching sexual stimuli. Homosexuals show a greater increase to male stimuli, heterosexuals to female stimuli, pedophiles to children, and so on.

Viewing Time

Zamansky (1956) showed overt male homosexuals and heterosexuals slides of men and women and noted the viewing time for each stimulus when the stimuli were presented in pairs. He found that homosexuals looked longer at the male figure whereas heterosexuals looked longer at the female figure. In male versus neutral pairs, the homosexuals preferred the male figure more than the heterosexuals. In female versus neutral pairs, the homosexuals preferred the neutral figure more, suggesting that homosexuals have an aversion to females.

PHYSIOGNOMIC QUALITIES

Berman and Freedman (1961) had psychologists write their clinical impression of sex offenders in jail and nonsexual offenders and found that the sex offenders received more negative and fewer positive statements. They then had the clinicians rate the photographs of sexual and nonsexual offenders from handsome to ugly, with the crime concealed. The sex offenders were rated significantly more ugly. (The same result was obtained with different judges when the crimes were not concealed.)

SUMMARY

A number of psychological techniques have been employed to detect homosexuality in subjects indirectly. Of the standard tests, only Wheeler's signs for the Rorschach and the *Mf* scale of the MMPI appear to have any validity. Much more fruitful appear to be the behavioral tests that assess pupil size, viewing time, and galvanic skin response to sexual stimuli. It would appear, therefore, that the use of standard psychological tests is of use only in retrospective study of data already collected. For current studies, behavioral tests would appear to be more valid.

REFERENCES

Aaronson, B.: A comparison of two MMPI measures of masculinity-femininity. *J Clin Psychol,* 15:48-50, 1959.

Aaronson, B., and Grumpelt, H.: Homosexuality and some MMPI measures of masculinity-femininity. *J Clin Psychol,* 17:245-247, 1961.

Anderson, D., and Seitz, F.: Rorschach diagnosis of homosexuality. *J Proj Tech,* 33:406-408, 1969.

Barker, A., Mathias, J., and Powers, C.: Drawing characteristics of male homosexuals. *J Clin Psychol,* 9:185-188, 1953.

Berman, L., and Freedman, L.: Clinical perception of sexual deviation. *J Psychol,* 52:157-160, 1961.

Brown, D., and Tolor, A.: Human figure drawings as indicators of sexual identification and inversion. *Percept Mot Skills,* 7:199-211, 1957.

Burton, A.: The use of the Mf scale of the MMPI as an aid in the diagnosis of sexual inversion. *J Psychol,* 24:161-164, 1947.

Carroll, J., and Fuller, G.: An MMPI comparison of three groups of criminals. *J Clin Psychol,* 27:240-242, 1971.

Chapman, L., and Chapman, J.: Illusory correlation as an obstacle to the use of valid psychodiagnostic signs. *J Abnorm Psychol,* 74:271-280, 1969.

Clarke, R.: The Slater selective vocabulary scale and male homosexuality. *Br J Med Psychol,* 38:339-340, 1965.

Coates, S.: Homosexuality and the Rorschach Test. *Br J Med Psychol,* 35:177-190, 1962.

Cowden, J., and Morse, E.: The relationship of defensiveness to responses on the Sex Inventory. *J Clin Psychol, 26*:505-509, 1970.
Cowden, J., and Pacht, A.: The Sex Inventory as a classification instrument for sex offenders. *J Clin Psychol, 25*:53-57, 1969.
Cutter, F.: Sex differentiation in figure drawings and overt deviation. *J Clin Psychol, 12*:369-372, 1956.
Darke, R., and Geil, G.: Homosexual activity. *J Nerv Ment Dis, 108*:217-240, 1948.
David, H., and Rabinowitz, W.: Szondi patterns in epileptic and homosexual males. *J Consult Psychol, 16*:247-250, 1952.
Davids, A., Joelson, M., and McArthur C.: Rorschach and TAT indices of homosexuality in overt homosexuals, neurotics, and normal males. *J Abnorm Soc Psychol, 53*:161-172, 1956.
Dean, R., and Richardson, H.: Analysis of MMPI profiles of forty college-educated overt homosexual males. *J Consult Psychol, 28*:483-486, 1964.
Dean, R., and Richardson, H.: On MMPI high-point codes of homosexual versus heterosexual males. *J Consult Psychol, 30*:558-560, 1966.
Feldman, M., MacCulloch, M., Mellor, V., and Pinschof, J.: The application of anticipatory avoidance learning to the treatment of homosexuality. *Behav Res Ther, 4*:289-299, 1966.
Fisher, G.: Relationship between diagnosis of neuropsychiatric disorder, sexual deviation, and the sex of the first-drawn person. *Percept Mot Skills, 9*:47-50, 1959.
Fisher, G.: Human figure drawing indices of sexual maladjustment in male felons. *J Proj Tech, 32*:81, 1968.
Fraas, L.: Sex of figure drawing in identifying practicing male homosexuals. *Psychol Rep, 27*:172-174, 1970.
Freund, K.: Diagnosing homo- or heterosexuality and erotic age-preferences by means of a psychophysiological test. *Behav Res Ther, 5*:209-228, 1967.
Geil, G.: The use of the Goodenough test for revealing male homosexuality. *J Clin Psychopath Psychother, 6*:307-321, 1944.
Goldfried, M.: On the diagnosis of homosexuality from the Rorschach. *J Consult Psychol, 30*:338-349, 1966.
Grams, A., and Rindler, L.: Signs of homosexuality in human-figure drawings. *J Consult Psychol, 22*:394, 1958.
Guertin, W., and Trembarth, W.: Card VI disturbance of the Rorschachs of sex offenders. *J Gen Psychol, 49*:221-227, 1953.
Hartman, B.: Comparison of selected experimental MMPI profiles of sexual deviates and sociopaths without sexual deviation. *Psychol Rep, 20*:234, 1967.
Hathaway, S.: Scales 5(Mf), 6(Pa) and 8(Sc). In Welsh, G. and Dahlstron, W. (Eds.): *Basic Readings on the MMPI in Psychology and Medicine.* Minneapolis, U of Minn Pr, 1956, pp. 104-111.
Haupt, T., and Allen, R.: A multivariate analysis of the variance of scale scores on the Sex Inventory, male form. *J Clin Psychol, 22*:387-395, 1966.

Hess, E., Seltzer, A., and Shillen, J.: Pupil response of hetero-homosexual males to pictures of men and women. *J Abnorm Psychol, 70*:165-168, 1965.

Hooker, E.: Male homosexuality in the Rorschach. *J Proj Tech, 22*:33-54, 1958.

Houston, L.: Vocational interest patterns of institutional youthful offenders as measured by a nonverbal battery. *J Clin Psychol, 21*:213-214, 1965.

Jensen, D., Prandoni, J., and Abudabbeh, N.: Figure drawings by sex offenders and a random sample of offenders. *Percept Mot Skills, 32*:295-300, 1971.

Krippner, S.: The identification of male homosexuality with the MMPI. *J Clin Psychol, 20*:159-161, 1964.

Levy, S.: Figure drawing as a projective test. In Abt, L., and Bellak, L. (Eds.): *Projective Psychology.* New York, Knopf, 1950, pp. 257-297.

Lindzey, G.: Seer versus sign. *J Exp Res Pers, 1*:17-26, 1965.

Lindzey, G., Tejessy, C., and Zamansky, H.: Thematic Apperception Test. *J Abnorm Soc Psychol, 57*:67-75, 1958.

Mainord, F.: A note on the use of figure drawing in the diagnosis of sexual inversion. *J Clin Psychol, 9*:188-189, 1953.

Marks, I., and Sartorius, N.: A contribution to the measurement of sexual attitude. *J Nerv Ment Dis, 145*:441-451, 1967.

Marsh, J., Hilliard, J., and Liechti, R.: A sexual deviation scale for the MMPI. *J Consult Psychol, 19*:55-59, 1955.

Nitsche, C., Robinson, J., and Parsons, E.: Homoesxuality and the Rorschach. *J Consult Psychol, 20*:196, 1956.

Panton, J.: MMPI profile configurations among crime classification groups. *J Clin Psychol, 14*:305-308, 1958.

Panton, J.: A new MMPI scale for the identification of homosexuality. *J Clin Psychol, 16*:17-21, 1960.

Peek, R., and Storms, L.: Validity of the Marsh-Hilliard-Liechti MMPI sexual deviation scale in a state hospital population. *J Consult Psychol, 20*:133-136, 1956.

Pustel, G., Sternlicht, M., and Deutsch, M.: Feminine tendencies in figure drawings by male homosexual retarded dyads. *J Clin Psychol, 27*:260-261, 1971.

Raychaudhuri, M., and Mukerji, K.: Rorschach differentials of homosexuality in male convicts. *J Pers Assess, 35*:22-26, 1970.

Schafer, R.: *Psychoanalytic Interpretation in Rorschach Testing.* New York, Grune, 1954.

Scott T., Wells, E., Wood, D., and Morgan, D.: Pupillary response and sexual interest re-examined. *J Clin Psychol, 23*:433-438, 1967.

Singer, M.: Comparison of indicators of homosexuality on the MMPI. *J Consult Clin Psychol, 34*:15-18, 1970.

Sipprelle, C., and Swensen, C.: Relationship of sexual adjustment to certain sex characteristics of human figure drawings. *J Consult Psychol, 20*:197-198, 1956.

Slater, E., and Slater, P.: A study in the assessment of homosexual traits. *Br J Med Psychol, 21*:61-74, 1947.

Solyom, L., and Beck, P.: GSR assessment of aberrant sexual behavior. *Int J Neuropsychiatry, 3*:52-59, 1967.

Thorne, F., and Haupt, T.: Objective measurement of sex attitudes and behavior in adult males. *J Clin Psychol, 22*:395-403, 1966.

Vilhotti, A.: An investigation of the use of the DAP in the diagnosis of homosexuality in mentally deficient males. *Am J Ment Def, 62*:708-711, 1958.

Walker, E.: The Terman-Miles "M-F" test and the prison classification program. *J Genet Psychol, 59*:27-40, 1941.

Wanderer, Z.: Validity of clinical judgments based on human figure drawings. *J Consult Clin Psychol, 33*:143-150, 1969.

Wattron, J.: Validity of the Marsh-Hilliard-Liechti MMPI sexual deviation scale in a state prison population. *J Consult Psychol, 22*:16, 1958.

Wheeler, W.: An analysis of Rorschach indices of male homosexuality. *Rorschach Res Exch, 13*:97-126, 1949.

Whitaker, L.: The use of an extended draw-a-person test to identify homosexual and effeminate men. *J Consult Psychol, 25*:482-485, 1961.

Yamahiro, R., and Griffith, R.: Validity of two indices of sexual deviancy. *J Clin Psychol, 16*:21-24, 1960.

Zamansky, H.: A technique for assessing homosexual tendencies. *J Pers, 24*:436-448, 1956.

Zucker, R., and Manosevitz, M.: MMPI patterns of overt male homosexuals. *J Consult Psychol, 30*:555-557, 1966.

CHAPTER 21

GENERAL STUDIES OF SEXUAL DEVIANTS

MANY THEORIES OF SEXUAL DEVIATION MAKE LITTLE OR NO DISTINCTION BETWEEN THE DIFFERENT DEVIATIONS and common etiologies are proposed for all deviations. Some research studies group together various kinds of sexual deviants and try to find characteristics that they share in common. This chapter will review these reports.

ETIOLOGICAL THEORIES

Learning Theory

McGuire, et al. (1965) have explored the idea that sexual variations are learned. They postulated that the learning takes place *after* the initial seduction or sexual experience which plays a role only in supplying a fantasy for later masturbation. Any stimulus which precedes ejaculation by the correct time interval should become more sexually exciting (by classical conditioning). This can happen accidentally (incidental stimuli in the place where one masturbates may become classically conditioned to sexual arousal) or deliberately (as when deliberate fantasies are used for masturbation). The latter situation is primarily responsible for the sexual deviations.

Why should the individual masturbate to his particular fantasy rather than to thoughts of heterosexual intercourse? McGuire, et al. suggested that the precipitating incident was the first actual experience, rather than a story that was read or heard. This gave the incident stronger stimulus value. As this stimulus became sexually exciting through association with masturbation, heterosexual stimuli were extinguished through lack of reinforcement.

Other factors influence this development. Many sexual deviants believe that a normal sex life is not possible for them because of early aversive heterosexual experiences or feelings of inadequacy. This belief often antedates the practice of the sexual deviation, although guilt from the deviation once it is learned reinforces the belief.

McGuire, et al. pointed out that their theory led to many predictions.

 1. The theory made no assumptions about previous sexual interest prior to the appearance of the deviation. Many deviants recalled heterosexual interest before the acquisition of the deviation.
 2. Any deviation could be acquired by this process.
 3. Any deviation acquired in this way should be extinguishable by deconditioning.
 4. The deviation was not extinguished by the guilt feeling since the pleasure from the deviant act came at a more effective moment with respect to the conditioning process.
 5. A deviant who masturbated to fantasies as his main sexual outlet should be more likely to develop other sexual deviations.
 6. Since females masturbated to orgasm less than males, females should be less likely to develop sexual deviations.
 7. Individuals who engaged in sexually deviant behavior during times of deprivation of heterosexual outlets would not be expected to become sexually deviant if their fantasies during the deviant acts were normally heterosexual.
 8. Even though psychopaths were supposedly poor learners, they might easily learn sexual deviations, since masturbation to fantasy was often practiced several times a week. Thus, the conditioning involved a lot of practice.

McGuire, et al. noted that not all of their patients fitted into this model. They felt that either these patients had forgotten their early (conditioning) experiences, or else they constituted an alternative kind of deviant.

Evans (1968) found some support for the ideas of McGuire, et al. by comparing the ease of deconditioning exhibitionism in a group of exhibitionists who masturbated to heterosexual fantasies and a group who masturbated to exhibitionistic fantasies. (The groups did not differ in their acting-out behavior.) The group who masturbated to heterosexual fantasies deconditioned faster.

Psychoanalytic Theories

Some psychoanalysts see sexual deviations as determined by neurotic motivations. Sexuality is seen as one area of functioning along with and as equally important as other areas.

The focus is thus upon the neurotic individual rather than the neurotic sexual activity.

Rubins (1969), for example, argued that where sexual functioning is unsettled, disturbances will be found in other areas of living. Correlations will be found between fluctuations in the deviant sexual activity and changes in the personality. Rubins combined this orientation with an emphasis on the social relationships of the sexual deviant. He noted how the deviant activity permitted a sexual relationship which might allow for closeness and distance simultaneously; how the deviation might permit satisfaction of expansive attitudes in an impersonal and mechanized activity without requiring the experiencing of the softer emotions demanded by intimate sexual intercourse; and how a deviation might be considered to be an alienated, distanced, benumbed, mechanized, or impersonal way of permitting the interpersonal sexual relationship by partially replacing its threatening emotional aspects.

An alternative view of the sexual deviations characterizes them as the "negative" of the neuroses. Instead they are diagnosed as primary character disorders. The sexual deviant expresses directly those impulses (fragmentary and infantile) which the neurotic represses and brings to expression only in symbolic form. The basic mechanism is that the Oedipal castration anxiety in the child is aroused by a phallic mother. The child obtains reassurance by either wishing to be the mother (transvestism); by displacing the imagined penis onto a symbolized object, thereby simultaneously affirming and denying its existence (fetishism); by reaffirming its presence and power through the reactions of others (exhibitionism); or by seeking visual images to displace the threatening mother image (voyeurism). Other psychoanalysts stress pregenital impulses and anxieties, such as those related to the breast rather than the penis.*

Ellis (1968) noted that the sexual deviant may be neurotic, psychotic, and so on, but not necessarily because of his sexual behavior. He might be disturbed aside from his sexual activities. Ellis argued that a behavior such as homosexuality per se was not sufficient to diagnose a person. However, acts such

*This concise summary is taken from Rubins (1969).

as homosexual pedophilia might be seen as indicative of psychological disturbance.

Sexual Deprivation

It has been argued that people turn to deviant sexual acts when deprived of their normal heterosexual outlets, as in those imprisoned. Hartman and Nicolay (1966) studied men being processed through a court psychiatric clinic and compared married men with pregnant wives to married men whose wives were not pregnant. Those with pregnant wives were more likely to have committed a sexual offense. The two groups did not differ in the number of previous arrests. Hartman and Nicolay suggested that a sexual offense may be precipitated by the sexual deprivation when a man's wife is pregnant or by stress caused by potential parenthood.

In a similar vein, Barber (1969) argued that the incidence of rape in Queensland, Australia, rose after and as a result of the closing of brothels there.

Pornography

A couple of studies have endeavored to see whether experience with pornography could be a contributing factor to the development of sexually deviant behavior.

Goldstein, et al. (1971) found that normal controls had had more experience with pornography during adolescence than sexual offenders (rapists and pedophiles), homosexuals, and transexuals in the community. In adulthood the sexual offenders and transexuals continued to have a lower exposure to pornography, but the homosexuals resembled the normal controls. As adolescents the controls and rapists were excited to masturbate by pornography more than the pedophiles and transexuals. In adulthood the controls and rapists were less excited by pornography while the excitement of the homosexuals rose. Goldstein, et al. concluded that there was no evidence for an association between adolescent experiences with pornography and the development of sexual deviation.

Cook, et al. (1971) studied the effects of pornography on sexual and nonsexual offenders. The immediate arousal to pornography was on the whole quite similar for both groups, and there were no differences between the different kinds of sexual offenders. Cook, et al. confirmed the finding of Goldstein, et al. that sexual offenders had less experience with pornography during their preadolescent and adolescent years. Prior to prison, there were no differences in exposure to pornography. After looking at pornography, the nonsexual offenders tended to have heterosexual relations more while the sexual offenders tended to masturbate more. Only four of the sixty-three sexual offenders said that seeing pornography encouraged the sexual offense.

Brain Damage

Kolarsky, et al. (1967) studied a group of epileptics and found that those who were psychosexually deviant were no more likely to have temporal lobe lesions than those who were not psychosexually deviant. However, the sexually deviant epileptics were more likely to know the date of the onset of the lesion, and the onset was earlier. Kolarsky, et al. concluded that sexual deviation was associated (in epileptics) with temporal lobe damage prior to the end of the first year of life.

Other Views

Storr (1957) argued that sexual deviants felt consciously or unconsciously less masculine than their fellows. In their lives they were often found to have been unable to compete with peers at school, to defend themselves when attacked, and so on. They developed a large amount of repressed aggression. They were often impotent, a result not so much of their fear of castration but of the feeling that they had been castrated already.

If they become fetishists, the fetish represents a means by which the patient can identify himself with someone more masculine. If they become homosexual, they are seeking a male who possesses the qualities that they feel they lack (a motive suggested by Karp, et al. [1970] for heterosexual choice of partners).

Storr also noted the fear of the mother. Sexual deviants do not become established as males with a separate sense of existence and a consciousness of their own potency. Because the men are not confident of their own masculinity, their power is felt by them to lie still with their phallic mother, and their task is to wrest it away from her. One way of overcoming the great mother is to identify with her, the method adopted by transvestites.

Hammer and Glueck (1957) identified and described the following psychodynamic patterns found in the male sexual offenders that they studied.

FACTOR I: PSYCHODYNAMIC PATTERNS. All of the sex offenders were found to have a similar pattern of psychosexual disturbance. They differed only in degree, not in kind. (1) They had a fear of sexual contact with females. The incest offenders were judged to have the most fear, the pedophiles a moderate amount, and the rapists least. (2) The Oedipal involvement of the sexual offenders led to the maternalization of the sexual object, or rather the maternal figure was sexualized. (3) The men had feelings of genital inadequacy, feelings that included castration anxiety, an emphasis on feminine identification, and anxiety concerning the assumption of the active male sexual role. The rapists showed least anxiety and the homosexual pedophiles most. The relatively lower castration anxiety of the rapists allowed them to overcompensate with overassertive and aggressive virility.

(Much of the supporting evidence that Hammer and Glueck used to support their conclusions came from interpretation of projective test data and is of dubious validity.)

FACTOR II: SCHIZOID-SCHIZOPHRENIC CONTINUUM. Some 65 percent to 90 percent of the sexual offenders were judged to be schizoid or schizophrenic. Most often the judgment was of incipient schizophrenia with the frank symptoms of schizophrenia absent. The prevalence of schizoid and schizophrenic withdrawal suggested the presence of a basic mistrust of personal relationships, which affected the men's psychosexual behavior. Hammer and Glueck felt that this basic mistrust was a result of the men's childhood home experiences, in particular rejecting, emotionally sterile, and traumatizing mothers.

The rapist feels rejected by his mother and as a result feels that he cannot be wanted or desired by any other woman. Thus, he attempts to command women with force. The male homosexual handles his interpersonal anxieties by choosing a sexual object who is as much like himself as possible. The pedophile has the most interpersonal anxiety. He is the victim either of fixation or of regression in his search for interpersonal security. For the pathologically inhibited sexual offender, there is only one sexual object less threatening than children, and this is a child within his own family.

FACTOR III: CONTROL OF IMPULSES. Sexual offenders also have lack of ego-strength and inadequate control of impulses. Rapists and pedophiles seem to have rigid control of weak control mechanisms. The control is inflexible and tightly spread so that impulses break through sporadically. The incest offenders seem to have inadequate control by a shattered ego.

A small proportion of sexual offenders seem able to exhibit relatively enduring hypervigilant controls, even over their responses to projective test stimuli. They have a massive fear of a breakthrough of forbidden impulses. Such constant vigil is impossible and occasional eruption of the impulse inevitably occurs.

FACTOR IV: CONCRETE ORIENTATION. The sexual offenders were judged to have a concrete orientation. They were relatively nonverbal on psychological tests and they had little introspective capacity. This might be a reflection of their schizoid/schizophrenic trend. They also had a reduced capacity for fantasy release and other sublimatory behavior, leaving them no other alternative to acting-out.*

Most of the authors whose work is reviewed in this book tend to see the sexual deviant as psychiatrically disturbed or as a criminal. A very different view is presented by Maslow (1942). Maslow studied females who scored either very high or very low on a test of self-esteem. He found that the women with high self-esteem (who approximate his idea of self-actualized people) tended to engage more in sexually deviant behavior than the women with low self-esteem. They did so out of curiosity, for experimentation and for fun (that is, because of growth needs). For Maslow, any person who is unable to experiment with unusual activities, including sexual behaviors, is constricted and cannot be self-actualized.*

---

*Hammer and Glueck noted the questionable validity of their data from projective tests, the fact that they assessed the psychodynamics of the sexual offenders after the sexual offense rather than before, and the possible confounding effect of the prison environment.

*Maslow noted that not all of his women with high self-esteem were psychologically healthy. Those who were insecure tended to resemble the classic Don Juan syndrome in which sexual conquest and sexual activity was used to establish feelings of esteem (that is, to satisfy deficiency needs).

RESEARCH ON SEXUAL DEVIANTS
Projective tests

Pascal and Herzberg (1952) compared nonsexual offenders and sexual offenders on their response to the Rorschach test. Each subject was given the test once in a standard fashion and then a second time during which he was asked to point out any male or female genitals seen on the cards. The groups did not differ in the total number of responses given during the standard administration, nor on the number of genitals seen in the modified administration. However, using the criteria of rejecting a card and the number of times a genital was seen in an unusual (in terms of statistical frequency) location on the card, Pascal and Herzberg were unable to distinguish the rapists from the nonsexual offenders, nor the pedophiles from the homosexuals. However, the rapists/nonsexual offenders differed significantly from the pedophiles/homosexuals. Thus, deviant sexual behavior seemed to be associated with deviant responding on the Rorschach Test.

Piotrowski and Abrahamsen (1952) hypothesized that if the Rorschach protocol contained more M responses than FM responses then the subject will become more restrained when intoxicated, whereas if there were more FM responses than M responses then the subject will become less restrained when intoxicated. In a study of a group of sexual offenders, an association was found between being intoxicated at the time of the sexual offense, and the presence of more FM responses in the Rorschach protocol.

Hammer (1957) gave the TAT, the Rorschach, the House-Tree-Person test, and the Blacky test to groups of sexual offenders (mainly rapists and pedophiles) and nonsexual offenders. Judges rated the castration anxiety from the protocols blindly, and the sexual offenders were found to have significantly more castration anxiety (confirming the psychoanalytic view of sexual deviancy). Hammer noted that the sexually deviant acts seemed to rid the individual of tension, was compulsive, and did not often give the individual any sexual pleasure.

Lindner (1953a) found no differences between homosexual and heterosexual sexual offenders on the Blacky test, but the sexual offenders as a group differed from nonsexual offenders on the standard scoring dimensions for the test. In a second study, Lindner (1953b) showed the same subjects incompleted pictures of sexually deviant acts and asked the subjects to guess what the pictures were about. The sexual offenders gave more sexually oriented responses and more aggressive responses than the nonsexual offenders. On a serial drawing test in which subjects were presented with drawings of sexual organs which got progressively clearer with successive pictures, the sexual offenders more quickly recognized the pictures and more often gave sexual identifications to the pictures. Lindner concluded that the sexual offenders had sexually oriented perceptual sensitization; that is, they are sexually oriented, and this orientation influences their perception of ambiguous stimuli.

Markey (1950) found no differences between boys arrested for sexual misconduct of various kinds and other delinquents in Rorschach measures of neurotic, psychotic, or favorable adjustment, although the sexual offenders tended to have more homosexual signs in their protocols. (Markey did not specify whose signs he utilized.)

Wagner (1963) gave the Hand Test to groups of male neurotics and male sexual deviants who were in therapy. The sexual deviants gave more responses in which the hand was in contact with a cylindrical object and more in which the hand was engaged in sexual activities. It appeared, therefore, that the sexual preoccupation of the sexual deviants influenced their responses, both directly and symbolically.

Sociological Variables

Gillin (1935) compared sexual offenders with murderers and reported that the sexual offenders more often had foreign-born parents, were raised more often on farms, had skilled fathers more often but their parents had lower incomes than those of the murderers, had parents who got on less well, lived longer with their parents, had less affection for their parents, had lower IQs, and were more often single.

Psychiatric Studies

Brancale, et al. (1952) found no association between the seriousness of the psychiatric disturbance of a group of sexual offenders and the seriousness of the sexual offense (although they did not define the concept of "seriousness").

Ruskin (1941) felt that the kind of sexual deviation engaged in by male psychiatric patients was related to their diagnosis. For example, schizophrenics and the mentally deficient were more likely to engage in homosexual acts and to molest women; psychopaths were more likely to be pedophiles and to rape women; those judged senile or with arteriosclerosis were more likely to be exhibitionists and pedophiles; those with organic psychoses were more likely to rape women, be voyeurs, or engage in bestiality, while the manic-depressives showed no preference for any particular deviation.

Ellis, et al. (1954) studied a group of sexual offenders and intercorrelated a number of variables over the subjects. The results were difficult to interpret. However, some differences were clear. The black offenders differed considerably from the white offenders: they were less psychologically disturbed, less deviated (although "deviation" was not defined by the authors), younger, and better socially adjusted. Young offenders differed in a similar fashion from old offenders. Deviated sexual offenders (again, "deviated" was not defined) were older, more likely to be recidivists, had fewer extenuating circumstances related to the sexual offense, and had severer psychological disturbance than the nondeviated sexual offenders.

Frosch and Bromberg (1939) reported on a sample of sexual offenders. In general, the pedophiles differed the most from the other sexual offenders. They tended to be diagnosed more often as psychopaths and neurotics, to be more likely to have a history of alcoholism, to be more likely to be under the influence of alcohol at the time of the sexual offense, to have the most maladjusted sexual lives, to be older, to be more often white, and to have the highest rates of recivism. The homosexual offenders resembled the pedophiles a little: they too tended to have a high incidence of neurosis, to have maladjusted sexual lives, and to be older. A history of alcohol abuse was also common in men arrested for forcible rape. In general, blacks were over-represented among the men. Religion, birthplace, and intellectual level did not seem to differentiate between the groups.

Glueck (1956) found psychotic tendencies to be most common in pedophile offenders than in rapists or nonsexual offenders.

The pedophiles were least often married and the nonsexual offenders most often married. The pedophiles mentioned sexual problems as their reason for not marrying more often than did the rapists.

The pedophiles were more feminine as children, more fantasy activity, and had fewer friends. The rapists resembled the nonsexual offenders on most variables examined, except for a very low level of fantasy behavior. Both sexual offense groups abused drugs less than the nonsexual offenders.

Cohen, et al. (1969) argued that the simple classification of deviants into the major categories was unsound. They took a group of rapists and pedophiles and had them complete a sociometric rating of their fellow offenders. The rapists did not differ from the pedophiles on this sociometric task. However, when Cohen, et al. classified the rapists and pedophiles according to the kind of offense, then significant differences were found.

The rapists were classified as (1) displaced-aggression type in which the intent of the act was primarily aggressive, with sexual feelings minimal or absent; (2) compensatory type in which sexual desires are predominant and the act compensates for feelings of sexual inadequacy; (3) sex-aggression-defusion type in which aggressive thoughts and feelings are crucial for the man in order to gain sexual arousal; and (4) impulse type in which neither sexual nor aggressive desires play a major role. The rape is usually carried out in the context of some other antisocial act. The pedophiles were classified as (1) fixated type, where the pedophile is socially comfortable only in the presence of children and has never developed mature relationships with peers; (2) the regressed type, where the pedophile maintains precarious relationships with peers but under stress (in particular direct confrontation of his sexual adequacy by an adult female) regresses in his object choice; and (3) aggressive type where aggressive impulses are strong and the victim is usually male.

Cohen, et al. hypothesized that the rapist-displaced-aggression type and the pedophile-regressed type should show the highest level of social skills since they have demonstrated higher levels of social adaptation. The sexual offenses for these men are more often reactive and experienced as dystonic. Analysis of the sociometric data supported this hypothesis. The displaced-aggression type of rapist was the most popular sociometric choice and the regressed pedophile followed close behind.

Galvanic Skin Response Studies

Tong (1960) studied mentally deficient male offenders and measured their GSR response to sexual and neutral words. The sexually deviant males reacted differently from other males to the sexual words. Tong attempted to present data to indicate that the response of the sexually deviant males to the sexual words resembled their response to mild stressors, and he argued that sexual stimuli constituted stress for the sexually deviant males.

Tong also found associations between Rorschach scores, the particular sexual offense, and GSR responses, but these results are difficult to interpret.

Conclusions

In general, the studies indicate that the rapist is psychologically the healthiest of the sexual offenders (that is, resembles the nonsexual offender most) whereas the pedophile offender is least psychologically healthy. However, the study by Cohen, et al. (1969) points to the danger in such overgeneralizations. Particular kinds of pedophiles and rapists may be exceptions to this general finding.

THE SEXUAL BEHAVIOR OF SEXUAL DEVIANTS

Gebhard, et al. (1965) compared sexual and nonsexual offenders, focusing primarily upon their sexual histories. Much of their work has been reviewed in the chapters on particular kinds of sexual deviants. However, some of their analyses result in more general conclusions.

They reported that sexual offenders were less likely to have juvenile records, and if they did have juvenile records the offenses were generally less serious and less violent. Those sexual offenders who used force and those whose sexual objects were children tended to have been convicted more than other offenders. The repetition of sexual offenses of the same type was common among the sexual offenders, especially those convicted of incest and homosexual offenses against adults. (About 80% of these repeated their offense.) The aggressors and homosexual offenders against children were least likely to repeat (only about 50% did so). Recividism for any offense was most common in the aggressors, exhibitionists, and voyeurs and least common for the incest offenders. On the whole, the sexual offenders tended to repeat the same kind of offense and to be less likely to use force with successive offenses.

Patterned offenders (those who repeat a succession of similar offenses) came from less favorable homes than incidental offenders. They engaged in more prepubertal sexual play, but after puberty developed more sexual anxiety, inhibitions, and worry. At the same time (perhaps because of less sexual activity and more restraint), they became more responsive to the sight and thought of females and became more preoccupied with the esoteric aspects of sex, as evidenced by their dreams and fantasies. They tended to experiment with mouth-genital contact, homosexuality, extramarital coitus, and animal contacts.

Specificity of the sexual offense was most common in homosexual and incest offenders and least common in the heterosexual aggressors, voyeurs, and exhibitionists. An association between exhibitionism and voyeurism was apparent: 43 percent of the voyeurs also had exhibited but no data were reported on the percentage of exhibitionists who also had been voyeurs.

Gebhard, et al. examined a number of variables for their association with sexual offenses. For example, impotence was most common in the incest offenders and least common in the heterosexual offenders. Witnessing parental coitus was least common in incest offenders and most common in the heterosexual aggressors. The intelligence scores ranged from being lowest in the voyeurs and heterosexual offenders and highest in the incest offenders and homosexual offenders.

The pedophiles were least often married and the nonsexual offenders most often married. The pedophiles mentioned sexual problems as their reason for not marrying more often than did the rapists.

The pedophiles were more feminine as children, engaged in more fantasy activity, and had fewer friends. The rapists resembled the nonsexual offenders on most variables examined, except for a very low level of fantasy behavior. Both sexual offense groups abused drugs less than the nonsexual offenders.

Overall, Gebhard, et al. concluded that the more "deviant" offenders stood out in contrast to the "garden variety" type. By deviant, Gebhard, et al. meant pedophiles and those using force. These offenders were more repetitive, more compulsive, more psychotic, and used drugs and alcohol more. These offenders had more difficulty admitting guilt for their actions.

Goldhirsh (1961) compared prisoners who had committed sexual offenses with other prisoners and found that the sexual offenders had more dreams with heterosexual content and more dreams in which sexual offenses were committed. (Goldhirsh included homosexual acts as sexual offenses.) Sexual behavior appeared, therefore, to be more important for the sexual offenders, since it figured so prominently in their dreams.

SEX DIFFERENCES IN SEXUAL DEVIATIONS

The majority of sexual deviants are male. Why is this so? The answer can be found in various places. First, legal procedures may differ for the sexes. For example, if a woman exposes herself at a window, any man looking may be arrested. If a woman sees a man exposing himself at a house window, again the man will probably be arrested. The prosecution of homosexual behavior has always been more vigorously pursued with male homosexuals than with female homosexuals.

The etiological theories of sexuality discussed above provide other answers. For example, the learning theory of McGuire, et al. (1965) predicted a sex difference in the incidence of sexually deviant behavior due to differences in the incidence of masturbation.

Psychoanalytic theory can also predict the differential incidence of sexual deviations for the sexes. The female child begins by being close to her mother, and in order to become someone who adopts the female role in the society she must identify with her mother. The boy has to switch his allegiance, from his mother to whom he was close as an infant to an identification with his father. The switch for the boy from mother to father means that he needs two healthy parents, and the switch itself is a process that can go wrong. If the father is for some reason an inadequate figure, the girl may still identify with her mother and learn the appropriate sexual role (although we might expect her heterosexual choices to be poor because of her inadequate father). The boy with an inadequate father either may fail to identify with his father or may identify with an inadequate figure and thus will be less likely to learn an appropriate sexual role. The boy needs two healthy parents whereas the girl needs only one if they are to learn the correct sexual role.

REFERENCES

Barber, R.: Prostitution and the increasing number of convictions for rape in Queensland. *Aust NZ J Criminol, 2*:169-174, 1969.

Brancale, R., Ellis, A., and Dorbar, R.: Psychiatric and psychological investigations of convicted sex offenders. *Am J Psychiatry, 109*:17-21, 1952.

Cohen, M., Seghorn, T., and Calmas, W.: Sociometric study of the sex offender. *J Abnorm Psychol, 74*:249-255, 1969.

Cook, R., Fosen, R., and Pacht, A.: Pornography and the sex offender. *J Appl Psychol, 55*:503-511, 1971.

Ellis, A.: Sexual manifestations of emotionally disturbed behavior. *Ann Am Acad Pol Soc Sci, 376*:96-105, 1968.

Ellis, A., Doobar, R., and Johnston, R.: Characteristics of convicted sex offenders. *J Soc Psychol, 40*:3-15, 1954.

Evans, D.: Masturbatory fantasy and sexual deviation. *Behav Res Ther, 6*:17-19, 1968.

Frosch, J., and Bromberg, W.: Sex offenders. *Am J Orthopsychiatry, 9*:761-776, 1939.

Gebhard, P., Gagnon, J., Pomeroy, W., and Christenson, C.: *Sex Offenders.* New York, Har-Row, 1965.

Gillin, J.: Social backgrounds of sex offenders and murderers. *Soc Forces, 14*:232-239, 1935.

Glueck, B.: Psychodynamic patterns in the homosexual sex offender. *Am J Psychiatry, 112*:584-590, 1956.

Goldhirsh, M.: Manifest content of dreams of convicted sex offenders. *J Abnorm Soc Psychol, 63*:643-645, 1961.

Goldstein, M. Kant, H., Jodd, L., Rice, C., and Green, R.: Experience with pornography. *Arch Sex Behav, 1*:1-15, 1971.

Hammer, E.: A psychoanalytic hypothesis concerning sex offenders. *J Clin Exp Psychopathol, 18*:177-184, 1957.

Hammer, E., and Glueck, B.: Psychodynamic patterns in sex offenders. *Psychiatr Q, 31*:325-345, 1957.

Hartman, A., and Nicolay, R.: Sexually deviant behavior in expectant fathers. *J Abnorm Psychol, 71*:232-234, 1966.

Karp, E., Jackson, J., and Lester, D.: Ideal self-fulfillment in mate selection. *J Marriage Fam, 32*:269-272, 1970.

Kolarsky, A., Freund, K., Machek, J., and Polak, O.: Male sexual deviation. *Arch Gen Psychiatry, 17*:735-743, 1967.

Lindner, H.: The Blacky pictures test. *J Proj Tech, 17*:79-84, 1953a.

Lindner, H.: Sexual responsiveness to perceptual tests in a group of sexual offenders. *J Pers, 21*:364-374, 1953b.

Markey, O.: A study of aggressive sex misbehavior in adolescents brought to juvenile court. *Am J Orthopsychiatry, 20*:719-731, 1950.

Maslow, A.: Self-esteem (dominance feeling) and sexuality in women. *J Soc Psychol, 16*:259-294, 1942.

McGuire, R., Carlisle, J., and Young, B.: Sexual deviations as conditioned behavior. *Behav Res Ther, 2*:185-190, 1965.

Pascal, G., and Herzerg, F.: The detection of deviant sexual practice from the Rorschach. *J Proj Tech, 16*:366-373, 1952.

Piotrowski, Z., and Abrahamsen, D.: Sexual crime, alcohol and the Rorschach test. *Psychiatr Q Suppl, 26*:248-260, 1952.

Rubins, J.: Sexual perversions. *Am J Psychoanal, 29*:94-105, 1969.

Ruskin, S.: Analysis of sex offenses among male psychiatric patients. *Am J Psychiatry, 97*:955-968, 1941.

Storr, A. The psychopathology of fetishism and transvestism. *J Anal Psychol, 2*:153-166, 1957.

Tong, J.: Galvanic skin response studies of sex responsiveness in sex offenders and others. *J Ment Sci, 106*:1475-1485, 1960.

Wagner, E.: Hand test content indicators of overt psychosexual maladjustment in neurotic males. *J Proj Tech, 27*:357-358, 1963.

SECTION VI

CONCLUSIONS

CHAPTER 22

REFLECTIONS

READERS OFTEN EXPECT AN AUTHOR TO COME UP WITH SOME NOVEL AND REMARKABLE CONCLUSION at the end of book, a synthesis of the studies that depicts them in a new light, or a new theory that makes all the facts fit into place. No such final chapter is possible for this book. The literature reviewed is considerable and, on occasion, the results of the research impressive. But the study of sexual deviation is nowhere nearly advanced enough for final conclusions to be drawn. All that is said must be tentative.

Rather, in this final chapter I shall try to suggest a few directions for future research and theorizing about the sexual deviations.

BIAS AND PREJUDICE

It is important to be aware of the degree of bias that is present in the research and theorizing about sexual deviations. Sexual deviations are considered to be antisocial or criminal acts or as signs of psychological disturbance by almost every writer on the topic. The diagnostic manual of the American Psychiatric Association places the sexual deviations as a separate diagnosis, but most psychiatrists would see sexual deviations as symptoms of some other underlying psychiatric disturbance. If a sexual deviant is found, he or she must be "cured" or treated so that he or she becomes "normal."

The lone contrary voice cited in this book is that of Abraham Maslow. Maslow noted that healthy, even self-actualized people (maybe, *especially* self-actualized people), behave in ways that sexual deviants do. And it is easy to find "normal" manifestations of sexually deviant behavior. Each of the sexual deviations can be found in less extreme forms in nearly all people. To take but one example here, fetishism can be seen as similar to the preference of people for sexual partners with particular qualities: beards, blue eyes, or well-developed breasts.

Maslow concluded his research into the sexual behavior of healthy women by noting that there is no such thing as a perverted behavior—there are only perverted individuals (Maslow, 1942). Investigators of sexual behavior can adopt either strategy: they can study a particular sexual behavior or they can study particular kinds of individuals. If an investigator chooses to study homosexuals who, for example, are arrested for soliciting people in public toilets, research may indicate a variety of disturbed behaviors in these men. However, similar disturbed behaviors might be found in people's begging for money in public places. We must remember that large numbers of homosexuals live ordinary lives, well out of the reach of legal authorities. An investigator who studies homosexuals arrested by the police may be learning little about homosexuality in general, in the same way that an investigator who studies criminals may learn about mankind in general.

Recent research is beginning to recognize this fact. The investigator of homosexuality now tries to recruit subjects for his research who are in the community and living ordinary lives, rather than homosexuals in jail or in psychotherapy. (However, usually the homosexuals are recruited from activist groups, and homosexuals in activist groups may not be typical of the average homosexual. Siegelman [1972] found that homosexuals in an homophile organization were more neurotic than homosexuals not in the organizations.)

For other sexual deviations, such efforts are not made. To take one example, research on incest uses the few cases that come to the attention of psychotherapists or legal authorities. According to the data collected by Gebhard, et al. (1965), some 4 percent of Americans have had incestuous experiences. The vast majority of these do not come to the attention of psychotherapists or police officers. What is especially intriguing is that research into incest has ignored the most common forms of incest, that between brother and sister and between distant relatives. Most of the research is on fathers who have had incestuous relations with their daughters and have been prosecuted for the offenses.

The alternative to studying particular individuals, usually psychologically disturbed or offenders of some kind, is to study the behavior. If we are interested in the attraction of relatives toward each other, the range of behaviors that we may investigate becomes broader and the kinds of people we study may be quite different than if we focus upon an extreme group. Cousins are often attracted to each other; brothers and sisters are sometimes (although often reaction formation seems more apparent). Parents often feel sexually aroused by their children. Mothers perhaps can achieve partial gratification for these desires. An investigator who studies sexual attraction between cousins will obtain very different findings from the investigator who studies incestuous fathers in jail for their acts.

Neither investigator, of course, will discover the "truth," but both sets of data are necessary for a balanced view of the behavior under investigation. The reader who has plowed through the chapters of this book must be aware of the unbalanced nature of the data collected and reviewed here.

The so-called sexual deviations are perhaps extreme manifestations of sexual behavior in which most humans engage. The research will be more useful if the continuum of the behaviors is recognized and if less extreme manifestations are also studied. Freund, et al. (1972) found that "normal" college males generalized their sexual attraction for females to young girls aged less than eleven (as measured by penile responses). These students were not pedophiles; the research shows that most people will generalize their sexual response to objects other than the most preferred.

RETROSPECTIVE VERSUS PROSPECTIVE RESEARCH

Virtually all of the research into antecedents of sexual choice is retrospective. Adult subjects are collected and asked about their childhoods and how they now feel about their parents. In order to be chosen as a subject, the sexual choice has to be firm. Researchers rarely study people ambivalent about their sexual orientation. Rather, they go to a homosexual activist group, for example, and recruit subjects.

To be sure, caveats can be found in the discussion of papers, cautioning the reader about trusting the recollections of the subjects. There may be memory failures; there may also be rationalizations and conscious and unconscious distortions. In the literature on transexuals, there are frequent references as to the doubtful validity of their reports. However, there is rarely an alternate source of data. Relatives and parents are not searched out and asked for their opinions.

It might be argued that sexual choice is a "sensitive" topic and makes it difficult to search out relatives. Such research, however, has been conducted for behaviors such as homicide, suicide, and schizophrenia. And the study need not be presented in a threatening form. Most parents are willing to talk about how their children behaved when young.

The failure to study the parents and the siblings of sexual deviants make the conclusions possible of doubtful validity. That female homosexuals, for example, feel babied more by their fathers than female heterosexuals is of interest. However, what would also be of interest is how the mother, father, and the brothers and sisters perceived the relationship between the father and his to-be-homosexual daughter.

This is not to deny the importance of the homosexual's current perception of the relationship. All that is meant is that the current perception may well not be an antecedent (and therefore a possible cause) of the present sexual choice.

There have been few follow-up studies of young children who engage in sexually deviant behaviors. There have been few follow-up studies of children who might show different sexual choices when adult, such as girls seen as "tomboys" or boys seen as "sissies." These kinds of studies would be so much more valuable than the research presently being conducted.

To take an example, there is some good evidence that homosexuals and heterosexuals may differ from each other endocrinologically. The evidence on endocrinological differences would be so much more valuable if endocrinological differences could be found in adolescence and childhood before sexual choices had been made.

METHODOLOGICAL INADEQUACIES

A review of research always uncovers methodological inadequacies. However, a couple of points are worth noting here. First, since most subjects for research on sexual choice will be found in mental health settings or prisons, they will probably be more disturbed than control groups. It is important to control for these differences in psychological disturbance. As Siegelman (1974) found, controlling for differences in neuroticism between homosexuals and heterosexuals eliminated the "classic" differences usually found in the parental constellation of homosexuals. It appears as if the "classic" picture may have been the result of a failure to control for differences in psychopathology.

This leads to the second point. Rubins (1969) noted that the families from which homosexuals are believed to come resemble the families from which self-mutilators, suicides, and schizophrenics are also supposed to come. If we are going to try to develop a theory of the causation of some particular sexual choice, then we must take care to indicate how the theory is unique to the particular behavior we are studying. In the research reviewed in Chapter 9 on the parents of homosexuals, only one study had attempted to do this.

THE ETIOLOGY OF SEXUAL CHOICE

Finally, it is worth noting that this review has uncovered a wide range of possible etiological factors determining sexual choice. There is some evidence from twin studies for a genetic component, although the data have not reached the level of complexity required before confidence can be placed in the results. There is some evidence for physiological, and in paticular endocrinological, factors. Here the current research is contradictory, but nonetheless suggestive of important differences.

Evidence on central nervous system involvement is quite poor. Evidence for the influence of the parents is good should the results be found to be reliable even when differences in psychopathology of the different groups being compared are held constant.

Finally, there are two powerful contrasting theoretical models available to give a broad framework for the development of sexual choice: Freud's psychoanalytic theory and the learning theory of McGuire, et al. (1965) which has moved well beyond the simple postulate of the importance of learning.

Research into sexual choice would seem to be on the threshold of great advances. Much of the present "knowledge" is clearly suspect and untrustworthy. However, adequate methodologies are now available and clear directions exist for the research to take. The next decade or two should witness a great increase in our understanding of the etiology of sexual choice.

REFERENCES

Freund, K., McKnight, C., Langevin, R., and Cibiri, S.: The female child as a surrogate object. *Arch Sex Behav, 2*:119-133, 1972.

Gebhard, P., Gagnon, J., Pomeroy, W., and Christenson, C.: *Sex Offenders.* New York, Har-Row, 1965.

Maslow, A.: Self-esteem (dominance-feeling) and sexuality in women. *J Soc Psychol, 16*:259-294, 1942.

McGuire, R., Carlisle, J., and Young, B.: Sexual deviations as conditioned behavior. *Behav Res Ther, 2*:185-190, 1965.

Rubins, J.: Sexual perversions. *Am J Psychoanal, 29*:94-105, 1969.

Siegelman, M.: Adjustment of male homosexuals and heterosexuals. *Arch Sex Behav, 2*:9-25, 1972.

Siegelman, M.: Parental background of male homosexuals and heterosexuals. *Arch Sex Behav, 3*:3-18, 1974.

NAME INDEX

Aaronson, B., 203, 206
Abe, K., 43, 44, 63, 73
Aberle, D., 129, 138, 139, 143
Abraham, K., 160, 165
Abrahamsen, D., 32, 34, 36, 216, 224
Abudabbeh, N., 207
Adamopoulos, D., 55, 122
Adams, M., 130, 143
Adler, K., 85, 87
Akesson, H., 184, 191
Alexander, D., 47, 55
Allen, R., 201, 207
Almansi, R., 22, 24
Amir, M., 28, 29, 36
Anderson, D., 196, 206
Andress, V., 108, 109
Apperson, L., 68, 73
Armon, V., 115, 116, 122
Athanasiou, R., 97, 109

Bagley, C., 141, 143
Baker, H., 40, 44
Balint, M., 164, 165
Ball, J., 53, 54
Ball, R., 18, 156
Barahal, H., 48, 54
Barber, R., 212, 223
Barker, A., 197, 198, 206
Barr, M., 40, 44, 176, 179
Barry, M., 131, 143
Bartelme, K., 157
Bartelt, C., 157
Beach, F., 138, 143
Beck, A., 75, 80
Beck, P., 204, 208
Bell, R., 72, 73
Bene, E., 68, 69, 73, 120, 122
Benjamin, H., 180, 187, 191
Bentler, P., 170-172, 179
Beran, L., 19, 21
Berl, S., 122
Berman, L., 204, 206
Bieber, I., 59, 62-65, 69-71, 73, 97, 109, 117, 118, 122
Bishop, M., 55
Blanchard, W., 35, 36
Blank, L., 16, 17
Block, D., 187, 191

Block, J., 64, 73, 106, 109
Blum, G. 133, 143
Blumer, D., 191
Bobrow, N., 47, 54
Botwinick, J., 91, 94
Braaten, L., 50, 54, 100, 101, 104, 109
Brancale, R., 7, 9, 17, 134, 143, 217, 223
Brawley, B., 53, 54
Brennan, J., 186, 187, 191
Brockopp, G., 19, 21
Bromberg, W., 14, 17, 134, 143, 146, 156, 218, 223
Bronfenbrenner, U., 143
Brown, D., 83, 87, 197, 206
Brown, J., 25, 26
Buckner, H., 176, 179
Burton, A., 32, 36, 203, 206
Buxbaum, E., 158, 165

Calmas, W., 223
Caprio, F., 13, 17
Carlisle, J., 18, 165, 223, 232
Carr, A., 44
Carrier, J., 81, 87
Carrol, J., 200, 206
Casler, L., 16, 17
Cassity, J., 154, 156
Castelnuovo-Tedesco, P., 92, 94
Cattell, R., 102, 109
Chang, J., 64, 73, 106, 109
Chapman, J., 195, 206
Chapman, L., 90, 195, 206
Chappell, D., 28, 30, 36
Chornyak, J., 50, 55
Christenson, C., 17, 21, 24, 36, 62, 87, 143, 156, 223, 232
Christodorescu, D., 183, 191
Christoffel, H., 13, 17
Cibiri, S., 156, 232
Clare, J., 122
Clark, T., 106, 109
Clarke, R., 43, 44, 58, 62, 68, 73, 105, 107, 110, 202, 206
Clifton, A., 26
Coates, S., 196, 206
Cohen, M., 219, 220, 223

233

Collins, M., 6, 17
Coppen, A., 49, 54
Cornelison, A., 144
Cook, R., 212, 223
Coron, M., 80
Costello, C., 17
Coult, A., 138, 142, 143
Cowden, J., 201, 206
Cowen, E., 151, 156
Crane, J., 87
Cubitt, G., 100-102, 109
Cupp, M., 45
Cutter, F., 199, 206

Dahlstrom, W., 207
Dank, B., 95, 109
Darke, R., 41, 44, 104, 109, 198, 206
Darling, C., 50, 54, 100, 101, 104, 109
Darwin, M., 145, 157
David, H., 197, 206
Davids, A., 197, 206
Davis, C., 94
Dean, R., 200, 203, 206
Deluca, J., 98, 104, 109
Devereux, G., 86, 87
Dewhurst, K., 52, 54
Dickey, B., 107, 109
Dingman, H., 45
Dingman, J., 55
Dittmar, F., 54
Doerr, P., 51, 54
Doidge, W., 101, 109
Doorbar, R., 185, 187, 191, 223
Dore, G., 55, 122
Duel, H. 54
Dutton, C., 145, 157

Edwards, D., 62, 73, 111, 122
Ehrhardt, A., 46, 54, 55
Eleston, M., 122
Ellis, A., 7, 9, 17, 106, 108, 109, 134, 143, 211, 218, 223
Elonen, A., 115, 122
Engel, G., 92, 94
Epstein, A., 160, 162, 165, 175, 179
Epstein, R., 54, 106, 109, 172, 179
Ericksen, C., 91, 94
Evans, D., 5-7, 12, 17, 210, 223
Evans, R., 43, 44, 49, 51, 54, 50, 60, 62, 66, 69-71, 73, 102, 103, 109

Falconer, M., 55
Feldman, M., 202, 206
Fenichel, O., 14, 17
Ferracuti, F., 29, 36
Fine, R., 97, 110
Fisher, G., 151, 156, 197, 206, 207
Fitch, J., 146, 148, 156
Fleck, S., 144
Flomenhaft, K., 144
Fosen, R., 223
Fox, J., 137, 143
Fraas, L., 198, 203, 207
Franzini, L., 109
Freedman, L., 204, 206
Freud, S., 137, 143
Freund, K., 150, 154, 156, 188, 191, 204, 207, 223, 229, 232
Friberg, R., 101, 102, 110
Frisbie, L., 11, 17, 146, 148, 156
Fromm, E., 115, 122
Frosch, J., 134, 143, 218, 223
Fuller, G., 200, 206

Gagnon, J., 17, 21, 24, 36, 62, 87, 143, 153, 156, 223, 232
Galbraith, H., 48, 54, 112, 122
Garst, J., 50, 54
Gebhard, P., 10, 13, 17, 19, 21, 23, 24, 33, 36, 58, 62, 82, 87, 128, 134, 141, 143, 152, 153, 156, 220, 223, 228, 232
Geil, G., 104, 109, 198, 206, 207
Geis, G., 36
Gelder, M., 26
Gendreau, P., 100-102, 109
Gentry, K., 110, 122
Gershwin, B., 122
Gershwin, P., 122
Giannell, A., 114, 122
Gibbens, T., 49, 54
Gibbins, R., 91, 94
Gillespie, J., 73, 110
Gillespie, W., 77, 80
Gillin, J., 217, 223
Gioscia, N., 82, 87
Glass, S., 50, 54
Glick, B., 88, 94
Gligor, A., 132, 136, 143
Glover, E., 164, 165
Glueck, B., 153, 156, 214, 218, 223
Goldfried, M., 195, 207
Goldhirsh, M., 221, 223
Goldner, N., 27, 32, 36
Goldstein, M., 212, 223
Goodwin, D., 87

Name Index

Goody, J., 127, 143, 144
Grams, A., 190, 207
Grant, V., 158, 161, 165
Grauer, D., 89, 94
Greaves, T., 142, 144
Green, R., 47, 54, 57, 61, 62, 99, 110, 182, 191, 223
Greene, R., 113, 116, 123
Greenstein, J., 63, 73
Griffith, R., 199, 208
Grumpelt, H., 203, 206
Grygier, T., 103, 110
Guertin, W., 196, 207
Guze, S., 85, 87

Hackfield, A., 52, 54
Hackett, T., 13, 17
Hamburger, C., 184, 191
Hammer, E., 31, 32, 36, 150, 156, 214, 216, 223
Hampson, J., 55
Hannum, T., 113, 122
Hartman, A., 212, 223
Hartman, B., 200, 207
Haselkorn, H., 98, 110
Hathaway, S., 203, 207
Haupt, T., 201, 207, 208
Hayes, F., 42, 45, 71, 73
Hemphill, R., 43, 44, 49, 52, 54
Hendryx, J., 55
Henry, A., 30, 36
Henry, G., 5, 17, 48, 54, 112, 122
Henslin, J., 36
Herzberg, F., 32, 36, 151, 156, 216, 224
Hess, E., 143, 204, 207
Heston, L., 39, 44
Hill, D., 55
Hilliard, J., 55, 207
Hirning, L., 155, 156
Hirsch, J., 144
Hobbs, G., 40, 44, 176, 179
Hodgson, R., 162, 165
Hoenig, J., 40, 44, 49, 54, 185, 188, 191
Holemon, E., 84, 87
Holtzman, W., 101, 109
Honigmann, J., 5, 17
Hooker, E., 83, 87, 103, 110, 196, 207
Hoopes, J., 184, 188, 191
Hooshmand, H., 53, 54
Hooton, E., 33, 36
Hopkins, J., 114-116, 122
Hoskins, R., 52, 55

Housden, J., 49, 55, 176, 179
Houston, L., 98, 100, 110, 198, 207
Howell, L., 151, 156
Humphreys, L., 85, 87
Hurwitz, I., 11, 18

Imielinski, K., 95, 110
Ismail, A., 55, 122

Jacks, I., 32, 36, 150, 156
Jackson, D., 171, 179
Jackson, J., 80, 223
James, W., 42, 44
Jensen, D., 197, 198, 207
Jodd, L., 223
Joelson, M., 206
Johnson, A., 131, 143
Johnston, R., 223
Jones, E., 157

Kallman, F., 39, 41, 43, 44
Kanin, E., 27, 36
Kant, H., 223
Kaplan, E., 76, 80
Karon, B., 94
Karp, E. 76, 80, 213, 223
Karpinski, E., 131, 145
Karpman, B., 14, 17, 154, 156
Katan, M., 164, 165
Kaufman, I., 130, 133, 144
Kaye, H., 116, 122
Kearney, T., 65, 73
Keiser, S., 121, 122
Kemph, J., 131, 141, 145
Kendrick, D., 43, 44, 58, 62, 68, 73, 105, 107, 110
Kenna, J., 191
Kenyon, F., 112-114, 116, 119, 120, 122
Kercher, G., 33, 36
Khan, M., 158, 165
Kinsey, A., 39, 50, 55, 71, 81, 87
Kirkham, G., 86, 87
Klaf, F., 94
Knight, R., 89, 94
Knorr, N., 191
Kockott, G., 54
Kogan, L., 122
Kolarsky, A., 213, 223
Kolb, L., 44
Kolodny, R., 50, 51, 53, 55
Kopp, S., 11, 17
Krazanowska, H., 129, 144

Krieger, M., 64, 73
Krippner, S., 199, 202, 207
Kuethe, J., 96, 110
Kurland, M., 152, 156
Kwawer, J., 80

Lamberd, W., 106, 110
Lang, T., 41, 43, 44
Langevin, R., 156, 191, 232
Leitch, A., 44, 54
Lester, D., 19, 21, 31, 32, 36, 80, 88, 94, 127, 134, 223
LeVine, R., 30, 36
Levy, S., 198, 207
Lewis, M., 59, 62, 68, 73, 99, 110
Lewis, V., 54
Leziak, K., 129, 144
Lidz, R., 121, 122
Lidz, T., 121, 122, 131, 144
Liechti, R., 55, 207
Lief, H., 52, 55
Lindner, H., 156, 216, 217, 223
Lindzey, G., 128, 129, 137, 144, 196, 197, 207
Linton, M., 109
Litman, R., 25, 26
Loney, J., 100, 110
Loraine, J., 51, 55, 113, 122
Lukianowicz, N., 170, 173-175, 179
Lyman, S., 90, 94

MacAlpine, I., 82, 87
MacCulloch, M., 206
Macdonald, J., 6, 7, 10, 11, 17, 28, 36
Machek, J., 223
Machotka, P., 132, 144
Machover, K., 94
Machover, S., 91, 94
Mainord, F., 197, 207
Manosevitz, M., 97, 100, 101, 110, 200, 208
Margolese, M., 51, 55
Marguis, D., 93, 94
Markey, O., 217, 223
Marks, I., 25, 26, 202, 207
Marsh, J., 52, 55, 188, 191, 199, 207
Marshall, J., 73, 110
Martin, C., 87
Martin, J., 133, 144
Masica, D., 47, 55
Maslow, A., 215, 223, 227, 228, 232
Masters, W., 55
Mathias, J., 206
Mathis, J., 6, 17

McAdoo, W., 68, 73
McArthur, C., 206
McCaghy, C., 14, 18, 148, 156
McCandless, B., 62, 73, 111, 122
McCawley, A., 10, 18
McClearn, G., 129, 144
McConaghy, N., 96, 110
McCord, J., 62, 73, 144
McCord, W., 57, 60, 62, 64, 67, 70, 73, 131, 144
McGuire, R., 12, 18, 162, 165, 209, 222, 223, 231, 232
McKerracher, D., 41, 44
McKnight, C., 156, 232
McLachlan, D., 170, 174, 176, 179
McLaughlin, J., 73, 110
Meerloo, J., 188, 191
Mellan, J., 156
Mellor, V., 206
Mendelsohn, F., 98, 100, 110
Mesnikoff, A., 39, 44
Meyer, J., 185, 187, 191
Middleton, P., 128, 144
Miller, D., 143
Miller, W., 113, 122
Mitchell, W., 53, 55
Mohr, J., 9, 11, 13, 18, 146, 147, 156
Money, J., 40, 45-48, 54, 55, 57, 61, 62, 87, 99, 110, 172, 179, 186, 187, 191
Monsour, J., 92, 94
Moore, S., 128, 144
Moos, M., 86, 87
Moran, P., 43, 44, 63, 73
Morgan, D., 208
Moroney, J., 102, 109
Morrow, J., 42, 45
Morse, E., 201, 206
Morton, N., 130, 144
Mosberg, L., 66, 73, 100, 107, 110
Mosher, D., 101, 105, 110
Mosier, H., 41, 45
Mukerji, K., 196, 208
Murdock, G., 127, 138, 144
Murphy, F., 52, 55
Murray, F., 19, 21
Myerhoff, B., 135, 144
Myerson, A., 50, 55
Myerson, P., 26

Nadler, R., 19, 21
Nagler, S., 160, 165
Nash, J., 42, 45, 71, 73
Nedoman, K., 40, 45, 49, 156
Neel, J., 130, 143, 144

Name Index

Neustadt, R., 50, 55
Newnham, W., 53, 55
Nicolay, R., 212, 223
Nitsche, C., 196, 207
Norman, J., 91, 94

Obendorf, C., 22, 24
O'Connor, P., 58, 62, 67, 73, 99, 106, 110
Oliver, W., 101, 105, 110
Opler, M., 65, 73
Ovesey, L., 77, 80

Pacht, A., 201, 206, 223
Palm, R., 32, 34, 36
Panton, J., 102, 199, 200, 207, 208
Pardes, H., 39, 45
Pare, C., 40, 45
Parsons, E., 207
Parsons, T., 139, 144
Pascal, G., 32, 36, 151, 156, 216, 224
Pauly, I., 180, 182, 184, 191
Payne, S., 160, 165
Peck, A., 144
Peek, R., 200, 208
Perdue, W., 32, 36
Pinschof, J., 206
Piotrowski, Z., 216, 224
Pirke, K., 54
Pittman, F., 144
Plumeau, F., 94
Polak, O., 223
Pollitt, E., 40, 45
Pomeroy, W., 17, 21, 24, 36, 62, 87, 143, 156, 185, 191, 223, 232
Pondelickova, J., 156
Powers, C., 206
Prandoni, J., 207
Primrose, C., 186, 191
Prince, C. V., 170, 171, 179
Pritchard, M., 40, 45
Pustel, G., 198, 208
Puzzo, F., 94

Rabinowitz, W., 197, 206
Raboch, J., 40, 45
Rachman, S., 26, 162, 165
Rainer, J., 44
Ramsay, R., 96, 110
Randell, J., 40, 45, 173, 176, 179
Rascovsky, A., 131, 144
Rascovsky, M., 131, 144
Raychaudhuri, M., 196, 208

Rees, D., 90
Reitzell, J., 91, 94
Resnick, H., 25, 26, 175, 179
Rhinehart, J., 128, 144
Rice, C., 223
Richardson, H., 200, 201, 203, 206
Rickels, N., 8, 12, 14, 18
Rindfuss, R., 42, 45
Rindler, L., 199, 207
Roberts, D., 130, 144
Robins, E., 110, 122
Robinson, J., 207
Rogers, E., 145, 157
Romm, E., 159, 160, 165
Rooth, G., 13, 18
Rosanoff, W., 52, 53, 55
Roseberg, J., 94
Rosenfeld, H., 88, 94
Rosenzweig, S., 52, 55
Ross, M., 98, 100, 110
Roth, L., 86, 87
Roth, R., 16, 17
Rubins, J., 69, 73, 106, 110, 211, 224, 231, 232
Ruskin, S., 218, 224

Sachs, L., 45
Sade, D., 129, 144
Saghir, M., 105, 106, 110, 119, 122
Salzman, L., 77, 80
Sartorius, N., 202, 207
Saul, L., 13, 18, 75, 80
Schafer, R., 196, 208
Schafer, S., 36
Schaffer, D., 121, 122
Schiffer, D., 108, 111
Schlegel, W., 12, 18
Schneider, D., 143
Schoenfeldt, L., 59, 62, 68, 73, 99, 110
Schroeder, T., 128, 144
Schull, W., 130, 144
Schwartz, D., 62, 73, 111, 122
Scott, L., 45
Scott, M., 90, 94
Scott, T., 204, 208
Seghorn, T., 223
Segner, L., 129, 137, 144
Seitz, F., 196, 206
Seliger, R., 156
Seligman, B., 139, 140, 144, 145
Selling, L., 11, 18, 53, 55
Seltzer, A., 207
Sevringhaus, E., 50, 55
Shaver, R., 97, 109

Sherman, R., 179
Shields, J., 39, 44
Shillen, J., 207
Shoor, M., 149, 157
Shore, M., 25, 26
Short, J., 30, 36
Siegel, L., 36
Siegelman, M., 57, 58, 62, 69, 73, 104, 111, 116, 122, 228, 231, 232
Silverman, D., 53, 55
Silverman, L., 78, 80
Simons, R., 45
Singer, M., 199, 203, 208
Sinnett, E., 94
Sipprelle, C., 198, 208
Sjostedt, E., 11, 18
Skipper, J., 14, 18
Slater, E., 43, 45, 202, 208
Slater, M., 139, 145
Slater, P., 202, 208
Sloane, P., 131, 145
Slotkin, J., 127, 145
Snortum, J., 73, 110
Socarides, C., 78, 80, 159, 164, 165
Solyom, L., 204, 208
Sonenschein, D., 83, 87
Speed, M., 157
Spencer, S., 49, 56, 58, 60, 62, 68, 73, 101, 106, 111
Steinberg, A., 144
Steinberg, J., 45
Steiner, B., 191
Stekel, W., 14, 18
Stephan, W., 59, 60, 62, 64, 68, 73
Sternlicht, M., 208
Stevens, S., 143
Stobin, E., 50, 54
Stoller, R., 40, 44, 169, 174, 179, 183, 191
Storms, L., 200, 208
Storr, A., 213, 224
Stricker, G., 151, 156, 157
Strickland, B., 111, 122
Stuart, J., 44, 54
Svalastoga, K., 30, 36
Swearingen, C., 25, 26
Swensen, C., 198, 208

Tagiuri, C., 144
Taylor, A., 170, 174, 176, 179
Taylor, C., 65, 73
Tejessy, C., 207
Tharp, R., 128, 145

Thompson, N., 59, 62, 64, 67, 73, 103, 108, 111, 115, 120, 122
Thorne, T., 201, 208
Tittle, C., 86, 87
Tolor, A., 197, 206
Tong, J., 219, 224
Toobert, S., 149, 157
Torda, C., 122
Toro, G., 55
Torr, J., 40, 44, 49, 54
Tremboth, W., 196, 207
Turner, R., 18, 156

Ullman, P., 66, 69, 74

Velzen, V., 96, 110
Verden, P., 62, 73, 144
Vetter, H., 92, 94
Vilhotti, A., 100, 111, 197, 208
Vogt, H., 54
Von Hentig, H., 30, 36

Wagner, E., 217, 224
Walbran, B., 110, 122
Walinder, J., 175, 179, 184, 191
Walker, C., 33, 36
Walker, E., 203, 208
Walters, R., 91, 94
Wanderer, Z., 198, 208
Wang, C., 172, 179
Wattron, J., 200, 208
Weich, M., 138, 145
Weinberg, M., 16, 18, 95, 111
Weinberg, S., 127, 132, 135, 145
Weingartner, H., 96, 110
Weisman, A., 25, 26
Weiss, J., 136, 145, 154, 157
Weissman, P., 77, 80, 161, 165
Wells, E., 208
Welsh, G., 207
West, D., 67, 74
Westermarck, E., 137, 145
Westoff, C., 42, 45
Wheeler, W., 195, 208
Whitaker, L., 198, 208
White, L., 140, 145
Wilber, C., 122
Williams, E., 52, 56
Wilson, M., 113, 116, 123
Winnicott, D., 158, 165
Winokur, G., 84, 87
Winter, W., 94

Name Index

Wolf, A., 137, 142, 145
Wolf, S., 191
Wolfgang, M., 29, 36
Wolitsky, C., 80
Wood, D., 208
Worchel, P., 64, 73
Worden, F., 188, 191
Wright, C., 50, 54, 56
Wulff, M., 158, 164, 165

Yalom, I., 22, 24
Yamahiro, R., 199, 208
Yazmajian, R., 173, 179

Yohe, C., 5, 18
Yorukoglu, A., 131, 141, 145
Youd, A., 191
Young, B., 18, 165, 223, 232

Zajac, A., 191
Zajac, Y., 191
Zamansky, H., 204, 207, 208
Zechnich, R., 10, 18
Zelin, M., 26
Zucker, R., 200, 208
Zuger, B., 48, 56

SUBJECT INDEX

A

Accidental death, 175
Active/passive role, 71, 83
Age, 95
Alcoholics, 5, 10, 23, 65
Alcoholism, 15, 28, 60, 91, 105, 216
Amorous fixation, 158
Anal intercourse, 29, 81, 146
Aversion to females, 97

B

Biochemical studies, 50
Birth order, 9, 15, 23, 57, 148, 187
Bisexual, 16
Bondage, 25
Brain damage, 7, 162, 175, 213, 218
Brothels, 212

C

Castration, 52, 76
Castration anxiety, 14, 22, 161, 164, 173, 211, 214
Character disorders, 211
Childhood, 8, 57ff
Chromosomes, 40
Colitis, 92
Creativity, 108
Cunnilingus, 29
Curiosity, 108

D

DAP test, 115, 197
Detection of the deviant, 195
Dissociative states, 186
Dreams, 222
Drug addiction, 15, 86, 105

E

Economic prosperity, 30
Effeminacy, 47, 84, 99, 169, 172, 182
Epileptics, 7
Exhibitionists, 5ff, 19, 23, 146, 147, 183, 211

F

Fathers, 9, 12, 133, 147, 170

Fear of pubic hair, 154
Fellatio, 29, 146
Felony rape, 29
Female homosexuality, 112ff
Fetishism, 25, 53, 158ff, 169, 189, 211, 213
Fixations, 75
Force, 6
Forced homosexuality, 85
Frotteurism, 13

G

Gag reflex, 82
Gang rape, 35
Genetic factors, 39, 176, 180
Grades, 100
GSR (galvanic skin response) 204, 220

H

Hanging, 175
Hermaphrodites, 47
Homosexuality, 13, 15, 25, 27, 32, 35, 37ff, 146, 175, 177, 183, 212, 213, 216
Hormones, 46, 113, 176, 180

I

Identification, 64, 75, 84, 173, 214
Impotence, 8, 13, 25, 50, 221
Incest, 127ff, 214, 221
Incestuous wishes, 78, 97
Incest taboo, 136ff
Insertor/insertee, 81
Intelligence, 9, 23, 32, 100, 147, 172, 187, 217, 221
Interests, 98
Inversion, 83

K

Kleptomania, 159
Klinefelter's syndrome, 40, 172, 180

L

Latent homosexuality, 77

Learning, 12, 161
Learning theory, 209
Lower animals, 129

M

Marriage, 95, 148, 219
Masculinity/femininity, 83, 101, 108, 186, 202
Masochism, 23, 25, 60, 76, 105, 163, 173, 188, 189
Masturbation, 6, 7, 9, 10, 23, 25, 50, 81, 118, 146, 160, 164, 177, 185, 210
Masturbatory guilt, 71
Menstruation, 15, 112
Migraine, 92
MMPI, 100, 113, 199
Mothers, 8, 12, 19, 32, 136, 147, 161, 174
Multiple intercourse, 29

N

Narcissism, 188
Neurosis, 7, 9, 92, 116, 210
Nudism, 16

O

Obscene telephone calls, 19
Offspring, 43, 130
Oral intercourse, 81

P

Pansexuals, 146
Paranoid delusions, 88
Parental age, 43
Parental loss, 63, 188
Parents, 15, 23, 63ff, 117, 181, 187
Pedophilia, 5, 31, 33, 53, 146ff, 212, 214, 216, 218, 219
Penis envy, 118
Penis volume, 204
Perceptual-cognitive maturity, 11
Physiognomy, 204
Physique, 33, 48, 112, 176
Pornography, 15, 23, 33, 98, 212
Pregnancy, 212
Projective tests, 195
Prostitution, 15
Pruritis ani, 82
Psychoanalytic views, 75, 154, 163, 173, 210
Psychological adjustment, 31, 100, 113, 150
Psychopaths, 210, 218

Psychosexual maturity, 31, 98, 214
Psychosis, 5, 7, 9
Pupil size, 204

R

Racial differences, 7, 28, 218
Rape, 13, 27ff, 150, 212, 214, 216, 218, 219
Recividism, 148, 221
Regression, 14
Repression, 14
Retardation, 5, 7, 10, 23, 218
Role playing, 99

S

Sadism, 23, 25, 60, 76, 105, 161, 173
Schizophrenia, 65, 90, 214, 218
Seasonal variation, 6, 28
Self-actualization, 215
Self-concept, 106
Sex ratio, 31, 41, 58, 148
Siblings, 9, 41, 148
Stammering, 10
Statutory rape, 27
Stripteasers, 14
Subculture of violence, 29
Suicide, 105
Szondi test, 197

T

TAT, 196
Temporal lobe damage, 53, 163
Territoriality, 86
Transitional objects, 158
Transexuals, 169, 172, 180ff, 212
Transvestism, 25, 49, 53, 169ff, 183, 189, 211
Turner's syndrome, 47
Twin studies, 39

U

Ulcer, 92, 93

V

Victim-precipitated acts, 7, 29
Violence, 28
Vocabulary, 202
Voyeurism, 8, 13, 19, 22ff, 211, 218

W

Weaning, 154
Wheeler's signs, 195
Wives, 9, 33, 34, 170, 174